CONNECTING YOUNG ADULTS AND LIBRARIES

A How-To-Do-It Manual

PATRICK JONES

HOW-TO-DO-IT MANUALS
FOR LIBRARIES
Number 19

Series Editor: Bill Katz

NEAL-SCHUMAN PUBLISHERS, INC.
New York, London

Published by Neal-Schuman Publishers, Inc.
100 Varick Street
New York, NY 10013

Printed and bound in the United States of America

Permissions

The following publishers and authors have generously given permission to reprint
excerpts from their copyrighted works:

Figure 2-1 from *Being Adolescent:* by Reed Larson and Mihaly Csikszentmihalyi.
Copyright © 1984 by Basic Books, Inc., a division of HarperCollins Publishers Inc.

Figures 4-5, 4-6, 5-5, 6-6, and 6-7 reprinted by permission of the Springfield (MA)
City Library, Springfield Library and Museums Association. Graphics prepared by Lynn
Walulak.

Figure 4-2, 5-6, and 6-10 reprinted by permission of Cuyahoga County (OH) Public
Library.

Library of Congress Cataloging-in-Publication Data

Jones, Patrick.
 Connecting young adults and libraries : a how-to-do-it manual /
Patrick Jones.
  p.   cm. — (How-to-do-it-manuals for libraries : no. 19)
 Includes bibliographical references and index.
 ISBN 1-55570-108-6
 1. Libraries, Young people's—Administration.   2. Libraries—
Special collections—Young adult literature.   3. Young adult
literature—Bibliography—Methodology.   4. Young adults—Books and
reading.   I. Title.   II. Series.{Z718.5.J66   1992
025.5′6—dc20   91-43720
                                                       CIP

TO ERICA

CONTENTS

ACKNOWLEDGMENTS

I would like to thank Cathy Hakala-Ausperk, Cynthia Glunt, and Brent Chartier for their contribution. I would also like to thank Jim Fish for hiring me for my first YA job and being supportive all during my tenure. The staff at the Tecumseh Branch Library and my new supervisor Michael Clegg were very supportive as I finished the book and started a new job at the same time. Finally, I would like to thank Janet Dickey, not just for her comments which helped me write the manuscript, but for showing every day that you do not need to be under 30, have long hair, or know a thing about Hulk Hogan to connect with young adults.

INTRODUCTION

In 1988 the National Center for Education Statistics released a Survey Report on young adult (YA) services and resources in America's public libraries. The report helped clarify a number of important issues in this area, but two of the study's findings were particularly revealing—and at the same time confusing—because they seemed to contradict each other strongly.

First, the study found that 25 percent of public library users are young adults—that is, one out of every four individuals who walks through the door of a public library is between the ages of 12 and 18 (using this general guideline for the YA age range). Anyone who has spent any time at a public library would not be surprised by this finding. The survey also revealed, however, that 89 percent of these same libraries do not have a professional librarian specifically dedicated to young adult services.

In business, this scenario would be hard to imagine. Would a business that could identify one quarter of its customers as a particular market segment not respond to this group directly? Other surveys have documented the wide use of libraries by children, and almost every public library of any size has responded by having at least one professional on staff with the title Children's Librarian (or the equivalent).

Yet, the same cannot be said with regard to YA staffing. Rather than asking such questions as, "How can we meet the needs of one fourth of our users?" or "Who has the proper training and attitude to provide this important service?" too often library administrators merely ask, "Okay, who has some extra time?" Even that question is asked only if a library is willing to assign a staff member to coordinate services to this user group. More often, the question is reduced to, "What are we going to do with all these kids?"

Connecting Young Adults and Libraries: A How-To-Do-It Manual is designed to help answer all these questions, but primarily the last one. For the most part, it is not intended for experienced YA librarians (at the 11 percent of libraries that have them), although they may find some useful tips for enhancing services within these pages. Instead, this book is primarily for staff at the other 89 percent of libraries who are trying to provide some level of quality YA service without the benefit of a YA professional: generalists; adult, children's, or general youth librarians; paraprofessionals; even clerical staff—all of whom may find themselves providing service to teenagers either by choice, order, or default.

Other groups who may find this manual useful are: new YA librarians, since library schools offer many courses on YA literature, but few on YA services; school librarians who work with YAs (who may get some new ideas for media centers even though the setting for most of the discussion is the public library); and library managers and administrators, who make the all-important decisions about where and how to allocate shrinking resources. Whoever the audience, the objective of this manual is to link the library's valuable resources with the country's most valuable resources, our youth.

This is not so much a book for reading from start to finish as it is a tool for building, fixing, or reconstructing YA services as needed. It is not a book about YA literature—there are already several fine titles in print that cover that subject sufficiently—but about connecting YAs with libraries. For some YAs, this will involve reading and enjoying YA literature, but for others it will not. Although there will be some discussion of YA collections, *Connecting Young Adults and Libraries* will deal primarily with strategies for implementing various services. The manual format allows each reader/user to choose the sections that address his or her library's particular needs and level of commitment to YA services. For some, the library's only commitment may be to providing information services while others realize, even in the absence of a YA librarian, that this is not enough. Regardless of the service level, *Connecting Young Adults and Libraries* contains sample documents, forms, and checklists that can be used and adapted in a variety of ways.

Chapters 1 and 2 discuss "stalking" YAs: who they are, what they are doing in libraries, why they need to be served, and the history of the hunt. Chapter 3 discusses the development of both print and nonprint YA collections. Chapter 4 examines different levels of service available to YAs, from reference services to more specialized services such as library instruction and booktalking. Chapters 5 and 6 look beyond day-to-day encounters with YAs toward making connections with schools and community organizations, and related programming. Chapter 7 discusses techniques for merchandising and marketing YA services. Chapter 8 moves beyond the strictly practical and looks into some larger questions about library service to YAs. The appendixes contain core collections with subject access and addresses of major YA publishers, as well as addresses of YA and professional magazines. A bibliography suggests further reading.

Connecting Young Adults and Libraries is a hybrid of research, experience, and intuition. It begins with a philosophy and an attitude: a YAttitude. A YAttitude recognizes the value of YAs, their right to library services, and the passion needed to serve them. Perhaps after using this manual and working with YAs, you will develop a YAttitude. Perhaps you already have one but lack the tools to put it into practice. In any case, lack of a healthy YAttitude will certainly hinder efforts to serve YAs.

For those of us who have a passion for serving YAs, the YAttitude and the tools are worth learning—not just because it is our job, but because it is an enjoyable and rewarding adventure.

1 "DO IT RIGHT"

1.1 OVERVIEW

The new director of a large suburban library visited all the branches in the system, meeting with staff and asking them about their concerns. One recurring concern was service to young adults. Some people thought the system did too much, while others believed it didn't do enough. It was clear to the new director that no one was sure what level of commitment the system had to YA, even though it had a history of YA excellence. Yet, the new director was facing hard choices given rising expectations, rising costs, and the increasing push to automate or re-automate library functions all in the face of falling revenues. After surveying the situation, the new director announced that "we will either do it right or we won't do it at all."

Across the country, other library directors are faced with similar choices. Many have invoked the Public Library Association's *Planning and Role Setting for Public Libraries*[1] method to help them prioritize. Refrains of

"We can't be all things to all people!"

"What are our roles?"

"Where have we been, where are we now, where do we want to be?"

echo in committees, task forces, subcommittees, and work groups facing this planning process. In some libraries, YA services are part of the discussion. Libraries choosing to devote extensive or even moderate effort to the roles of:

• Reference library
• Popular materials library
• Formal educational support center
• Community activity center

are choosing roles that include YA services. Choosing roles is choosing a potential audience. The problem with the YA clientele is that serving it is a lot like cutting the federal deficit—everyone knows something needs to be done, but no one is quite sure what.

CHRONOLOGY OF IMPORTANT YA DOCUMENTS AND EVENTS

1929 Formation of Young People's Reading Roundtable, part of ALA's Children's Library Association

1941 Roundtable becomes part of ALA'S Division of Libraries for Children and Young People

1949 Roundtable becomes a section called the Association of Young People's Librarians

1958 Section becomes the Young Adult Services Division (YASD)

1960 ALA issues *Young Adult Services in the Public Library* from its Committee of Standards for Work with Young Adults

1968 *Library Trends* publishes issue called "Young Adult Services in the Public Library," which provides an excellent overview of the status of YA services entering the 1970s

1978 YASD publishes *Directions for Library Services to Young Adults* to provide the profession with a document to help them plan services

1979 Libraries Unlimited publishes *Libraries and Young Adults*, which provides an excellent overview of services entering the 1980s

1988 *Library Trends* publishes another YA-dedicated issue, "Library Services to Youth: Preparing for the Future," which covers various issues from the 1980s and looks into the next decade

1.2 A SHORT HISTORY

The history of young adult services in libraries is an interesting one, with two broad themes. First, there is a huge gap between what libraries "know they should do" and what they do. This gap is caused by the factors that separate most library dreams from library reality, but with YA there seems to be a deeper philosophical question underneath: should YAs be treated as a special group? Some libraries have a long history of recognizing YAs as special, while other systems—large public library systems—have been unwilling to do so. The logic of history shows that to admit that YA is a special population is to admit that it needs a special service, which means special staff and collections.

The other theme is that YA services in libraries mirror what is happening with YAs in the nation. Just as each decade has seen different kinds of teenagers and teenage problems, every ten years something major has happened to YAs' library services. Examining each of these documents or events, it is easy to see where young adult services has been. The early drive was just to establish and recognize YA as a specialized service. This specialization was characterized by:

- Specialists serving YAs
- A separate professional association/division
- Separate YA collections and budgets
- Separate YA programs and services

By the late 1960s social changes in the country were being reflected in library service and the literature. With the publication of such YA novels as S.E. Hinton's *The Outsiders* and Paul Zindel's *The Pigman*, it became obvious that YA was a very specialized form of literature and not just children's books for older readers. Figure 1-1 summarizes an article from *Library Trends* by Edwin Castagna, "YA Services on the Public Library Organization Chart," providing an overview of then current services.[2]

Things were a bit different by the late 1970s when JoAnn Rogers edited *Libraries and Young Adults: Media, Services and Librarianship*. It is interesting to note the first word in the subtitle is "media," although there is only one article about nonprint media. YA novels were continuing to gain in popularity and acceptance, as were paperbacks. The book covered all the major issues of the times. Ms. Rogers contributed an article called "Trends and Issues in

Young Adult Services," summing up where YA was and where it was headed.[3] (Figure 1-2)

Around the same time, Professor Thomas Downen of the University of Michigan surveyed 254 public libraries.[4] He asked the directors of these systems to express their opinions not about the current state of YA services, but about its future. They were asked to imagine both the desirability and the probability of various YA services in the year 1993. Since that year is almost upon us, before looking at the state of the art, let's look at what library directors thought it would be at this time. (Figure 1-3)

1.3 STATE OF THE ART: STATISTICS

By the late 1980s, the large national survey that both Castagna and Rogers had called for was finally achieved by the National Center for Education Statistics.[5] The results were based on answers from over 800 libraries and were quite different from what Castagna had imagined, and what Rogers had hoped, and were closer to Downen's findings of the "probable" as opposed to the "desirable." (Figure 1-4)

Although Castagna and Rogers were correct about libraries moving toward specialized YA areas, with 84 percent of the libraries reporting separate YA sections, the specialized staffing for these sections is not available. Rather than being served by a YA specialist, 89 percent of libraries use other staff (see Appendix A for charts of survey results). A note about that statistic: it represents someone with the title "YA librarian." An interesting follow-up would be finding out how many of those YA librarians do full-time YA work. For example, almost every branch of the Cuyahoga County Public Library in Cleveland has a YA librarian, but in all but five branches they are part-time. The reality there and in other libraries across the country is that the YA librarian is often "pulled" to cover the adult or children's reference desk.

The survey reported *when* YAs would most likely be in the public library—not surprisingly, after school, evenings, and on weekends. The most interesting statistic is the dramatic difference between use of libraries with and without a YA librarian. Over 90 percent of libraries with a YA librarian report "moderate to heavy use" after school, while only 74 percent of those without one

---

FIGURE 1-1   YA SERVICES IN 1969

Summary of "YA Services on the Public Library Organization Chart" by Edwin Castagna

Surveyed: 32 libraries in 19 states.

Findings:

*27 libraries had YA coordinators or supervisors, indicating "an overwhelming consensus on the importance of work with young adults."

*About half of these people reported directly to either the library director or assistant director, indicating "the importance many administrators attach to young adult service."

*17 reported a separate YA materials budget.

*21 reported special YA collections in the central library and 22 collections in the branches.

FIGURE 1-2 YA SERVICES IN 1979

Summary of "Trends and Issues in Young Adult Services" by JoAnn Rogers (1979).

Rogers wrote, "In the absence of a much-needed national survey of public library services for young adults, identifying meaningful trends for this age group is a difficult task." She relied on reviews of the literature and news from state/national associations.

Findings:

*Most libraries have a separate "space" to attract YAs.

*Institutional support for YA services has not kept pace with making YA service a more dynamic part of the total library program.

*Expanded coverage of YA issues in library literature reflects more recognition of the importance of YA work and more emphasis on YA services in public libraries.

*Libraries are accepting some responsibility for responding to the recreational needs of adolescents and are attempting to determine other needs to which the library might respond.

*Helping the young person to communicate needs to a library professional is a current focus of young adult work.

FIGURE 1-3 YA SERVICES IN 1993

Summary of survey by Professor Thomas Downen, University of Michigan.

Surveyed: 234 library directors of systems serving at least 100,000 people.

*81% said the continuation and expansion of YA service was desirable, but only 41% said it was probable this would occur in the future.

*63% thought that YA being nonexistent in 1993 was undesirable and 51% thought it was improbable.

*79% thought it was desirable to move away from programming and toward a "general education for lifetime use of libraries."

*99% felt it was desirable and 80% thought it was probable that there would be a reemphasis on reading for enjoyment.

*Increased library instruction was thought desirable by 90% of respondents but probable by only 52%.

*Paperbacks in YA collections were seen as desirable by only 62% and probable by just 58%.

*Continuing education related to YA services was seen as desirable by 83% but probable by only 39%.

*Merging YA into Children's Departments was seen as both undesirable (94%) and improbable (81%).

FIGURE 1-4 SUMMARY OF NCES SURVEY

Summary of National Center for Education Statistics Survey Report: *Services and Resources for Young Adults in Public Libraries* (1988)

Libraries surveyed: 846

*One out of every four public library patrons is a YA (between the age of 12 and 18).

*Moderate and heavy use of public libraries by YAs is mostly after school (76%).

*65% of libraries reported "heavy or moderate use" of services to assist YAs with school assignments.

*76% of libraries reported "heavy or moderate use" by YAs loaning books/other printed materials.

*Only 11 percent of public libraries even have a young adult librarian.

*Over 40% of libraries do not have access to assistance from a coordinator or consultant.

*Over 80% of libraries require no continuing YA training.

*84% of libraries offer a section or collection of materials designed for YAs.

*This collection is primarily in hardback (60%), fiction (73%), and made up for juvenile/young adult materials (85%).

*55% of libraries indicate an increase in services to YAs.

*The major barrier to YA use of libraries was seen by 87% of libraries as competition from other activities.

The report concluded that libraries with young adult librarians are more likely to report modern or heavy use by YA after school than libraries that do not have a YA librarian.

report this level of use. In the evening hours, the difference is 79 percent for libraries with a YA librarian, but only 50 percent for those without.

Once in the library, *where* YAs go for help is again not surprising. They seem to bring forth a key point: YAs do not want to be considered children, as demonstrated by the small number who use the children's area. Finally, *what* services YAs use in the public library was reported. The services reporting the most moderate to heavy use were:

1. Loan books/printed materials (77%)
2. Assistance with school assignments (65%)
3. Study space (60%)
4. Assistance with independent needs (40%)
5. College and career information (40%)

In all cases, although some more so than others, those libraries with YA staff reported greater use.

This survey demonstrates the contradiction of YA services. YAs are in libraries and are using them, but they use them more when a YA librarian is present. It is clear that YA services are best with YA staff, but it is still the generalists who serve this special population. Libraries are facing the dilemma described by the library director at the beginning of this chapter: a desire to do YA services "right" but not enough YA staff (or staff with the proper training and tools) to indeed do it right.

In most libraries, "doing it right" would mean giving YA the same status as children's services:

• Recognizing service as unique so YA staff does primarily YA work
• Hiring and/or training specialized staff
• Supporting outreach activities
• Supporting cooperative programming
• Supporting after school programming

But the report seems to suggest it won't be done right. Factors that inhibit an increase in YA services include:

• A current trend toward generalization in all service areas
• More resources allocated to automation
• A trend toward building empowerment and reducing centralization and coordinators

- A "Give 'em what they want" collection philosophy which doesn't require subject/age level specialization
- Low priority for services with smaller/special audiences such as YA, which covers only a six year period
- Large systems that are setting an example by eliminating and reducing services to YA—others follow that lead
- Erroneous perception that YAs lack interest and therefore don't need service
- Lack of qualified YA librarians
- General trend in the society that undervalues YAs.

There is another more basic argument: YAs don't deserve a special service. Some librarians argue that "we have many special populations and we can't serve them all," or "YAs are just old children, so let the J staff handle them," or "YAs primarily use reference materials, so let the adult staff handle them," or "YAs are just like any other patron and we serve all patrons equally." But are YAs just like any other patrons?

1.4 WHY YA?

Why should librarians support YA services? Why should there be either a formal YA program or at least a training program for generalists to help them do it right? Because:

1. Today's patrons are tomorrow's voters and taxpayers.
2. It will help encourage an individual's habit of using the library learned in childhood and support it until adulthood.
3. If patrons are "lost" during their YA years, they often do not return to libraries or sustain literacy.
4. Libraries supplement other educational, recreational, social, and cultural institutions.
5. Staff stress can be reduced by serving YAs rather than "tolerating them."
6. It is more productive to act rather than react to situations involving teenagers.
7. It helps students use the vast resources purchased by libraries for their homework assignments.
8. Community partnerships and cooperative relationships are a vital part of serving this underserved age group.
9. Providing staff with specialized skills and knowledge enables them to meet this age group's special needs.

10. Providing materials and services fosters library use.
11. Most library resources are not available to young people elsewhere.
12. Because youth needs us.

Libraries cultivate and nurture children's reading and library use. Tremendous energy, time, and resources are put into building specialized children's collections and programs. Children who come into libraries soon learn they are special. Then, they enter junior high and quite suddenly they are ignored or merely tolerated. The responsibility libraries must feel to offer youth the chance to love reading and libraries should not disappear as the child ages.

There are several barriers discouraging YAs from becoming library users. The NCES report identifies some barriers that may be beyond the library's control, while others could be removed by innovative services. If YAs were surveyed, perhaps they would add another: library staff. The problem with some staff is simple: they just don't like teenagers. It is doubtful if this or any other book will help them get over that feeling. Most staff do want to help teenagers, but just don't have the tools. Most want to see the YAs find the information they need, get turned onto libraries, and have a positive library experience. The key is how well staff members provide services and break down barriers. The purpose of this book, then, is to break down barriers and do the job of connecting young adults and libraries.

ENDNOTES

1. Charles McClure et al., *Planning and Role Setting for Public Libraries: A Manual of Options and Procedures,* Chicago: American Library Association, 1987.
2. Edwin Castagna, "Young Adult Service on the Public Library Organization Chart," *Library Trends* 17,2 (October 1968): 132-139.
3. JoAnn Rogers, ed., "Trends and Issues in Young Adult Services," *Libraries and Young Adults: Media, Services and Librarianship*, Littleton, CO: Libraries Unlimited, 1979, 67-74.
4. Thomas Wm. Downen, "YA Services: 1993," unpublished paper, 1979?.
5. National Center for Education Statistics, *Services and Resources for Young Adults in Public Libraries,* Washington, DC: Government Printing Office, July 1988.

2 YOUNG ADULTS IN LIBRARIES

2.1 CONTRADICTIONS

Connecting Young Adults and Libraries is about serving YAs. Providing outstanding service means those currently using your library will have a positive experience and will create more demand in the future. A positive library experience would mean that YAs find what they need, don't feel frustrated, feel they have been helped (not hindered), and want to come back. Yet, at the same time, many staff members think there are already too many YAs in the library. They probably refer to them as "those kids," or if you are assigned any YA responsibility then it becomes "those kids of yours." Whoever is assigned YA tasks immediately begins to hear that possessive pronoun from colleagues. Because it is your task, everyone else is relieved, for now the YAs are your "problem."

This core contradiction is not the only one in YA services. Let's look at some others:

1. Libraries' most obvious priority is promoting reading, but during the YA years, many individuals either stop reading for pleasure or assign it a lower priority.
2. Libraries are about research but for many YAs, doing research for their school term papers is about the worst thing they will ever experience. Many will associate libraries with a negative rather than positive experience.
3. Libraries are about programs, but as the National Center for Education Statistics (NCES) report indicated, the main barrier for most YAs is competition from other programs or activities.
4. Libraries are like schools—run by adults with lots of rules, but the school experience is not pleasant for many YAs. Adults and their rules are a root cause of dissatisfaction.
5. Libraries are about limits—we claim access, but to a lot of YAs libraries are in the limiting business. We limit what books people can check out, how many they check out, when they are due back, how they can behave in the building, how many people can sit at one table, etc. Libraries are filled with limits and the essence of the YA experience is testing limits.

Consequently, the very group we want to serve, in many cases and for many reasons, doesn't want to be served. As the NCES reported, many YAs are in libraries seeking assistance and checking out materials because they must do so to do well at their job, which is making it through school.

2.2 PERCEPTIONS

The contradictions above are based on some rather broad generalizations about libraries and YAs. They indicate different sets of priorities. Let's look at some more generalizations. If we asked librarians to make a list of stereotypical characteristics of teenagers what might they come up with?

STEREOTYPES OF YAs HELD BY LIBRARIANS

1. Loud and obnoxious
2. Full of energy and enthusiasm
3. Rushed
4. Disorganized and chaotic
5. Emotional
6. Flip and disrespectful
7. Unpredictable
8. Physical/sexual
9. Concerned with "hip" or cool
10. FUN!!
11. Tuned into audiovisual media
12. Travel in packs
13. Destructive
14. Dangerous
15. Weird looking
16. Smartalecks
17. Pressured
18. Not interested in libraries.

Now, what if we asked YAs to make the same kind of list about us?

STEREOTYPES OF LIBRARIANS HELD BY YAs

1. Shhhh! Obsessed with quiet
2. Dull and staid
3. Slow people/slow computers/slow systems
4. Anal-retentive detail freaks
5. Cold and uncaring about anything but order
6. Solemn
7. Rigid
8. Intellectual/neutered
9. Out of touch with the times
10. BORING!

11. Bookworms
12. Can't deal with more than one person at a time
13. Overprotective of their precious books
14. Weaklings
15. Women with buns; men with silly ties
16. Serious
17. Laid back
18. Not interested in teenagers

Even for staff with a good YAttitude, there are barriers to overcome based on the nature of the relationship. There are not just two different sets of perceptions, but two totally different worlds. Librarians and YAs have different sets of values, priorities, norms, and even to some degree totally different languages—when YAs use slang we are amazed they expect us to know what it means, but when we toss out terms like "bibliographic record" we wonder why they don't understand us.

Where is the common ground? If our two worlds are so different, why do they intersect? Simple necessity is the answer. We have a resource called information. We have it, control it, and provide access to it—and they need it. Sometimes they need it to do their jobs, sometimes to kill some time, and sometimes to save their lives. The element of power is inherent here. Because we have information they need and they have to go through us to get it, libraries have some measure of power over YAs.

Assumption: many YAs don't want to be in libraries. They are there because they have to be: it is not a matter of their choice. They have to come to the library to find information they aren't interested in to write a paper they don't want to write to hand in to a teacher they don't even like to get a grade in a class they can't stand so they can graduate from the school which they loathe so they can get away from their parents who they also might just loathe at any given moment. Many come to the library, then, with more than just a notebook and pencil (which many will forget and ask you for); many come with a negative attitude. It's the attitude anyone might have when forced to be someplace you really don't want to be. Even in the summer or after school, YAs may be hanging out in groups looking at magazines because they don't have any other place to go. Many YAs come to us out of obligation or boredom: not exactly the best start to a successful relationship.

When they get to the library, what do they find? Often an overworked staff without enough resources to do their jobs well, feeling burnt out from too many reference questions, and frustrated from too few reference sources. They find a librarian sitting at a desk waiting grimly for the next patron or problem.

Then in walks the 16 year old with a purple Mohawk thirty minutes before closing. He would rather be anywhere else in the world, but needs (by tomorrow) a term paper on the uses of religious symbolism in the plays of Edward Albee. He can't figure out how the computer catalog works, but after he and his friends have a good time laughing about it, he comes to the reference desk to ask for help. It would not be surprising if the librarian at the reference desk failed to act as a bridge bringing this hypothetical young man into the world of information. High stress levels create barriers and no connection is made.

2.3 STRATEGIES

What strategies can be used to reduce the tension and stress? Let's look at some day-to-day over-the-desk strategies for serving YAs and some strategies for dealing with "problem" groups that will forge a relationship between librarians and YAs.

Listen: Hear what the YA means rather than just what is said. Answer the question with your ears first, then your lips. There will be a lot of "static" in the communication so you will have to work hard to really listen for the question.

Cooperate: Remember that you each need something. They need the information and you need to help them. Work with them, not against them. Approach the question as a problem you are going to solve together. You have to clarify the information you need to do this and what they can do to help you.

Establish YA relationships: If YAs travel in groups, then the group has a leader who is usually easy to spot. Direct your energies toward meeting this person—getting a name and whatever else he or she is willing to tell you. If you can get a group leader on "your side," then peer pressure may help control behavior problems and increase levels of communication.

Establish outside relationships: Not just with the YAs, but with schools and the police department. If you are having problems, tell them your concerns, and your library's policies. Schools might want to make you the assistant truant officer, which is not your role.

Be firm, fair and consistent: Don't treat the rockers and the preppies differently. Give everyone the same fair choice: either modify behavior (sit down, shut up, whatever) or leave. Tell them you don't want to kick them out, but they will be choosing to leave if they don't modify inappropriate behavior. Finally, everyone on staff needs a clear understanding of what the limits are: of what is allowed and not allowed. The rules can't change from day-to-day. That is why it is best for one or two people to be responsible for dealing with YAs so the same message is consistently transmitted.

Be creative: YAs' problem behavior results from the powderkeg of too much energy combined with too much boredom. Use your collection, your computers, your audio and visual media, and your other resources to channel YAs into productive activities.

Keep your cool: The two worst things you can do are get angry or powertrip. When you get angry, they "win." Sometimes part of the game is testing the limits to see what they can say or do to upset you. Reacting with anger provides a payoff for undesirable behavior. Second, the dynamics of the situation give you "power" over them. If you abuse your power (throwing them out arbitrarily, for example), then you are setting up a dangerous situation. Never humiliate or embarrass a YA. If you are angry or authoritarian you are creating a situation where somebody—either you or the YA—always loses.

Don't take it personally: Part of testing limits is seeing what things can be said. It is a natural YA tendency to want to shock. Probably they will try it on you. Fine. It has nothing to do with you—but if you overreact it sets up another situation down the road.

Develop mutual understanding: Empathize with their situation and try to understand "where they are coming from." If you pick up signals that a YA is in a hurry, then take shortcuts. You need to understand not only what information is needed, but also the best way to get it based on a particular YA's situation.

Be accepting: Most reference policies have a statement that school assignments should be treated like any other reference question. That policy has to be practiced.

Avoid stereotyping YAs: Remember that the list at the beginning of this chapter was an awareness exercise, not a list of actual traits.

Avoid stereotyping yourself: You are who you are. If you don't want YAs to treat you like a stereotype, then don't behave like one. If you want to spend your time saying "shhhhh," then don't expect to make good connections with YAs.

Be nonjudgmental: Just because a young man has long hair doesn't mean he wants books on sex, drugs, or rock 'n' roll. Wait until you hear the question before you come up with the answer.

Be enthusiastic: Just because you've answered a particular reference question 20 times, doesn't mean it is not new to the person asking it. If you are not enthusiastic about libraries, then what message does that send to the YA?

Watch your face: Smart YAs know the librarians to avoid—they recognize the ones whose faces start to get tight the minute teens walk through the door. If you've given your "good face" to a business patron, and then a YA walks up, the same nonverbal signals have to be transmitted. Think how young people feel seeing you joking, chatting, and being very attentive to an adult, and turning into a frowning "nightmare librarian from hell" when they walk up to the desk.

Lighten up: Sometimes YAs seem serious or awkward but underneath there is often casualness, lightness. If we come across as always putting things ahead of people, order ahead of everything, we turn off YAs. Kids make mistakes: they do a lot of dumb stuff which is not the end of the world, the Dewey Decimal system, or even of your library. If we over-react to every infraction, then connections become hard to make. Having a sense of humor is the single best way to connect with YAs. It is not a matter of being funny, just not being too serious. The stress we feel from YAs doesn't come from them, but from ourselves.

Share, don't teach: Information and library resources are for everyone. Again, the dynamics of the relationship put YAs almost in a subservient position, so we should share our knowledge in such a way as to build some equity that empowers them in the relationship. We are already authority figures; we don't have to act authoritarian.

Project/remember: Think back to when you were doing term papers. Was it your first time in a library? Was it the first time you needed to ask for help? Didn't you have other things on your mind and other priorities? Maybe you didn't look like that kid with the Mohawk standing across from you now, but underneath there is the quintessential experience of adolescence that manifests itself differently but also remains the same.

Be tolerant: Face facts: it is not just that YAs are loud (which they are) but that any group of people interacting in your library is going to make noise. Libraries tolerate babies crying, preschoolers screaming happily after story hour, senior citizens talking about the program they have just left, and even a group of staff gathered around a desk, but two YAs get together and criticism seems to double.

Develop a YAttitude: Recognize that a lot of the things they do are things that kids do because they are kids. Recognize that they wouldn't be in the library unless they needed either our help or our resources, so we have an obligation to meet that need.

These strategies won't work in every situation. They are general guidelines for improving the connection between YAs and libraries. There will be YAs you can't reach. There are YAs who are hostile, even nasty, to you despite your best efforts. They may be carrying more emotional baggage with them than you can readily imagine. Chances are you won't be getting through to seriously troubled YAs—their parents and teachers probably can't either. Nevertheless, the strategies here may help smooth your dealings with most of the YAs who come to your library.

2.4 BEHAVIOR

When your library automated, probably (hopefully) a great deal of thought, time, and planning went into implementing the change. For everyone on the staff, automation meant a change in job, for some slight, for others even job elimination. During the automation process, the staff probably experienced a higher level of stress, behaving perhaps with a little hostility or impatience. Change does that to people. Now, think back to when your entire world was changing—all of your relationships, your body, your voice, everything. Remember feeling differently about every single person you interacted with on a given day? That's adolescence.

There is a mountain of literature about adolescent psychology—from scholarly tomes to pop psych to books written for teens. The common theme, of course, is change. No longer are they children, not yet are they adults. Instead they inhabit a shifting state of transformation. It is during these same years that YAs must make choices about their futures, their sexuality, their relationships. These choices have always been there, but in the 1990s YAs have more pressures, more roadblocks, and more dangerous detours. No one would want to be 15 again.

To understand more, take a brief look into the world of adolescent psychology. There are various ways to approach this subject. Our main concern is what young people do in the library (our environment), but by looking at YAs' other interests and involvements, we can begin to understand what makes them tick. Figure 2-1, taken from *Being Adolescent* by adolescent psychologists Reed Larson and Mihaly Csikszentmihalyi, shows how YAs spend their time.[1]

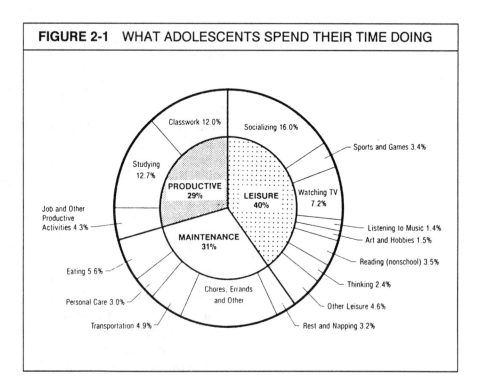

FIGURE 2-1   WHAT ADOLESCENTS SPEND THEIR TIME DOING

2.5 DEVELOPMENTAL TASKS

All the behaviors that drive us crazy about YAs (and make us like them) stem from the developmental tasks essential to adolescence: emotional, social, sexual, intellectual, and psychological changes. Different writers define them in different ways. For our purposes, we will define four of these tasks, and look at what types of programs, services, and resources libraries can develop to meet the needs associated with each task.

Gaining Independence: From birth, children depend upon their parents. During the YA years this basic relationship is challenged and changed as teens learn to do things on their own. Each step is a step away from dependence: from the first time they stay home alone to their first dates. Part of achieving independence is learning responsibility, and part is acting rebelliously. Perhaps rebellion is the most noticeable YA trait.

Library responses:

1. Library cards: All YAs should have their own cards so they can check out materials independent of their parents. This helps them learn about responsibility. At the beginning of each school year, campaigns should be launched in cooperation with schools to get every YA registered for a card.
2. Library instruction: By teaching YAs how to use our resources effectively, we allow them to work independently of us and of their parents. Instruction can help YAs learn about decision making (which resources to use) and time management.
3. Volunteerism: A teen volunteer program gives YAs a chance to experience the independence of working for someone who is not a family member.
4. Advisory groups: Advisory groups provide teens with a forum to learn decision-making skills, take on new responsibilities and participate in different programs and projects.
5. Music collection: Rap music isn't popular just because of the booming backing tracks. For many white suburban YAs, listening to rap is wearing their rebellion badge. That's nothing new; music has been a channel for teen rebellion for years. The change in the 1990s, however, is that music has become more controversial as YAs seek alternatives to the "top 40" mainstream and listen to more rap and thrash. One of the prime "declarations of independence" for a YA is to get control of his

or her own stereo system. There's probably no redder flag to wave in front of a teen than to say "turn that music down."

Managing Excitement: Because everything changes, everything is possible. Physical changes have wrought emotional changes and now the world is a more exciting (and scary) place with many more possibilities, opportunities, and dangers. Excitement manifests itself in abundance of energy, wild enthusiasm, good humor, bad pranks, vandalism, and the desire to be on-the-move.

Library responses:

1. Programming: Programs can offer teens a chance to participate rather than react passively. They can generate enthusiasm and channel energy into productive pursuits.
2. A YA Area: YAs need their own space, not just a collection of YA books. Not only does a YA area answer the need for independence (their own room), it can also be the place where exciting things happen. From the staff's perspective, a YA area means YAs will congregate there rather than spreading their potentially disruptive energy through the entire building. This area needs good materials, comfortable chairs organized so socializing can occur, and a welcoming atmosphere created by posters and appropriate decoration.
3. Magazines: Because YA attention span is short, magazines are a desirable reading format. In addition, magazines are current so they cover what is "hot," are full of photos, and meet the need for short bursts of information and/or leisure reading.
4. Games: YA areas should have board games and/or computer games. There's the excitement of winning, playing, interacting. Games speak to the YA need "to do." Games are social in nature, require mind energy, and offer opportunities for laughs, and some structured acting up.
5. Adjust expectations: You cannot expect a group of YAs full of pent-up energy from a day of school to walk into the library and be perfectly still and quiet. There are limits and there are realistic expectations, but if the expectations are not flexible, then an impossible situation is being created for both you and the YAs.

Searching for Identity: "Who am I?" is the basic YA question. Teens define themselves in many ways: some try to be as similar to everyone else as possible; some try to be as unique as possible. The search for identity brings on even more changes as YAs attempt to say, scream, or whisper in what they say, wear, do, and read the answers to this question of "who am I?"

Library responses

1. Readers advisory: What people read helps to define them. By helping YAs match their interests with the library's collections, you are helping them establish an identity. First, you are reinforcing their self-images as readers, but perhaps also certain kinds of reader. The Stephen King fan is a special breed, and by nurturing this kind of bent you might make a real connection with a YA.

2. Share interests: Not every single thing YAs are interested in is totally alien to you. Often YAs feel some doubts about the things they like or don't like, especially if those things are outside the YA mainstream. A library I worked in was frequented by a bunch of adolescent boys who were interested in professional wrestling. Since this was an interest I shared, I think some of these YAs realized that it wasn't such a weird thing to like, and the shared interest helped establish a rapport.

3. Writing programs: Offering YAs an opportunity to express themselves creatively on paper is a fantastic way to meet their developmental needs. Through writing, YAs explore themselves. You will be amazed, even shocked, at the things they come out with. Many YAs find their "darkside" when they pick up a pen.

4. Artist's programs: The same can happen when they pick up a paint brush, or a camera. Working with schools to develop a student art show might involve even more YAs than a writing program. Art, however, should be broadly defined to include all the kinds of art YAs like and use to define themselves: comics, cartoons, album cover design, fashion, graffiti, video, collage, even skateboard decoration.

5. Individualize: The best thing about being a YA librarian is getting paid to sit and talk with and listen to YAs. The most difficult thing for a non-YA librarian is finding time to do this. Not only is there not enough time, there are often too many people. Because YAs often travels in packs, it is hard to get to know individuals. Some YAs will respond to you immediately, while others are harder to reach. During a reference interview there really isn't time to learn anything, except perhaps a name. But that's a big thing. If you can learn the names of the young people who frequent your building, that is a good first step. Getting to know names, faces, and personalities of even a few

YAs makes it harder to stereotype and easier to accept them as valuable individuals.

Seeking Acceptance: Because the YA seeks independence, looks for excitement (but sometimes only finds trouble), and tries to develop an identity, the last developmental task is learning to find acceptance. As they are redefining themselves and their relationships, they make mistakes—most of them small, a few of them big. Because they lack experience they also lack the perspective to see the true magnitude of a particular mistake. Because they try so hard to develop and carry off a self, it is a fragile thing, under constant attack from outside and inside.

Library responses:

1. Space: Not so much physical space, as psychological space. The most basic thing any library can provide is a place for people to sit and think. Sometimes that is all a YA really needs and wants from us—some place just to be left alone. When we provide the space, then we must be careful not to invade it. If a YA is in the building during a school morning watching filmstrips in the children's room, then that YA is staking out a comfortable space for whatever reason.
2. Positive experience: A YA who comes to the library and finds unfriendly service, no information on hot topics, and frustrating technology will have a negative library experience. The tone needs to be set for all patrons, but especially for the YA, that the library is a place where they can "win." It is a place that is inviting with people so helpful that they don't end up frustrated. YAs are so self-conscious that any sort of rudeness they take very personally and remember. They will also think it is their fault somehow. They'll leave with the thought: "all I wanted was help on my term paper, but this. . ." Because the ego is fragile, it is often displayed with macho bravado or extreme shyness—neither of these traits are the easiest to work with in a reference interview. We are accepting by being inviting and helpful.
3. "Deal with it": YAs are sometimes going to hurl chess pieces across the room, and they will rip out pictures from magazines. This *behavior* is unacceptable, but the young person exhibiting it is not. This is the message that must be conveyed. Correct the behavior, not the person.
4. Outreach: There are lots of YAs who may never come into a library or if they do they aren't noticed. They are the YAs who

don't get into the honors class, don't write or draw and don't hang out in front of the building smoking. The only way to meet this large group is to get into the schools or get the schools into our libraries. We need to tell these YAs about what we do and what we have and that they are welcome.

5. Meeting special needs: Everyone is accepted. YAs who can't read are welcomed into the library. So are YAs who don't speak English or can't speak at all. Those serving YAs need always to be conscious of the fact that there is no average YA, and all sorts of teenagers have special needs. If librarians can't answer these needs (literacy training for out-of-school YAs for example) then they should be aware of the resources in the community which can meet these needs.

2.6 LEVELS OF RESPONSE

All libraries already have YAs. The NCES survey described the services YAs used the most. If serving YAs fits into your library's role, then you need to assess current conditions. The question becomes: given limited resources, at what level can the library respond? To help you get the right answers, use the survey forms in Figures 2-2 and 2-3, which will help you evaluate your library and your audience.

Where do you want to be? Your self-assessment has revealed the strong and weak points of your service. Now develop a YA service plan to focus your resources on specific areas where you wish to see improvement. A sample plan sets down on paper what, when, and how much you want to accomplish [Figure 2-4].

Connecting YAs and libraries is a task full of contradictions. You can develop library instruction and measure its effectiveness, but you can't know if it actually saved YAs time and helped them write better papers. Collections are easier to measure, but circulation only measures the number of books checked out, not the number read or enjoyed. The final contradiction is that even when you improve service, you can't measure exactly how much you've improved service to the YAs. So even though you plan for YAs and measure services for them, it is only by talking with individual YAs that you really learn if you've made the connection.

ENDNOTE

1. Reed Larson and Mihaly Csikszentmihalyi, *Being Adolescent,* New York: Basic Books, 1984.

FIGURE 2-2   SELF-EVALUATION SURVEY FORM

Answer yes or no to each of the following questions. For each yes answer, consider at what level (high, medium, or low) the library provides the particular service or resource. For each no answer, consider whether it is a necessary service or resource and, if so, at what level it should be provided. This is a short exercise: it is not meant to be cover all the possible avenues for YA services.

The Basics:

1. Can YAs have their own library card?
2. Is there an area of the library for YAs?
3. Is any area, collection, or format restricted?
4. Is YA a defined user group in library statistics?
5. Is there a perceived "problem" with YAs?
6. Is there a perceived need for YA services?

The Collections:

1. Is there a separate book collection?
2. Does it have recreational reading materials?
3. Does it have informational reading materials?
4. Does the library have sufficient materials to assist YAs in completing homework assignments?
5. Is there a separate magazine collection?
6. Are there nonprint materials available?

The Services:

1. Do YAs receive quality reference services?
2. Do YAs receive quality readers advisory service?
3. Is there a library orientation program?
4. Is there a library instruction program?
5. Is there a booktalking program?
6. Is staff trained in serving YAs?

The Connections:

1. Is there a working relationship with schools?
2. Do school groups visit the library?
3. Does library staff visit schools?
4. Is there a working relationship with youth serving agencies?

The Programs:

1. Is there a need for YA programming?
2. Are programs planned for YAs?
3. Are programs planned in cooperation with YAs, schools, outside agencies?
4. Have past YA programs been successful?

FIGURE 2-3 YA USER SURVEY

---

1. Which of these describes your use of the library?

[ ] 3 times/more a week [ ]twice a week
[ ] once a week   [ ]twice a month
[ ] once a month   [ ]less than once a month

2. Do you have a library card? [ ]yes [ ]no [ ]lost it

3. Pick a number from the scale to describe how often you visit the library to do the things listed below.
1 = frequently   2 = sometimes   3 = seldom   4 = never

[ ] complete homework assignments
[ ] checkout materials to use for homework
[ ] checkout materials to read for fun
[ ] checkout materials to read for information
[ ] checkout tapes, cds, or records
[ ] checkout videotapes
[ ] meet and talk with friends
[ ] attend a library program
[ ] study
[ ] use equipment (copies, computer, typewriter)
[ ] other

4. Pick a number from the scale to describe the following at this library.
1 = excellent 2 = good 3 = okay 4 = not so good 5 = poor

[ ] choice of books
[ ] choice of reference books and indexes
[ ] choice of magazines and newspapers
[ ] choice of records, tapes, and cds
[ ] choice of video tapes
[ ] staff helpful finding materials for homework
[ ] staff helpful finding books to read for fun
[ ] library programs
[ ] computers and other equipment
[ ] YA area

5. If you don't often use the library, why not?

[ ] unable to get to the library
[ ] not enough time/too much else to do
[ ] nothing that interests me
[ ] don't need it
[ ] bad experiences in the past with library staff

6. Please tell us:

[ ]male [ ]female [ ]age [ ]grade

FIGURE 2-4 SERVICE PLAN

GOAL: To increase during the year _____ use of the library by young adults.

I. Assessment

  A. Evaluate current services and resources

  B. Identify needs of YA population
    1. Survey of YAs
    2. Survey of staff

II. Collection development

  A. Fiction
    1. Increase purchase of popular paperback titles/series/comics by _____
    2. Decrease purchase of hardbacks by _____

  B. Non-fiction
    1. Decrease purchase of reference books by _____
    2. Increase purchase of multiple copies about "hot topics" by _____

  C. Other
    1. Increase purchase of magazines by _____
    2. Decrease purchase of records by _____ and increase purchase of cds by _____

  D. Merchandising
    1. Weed collection by _____
    2. Reorganize to increase display space by _____

III. Services

  A. Schools
    1. Meet with teachers/librarian
    2. Increase tours/instruction by _____
    3. Increase library card registration of YAs by _____

  B. Programs
    1. Organize YA advisory group
    2. Plan at least _____ cooperative programs

IV. Evaluate

  A. Formal
    1. Increase in YA circulation by _____
    2. Increase in YA program (programs, tours, instruction, booktalks, etc.) _____
    3. Increase in YA library cards: _____

  B. Informal
    1. Staff perceptions/comments
    2. Letters/calls from outside sources

3 YOUNG ADULT COLLECTIONS

This section is not about YA literature. The bibliography at the end of this book lists the best sources for learning about that. Most titles cover the history of the literature, discuss major trends, and list significant titles. Donelson and Nilsen's *Literature for Today's Young Adult*[1] and Cline and McBride's *A Guide to Literature for Young Adults*[2] are probably the two best books of this type. Both have been used in library schools and in education courses as textbooks. Although both have sections which discuss "use" of YA literature which librarians might find practical, their focus is more academic, analyzing the literature and related issues.

The few library school courses with "young adult" in the title almost exclusively concern young adult literature. There might be a session on booktalking and some discussion of popular trends, but most of the time is spent discussing classic YA literature. Such courses aren't especially helpful in selecting, promoting, and managing YA collections. Collection use by YAs is not synonymous with YA literature.

YA literature commentator Patty Campbell wrote in her last "YA Perplex" column for *Wilson Library Bulletin* that:

> Young adult literature is alive and well in the bookstores, but it is a different young adult literature . . . Nowadays every B. Dalton and Walden's has its section labeled "Young Adult," but the books that are found there are of far lower quality and aimed at much younger readers than those that are found on the similarly labeled shelves in public libraries. With the exception of Judy Blume, their Big Names are not our Big Names. The whole field has become strangely bifurcated and we seem to be moving in the direction of two separate literatures.[3]

It could be argued that there are really four separate bodies—literature, books, information sources, and products. Of these subsets, perhaps YA literature is the smallest if it is defined as well-written novels in hardback format, which show up in our reviewing sources. That YA literature is studied in library school and put on the *Best Books for Young Adults* list, but it is not primarily what YAs read. YA books—defined as the mass market paperbacks that glut bookstores and libraries—are more popular. There are also YA products which we (and YAs) recognize instantly: series romances which are sold, not because they are good books, but because they bear a certain brand name (*Sweet Valley High,* etc.). The printed materials most often used by YAs are information sources (books, articles, etc.), which are a means to an end. Further, perhaps the most popular YA items in libraries are often

READING SURVEY #1

AUTHOR:
Constance Mellon
SOURCE:
School Library Journal (February 1987)
AUDIENCE:
Rural high school students

RESULTS:

1. Do you read in your spare time?

boys: 72%
girls: 92%

2. What materials do you choose for leisure reading? (top responses only)

Boys:
72% magazines
68% sports/sports biographies
54% comic books

Girls:
90% romance
73% mysteries
73% magazines

not even books: many more YAs are interested in the new Madonna CD or wrestling videotape than in Cynthia Voigt's most recent sure-to-be "Best Book" book.

3.1 READING INTERESTS

Despite all the print space given to YA literature, books are not the primary reading materials for YAs—periodicals are. A variety of reading interests surveys have revealed this and other facts as well.

READING SURVEYS:

1. *Who reads?*
   Survey 1 shows two important statistics: first, that it is primarily girls who read. This is not surprising. Reading is considered a "non-macho" activity by most male YAs, and since most boys are defining themselves within a "macho" model, reading is often disdained. Young men who read are "nerds" and the peer pressure against being a reader, while not intense, is not negligible. The sheer physical aspect of being an adolescent boy also works against "passive" activities such as reading.
2. *What is read (format)?*
   Surveys 1 and 2 both show the preference for periodicals. Survey 2 seems to indicate that this preference increases as YAs get older and develop more awareness of the world around them. They acquire more interests, so while a younger YA might look through only one or two magazines, older YAs might find something of interest in several YA magazines as well as adult ones. As YAs grow older, there are more demands on their time. Magazines provide a "quick fix." Survey 3 demonstrates this same curve and a related declining interest in novels as YAs grow older. For all grades, however, the preference for magazines is clear and consistent. This is also the finding in Survey 4 by Obert.
3. *What is read (subject)?*
   Surveys 3 and 4 begin to explore the genres that interest those teens reading books. Although not divided by gender, one could make some assumptions. It is interesting to note the sharp decline of interest in humor books as YAs get older and the staggering difference in the popularity of romance between the two surveys. The Obert survey was conducted in 1986, which

READING SURVEY #2

AUTHOR:
Betty-Kay Williams Murray
SOURCE:
in *Meeting the Challenge: Library Services to Young Adults*, edited by A. Gagnon. Ottawa, Canada: Canadian Library Association, 1985: 55-66
AUDIENCE:
YAs surveyed in schools, libraries, and malls

RESULTS:

Most frequently read formats:

Newspapers: 71%

Magazines:
35.9% (grades 7-8)
42.7% (grades 9-10)
44.4% (grades 11-12)

Books:
29.6% (boys)
42.0% (girls)

42.5% paperbacks
11.5% hardbacks
46.3% doesn't matter

was a peak time for series romances, while the Cornelius survey was done in 1990, when these books began to decline in popularity. It is interesting that in both surveys, science fiction seems to have carved out a small niche.

4. *Why is it read?*
Survey 5 investigates what YAs liked about books. Based on results from students participating in a special reading program the findings are not surprising.

5. *How is it chosen?*
Survey 6 is bad news for librarians. It indicates that only a small number of YAs look for advice from librarians. Not surprisingly, they look to their peers—not only because it is easier, but probably because the information is better. YAs trust visual clues and their own instincts, and browsing is the preferred choosing technique.

DESIGNING A READING INTEREST SURVEY

Maybe your community is different. Maybe there is real interest in science fiction; maybe there are more male readers. The only way to document is to develop and distribute a reading interest survey such as the one shown in Figure 3-1. Doing this requires six steps:

1. State the objectives of the survey. (What do you want to learn?)
2. Design the survey. (How will you learn it?)
3. Distribute the survey. (Who will complete the survey and when/where will it be used?)
4. Tabulate the survey. (What did you find out?)
5. Analyze the survey. (What did you learn?)
6. Take action. (What will you do?)

Your results will guide you in setting collection development priorities. This survey can't be a one-time thing, since reading interests change over time. You can distribute to every single YA in the community through the schools or hand it out more randomly. Either way, it will provide you with some data to make hard choices necessary to develop a YA collection.

3.2 CHOICES AND PRIORITIES

A basic question is, "What kind of YA collection do you want?" A YA section is usually small enough to be modified in a short period

READING SURVEY #3

AUTHOR:
Marcia Cornelius
SOURCE:
Unpublished (1990 survey)
AUDIENCE:
Suburban students grades 7-12

RESULTS:

Most frequently read formats:

Newspapers:
10% (all grades)
.4% (grades 7-8)
11% (grades 9-10)
14% (grades 11-12)

Magazines:
60% (all grades)
55% (grades 7-8)
54% (grades 9-10)
65% (grades 11-12)

Novels:
20% (all grades)
30% (grades 7-8)
20% (grades 9-10)
15% (grades 11-12)

Subjects:
(all grades)
28% adventure
23% mystery
18% romance
10% science fiction
7% fantasy
6% drama/realistic
4% biography
4% nonfiction

FIGURE 3-1   READING INTEREST SURVEY

AGE___   SCHOOL:_____   GRADE:___   MALE( ) FEMALE( )

We are interested in providing YOU with the very best reading materials. Please help us do that by telling us what YOU like and what you WANT to see us have.

1. Which of these is your favorite:
    [ ] newspapers
    [ ] magazines
    [ ] fiction
    [ ] nonfiction
    [ ] comic books
    [ ] biographies

2. Which type of fiction do you like most:
    [ ] horror
    [ ] romance
    [ ] adventure
    [ ] sports
    [ ] science fiction
    [ ] fantasy
    [ ] mystery/thriller
    [ ] humor
    [ ] historical
    [ ] teen problems
    [ ] other:_____

3. Which type of nonfiction do you like most:
    [ ] supernatural
    [ ] health
    [ ] music, television and movies
    [ ] sports
    [ ] history
    [ ] poetry
    [ ] science
    [ ] "coping" with teen problems
    [ ] religion
    [ ] true crime
    [ ] other:_____

4. How do you get materials to read?
    [ ]buy them [ ]public library [ ]school library

5. How do you choose what to read?
    [ ]friend [ ]librarian [ ]teacher [ ]browsing
    [ ]other:_____

READING SURVEY #4

AUTHOR:
Beverly Obert
SOURCE:
Illinois Libraries (January 1988):
46-53
AUDIENCE:
Rural students grades 7-12

RESULTS:

1. Which kind of books do you list to read most?

Romance:
70% (grade 7)
66% (grade 9)
76% (grade 11)

Sci fi/fantasy:
18% (grade 7)
9% (grade 9)
7% (grade 11)

Historical fiction:
0% (grade 7)
7% (grade 9)
3% (grades 11)

Adventure/mystery:
26% (grade 7)
27% (grade 9)
28% (grade 11)

Humor:
28% (grade 7)
2% (grade 9)
3% (grade 3)

Animals:
14% (grade 7)
2% (grade 9)
0% (grade 11)

2. Which of these do you like to read very much?

Comic books:
14% (grade 7)
7% (grade 9)
16% (grade 11)

Magazines:
44% (grade 7)
66% (grade 9)
69% (grade 11)

Newspapers:
12% (grade 7)
20% (grade 9)
21% (grade 11)

of time to reflect your particular vision. Your vision may be influenced by:

1. Library's total collection development philosophy.
2. Quality and quantity of school library collections.
3. Budget, space, and staff available.
4. Reading interest of YAs in your community.
5. Your own professional values.
6. What needs that collection should meet.
7. Your goals for the collection.
8. The roles the library has chosen for itself.

To realize your vision for the collection, you need to set priorities, because everything can't be done at once. A "balanced collection" is usually desirable, but if you really want to set priorities and concentrate efforts, funds, and space on particular areas, the collection will be out of balance. The whole battle about collection balance (popularity vs. quality; breadth vs. depth) involves some basic philosophical issues. Lets look at some of the choices with emphasis on the YA aspects. After each choice are a series of questions to use as a self-evaluation tool.

CHOICES

Popularity vs. Quality: The oldest debate needs to be settled first. Here are a few questions to consider:

• Do you buy series paperbacks?
• Do you buy multiple copies of some titles?
• Given money to buy only one book and a choice between a popular book and a quality one, which one would you choose?

Circulation vs. Standards: Does the library have a "responsibility" to provide YAs with materials of only high literary quality? Is it easier to quantify (perhaps in an annual report) an increase in circulation or literary standards being upheld?

• How do you measure a book's value?
• Is "will it move" the only selection criterion?
• Will a book's appearance on a "best books" list merit its purchase and place on the shelf?

Permanency vs. Immediacy: What should the turnover rate be in a YA collection? Should it be stocked with long-lasting hardbacks

READING SURVEY #5

AUTHOR:
Barbara Samuels
SOURCE:
Journal of Reading (May 1989)
AUDIENCE: YAs in "Young Adult Choice" reading program

RESULTS:

What did you like about this book?

18% subject matter
15% genre
14% characters
14% it was interesting
11% it was real
9% author's style
5% related to me
4% illustrations

that will last decades and create a permanent YA collection? Or should the collection be based on paperbacks that meet immediate reading interests but won't survive more than two years?

- Are hardbacks the exception or the rule?
- If you didn't buy a certain hardback, would anyone miss it?
- Should you continuously replace lost/stolen/damaged paperbacks?

Recreational vs. Educational: This choice goes back to the roles librarians choose. The decision also hinges on the state of the school libraries.

- Do the school libraries have strong collections?
- Does the adult/reference department buy sufficient copies of materials needed by YAs?
- Do you shelve any YA nonfiction in the YA area?

Professional vs. Prudent: Another old debate about professional values, personal opinions, and community standards. The bottom line: do you buy YA materials that you (and most adults) object to, but YAs love?

- Do you buy rap music?
- Would you buy a professional wrestling magazine which had pictures of a wrestler bleeding?
- Do you buy Stephen King for the YA collection?

Librarian vs. Book Buyer: If your focus is popular reading, then have you forsaken your "professionalism" to become a glorified Walden's book buyer? A group of YAs could probably select a more responsive collection than many librarians charged with developing YA collections.

- What parts of YA book selection take some degree of professional judgement?
- Is the best selector one who selects the most "best books" titles or the one who selects all the YA best sellers?
- Does being a librarian hinder the development of YA collections due to prejudices about what YAs "should" read?

These questions were designed to help you think about the different choices and prejudices in YA collections. More than any other library service, YA services are anchored by both knowledge

READING SURVEY #6

AUTHOR:
Donald Gallo
SOURCE:
American Libraries (November 1985)
AUDIENCE:
Students grades 4-12 in Connecticut

RESULTS:

Who turns young people on to new books?

Friends suggestion:
42% (grades 7-9)
38% (grades 10-12)

Browsing in store:
28% (grades 7-9)
31% (grades 10-12)

Browsing in library:
27% (grades 7-9)
18% (grades 10-12)

Store display:
7% (grades 7-9)
8% (grades 10-12)

Library display:
5% (grades 7-9)
5% (grades 10-12)

Librarians:
4% (grades 7-9)
2% (grades 10-12)

and attitude. Your attitude about what a library could and should mean in terms of its collection for YAs probably came out in answering these questions.

SETTING PRIORITIES

Part of your vision is probably tied to unlimited funds. Since that is never a reality, the choices you make are the first step in setting priorities. After defining what is important to you, you need to link your choices to budget allocations. The smaller the budget, the more important priority setting becomes. For example, if given $1,000 to spend on YA materials (an insult to some; a dream to others), what would you do with it? Figure 3-2 lists a few possible options. After doing this exercise, you may be surprised at the results. Perhaps it's not necessary to buy any of some types of materials. Realistically, for example, taking $75 from the book budget and spending it on magazines probably means buying five fewer hardbacks in exchange for at least five magazine subscriptions. With a small collection, a change in focus can really have impact, which you hope will be noticed by the ones it is designed to attract to the library.

3.3 FICTION

The lifeblood of any YA department is normally the fiction collection. YAs use nonfiction books from other parts of the library, but most who are looking for recreational or assigned fiction reading end up in the YA area. Knowing YA fiction becomes more difficult as publishers change, series stop then start, and one year's trend is stone dead by the next year. Here are some suggestions, trends, and ideas for developing YA collections. For more comprehensive reference, a core collection is listed in Appendixes B and C and includes bibliographic information.

HARDBACKS

If we gave the book selection task over to a YA, how many (if any) hardback fiction titles would that YA select? Bookstores don't stock them, reading interest surveys and casual observation show most YAs don't read them, yet libraries buy them. Why? Some of the arguments in favor of YA fiction in hardbacks:

FIGURE 3-2 PRIORITIES EXERCISE

BUDGET: $1,000

Break down this amount into categories and sub-categories.

PRINT: _____

NONPRINT: _____

I. PRINT:
    BOOKS
    MAGAZINES   _____
    OTHER   _____

    A. BOOKS:
        FICTION
        NONFICTION   _____

        1. FICTION:
           HARDBACKS
           PAPERBACKS   _____

        2. NONFICTION:
           INFORMATION   _____
           RECREATION   _____
           EDUCATION   _____
           REFERENCE   _____

    B. MAGAZINES   _____

II. NON-PRINT:

    A. LISTENING:
        RECORDS
        TAPES   _____
        CDs   _____

    B. VIEWING:
        INFORMATION
        RECREATION   _____
        EDUCATION   _____

    C. SOFTWARE:
        RECREATION
        EDUCATION   _____

Inertia: "We've always bought them." Because it has always been done, it's hard to stop doing it.

Values: Some librarians don't believe libraries should even have paperbacks.

Reviews: The major journals don't review most paperbacks, so they must not be important.

Balance: "We're a library, not a bookstore."

Only format: Some YA authors never get paperbacked.

Book lists: Try to find original paperbacks on any YALSA-produced list. The professional prejudice is still for hardbacks.

Permanency: Because it is a library, the assumption is that we buy books not just for now, but forever.

Shelf life: A hardback has more "value" because it will last longer.

Impatience: Since the hardbacks are reviewed, rather than waiting for the paperback, we snap up the book immediately so we have it.

Responsibility: Many first time writers come out in hardback, and many libraries feel a responsibility to purchase these writers.

Prejudice: Books that come out only in paperback, the logic goes, are "trash" and not worthy of a library's money.

Inertia (again): Publishers keep publishing, so libraries keep buying.

Following are some of the arguments against YA fiction in hardbacks:

Inertia: The fact that it has always been done doesn't make it right.

Value: Rather than placing a value on format or the quality of what is read, the value should be on reading—period.

Reviews: *VOYA* and other journals are getting much better about reviewing paperback originals and listing reprints, although a review is not always necessary. When a new Christopher Pike or

Sweet Valley High paperback is out you don't need a review to purchase it.

Balance: Maybe you can't really balance a YA collection. By balancing it, you dilute the impact it might have.

Format: True, many books do come out in hardback only. Also, many come out in paper only. The choice, then, is determined not so much by format as by content.

Lists: Many who sit on YALSA book committees are library oriented and are prejudiced against paperbacks. Publishers and librarians who care about these lists need to lobby for the inclusion of paperback originals.

Permanency: YA collections are not like the children's room, where mothers will tell six-year-olds about books they read when they were children. The nature of the parent-child relationship in the teen years doesn't usually include recommending books. Ask yourself whether you need even YA classics in hardback, or if multiple paperback copies will do.

Shelf life: A hardback does have a longer shelf life—often because that is where the book is most of the time—sitting on a shelf.

Impatience: There is no *New York Times* bestseller list for YA hardback fiction, so if you don't buy it right away, no one will notice.

Responsibility: A tough call. If people had passed up books by fine new writers like Bruce Brooks, Chris Crutcher and Joyce Sweeney because they first came out in hardback, would they ever have gotten into paperbacks and reached the wide audience they deserve?

Inertia (again): If libraries stopped buying, would publishers stop publishing?

After reviewing all the arguments pro and con, some libraries still will not want to stop buying hardbacks. In a large library system perhaps the main library could keep up with hardbacks while the branches reallocate their money to paperbacks and magazines. If you cannot stop buying hardbacks altogether, then what criteria should you look for?

Author: If it is Peck, Hinton, Cormier, or Duncan, buy it. If the author is always showing up on lists and has mass appeal, take the plunge. If it's an adult author with YA appeal like King or Koontz, then the YAs will know about it and you'll need to have it.

Controversy: If it is getting wildly mixed reviews (*Weetzie Bat*), then it is worth a look and maybe a purchase.

On a list: If it is on a YALSA list, then it should at least be considered.

Built-in audience: Despite the format, some hardbacks have built in audiences because of the subject.

Great cover: If you can actually examine the book, the cover might be a selling point. "You can't judge a book by its cover," but for YAs it can affect popularity.

Too good: Then a book like *The Silver Kiss* by Annette Curtis Klause comes out and blows all these reasons away. If a book is getting praised everywhere like this one, then despite its format it will find an audience.

The smaller the budget, the harder you look at each purchase. If you spend $16, how can you justify it? If every book has to earn its place on the shelf, then the question is: what can a certain hardback bring to your collection, your YA population, and your circulation that several paperbacks or a magazine subscription cannot?

PAPERBACKS
The advantages to a primarily paperback YA fiction collection are numerous, including:

Preferred format: For reading in the library, for checking out, for hiding in textbooks, for all sorts of reasons both licit and illicit.

Multiple copy option: The low cost means more copies of a hot title.

Meet fluctuating demand: All those *New Kids on the Block* paperbacks you bought a year ago no one wants to touch now. But because publishers use paperback to latch onto fads, libraries follow.

Cost: Is it more costly to buy and replace five copies of a title in paperback or to keep a reserve list for the hardback copy?

Shelving: Paperbacks are the cornerstone of merchandising because of their size; you can cram more of them attractively into a small area.

Covers and blurbs: It seems hardback covers are designed to interest readers, while paperback covers are designed to excite them.

Every month about 50 mass market YA paperbacks are published: some are originals, some reprints, and the rest part of a series. In addition, mass market adult, humor, science fiction/fantasy, and movie tie-in titles are published that have YA appeal. There are titles in need of replacing due to theft or damage, books on reading lists, and older titles of popular authors which can be purchased.

Let's look at some of the more popular types of series and genres currently available. Although the market changes and changes fast, the categories outlined below seem to remain fairly consistent in their popularity.

TYPES OF SERIES

Girls' romances: The boom is certainly over as many of the old standbys (*Cheerleaders, Couples,* etc) have ceased publication, and even those hanging on don't seem to dominate the market as they once did. These can be divided into several subcategories:

* **Older teens:** *Portraits, Freshman Dorm* and several others not only focus on older characters, but the books themselves are longer. Because the characters are older, the situations are slightly more mature, but not much. For the teen who is past *Sweet Valley High (SVH)* but not yet into *Forever* or Norma Klein.
* **Younger teens:** These are not mass market but trade size books. These are probably a hotter market now than YA series. The "big ones" are *Babysitters Club* and *Sweet Valley Twins (SVT).* Readers tend to be pre-teens but they concern us because it shows how kids get "hooked" on series earlier than ever before. The creation of *Sweet Valley Kids (SVK)* for grade-schoolers makes one wonder if *Sweet Valley Babies (SVB)* or *Sweet Valley Embryos (SVE)* can be far behind.

- **Romance plus:** *SVH* is now concerning itself with issues weightier than "the big dance." The message of *SVH* used to be "a boyfriend solves everything." Nevertheless, a recent trend in books about girls with interests beyond boys seems to have petered out. Series like *Blue Ribbon* or *Silver Skates* presented girls interested in other things too.
- **Realism:** The *Nowhere High* series and the new *Hotline* series are an attempt to mix series and soap opera settings with larger issues. Both of these series move romance off the front burner, and often off the page completely.
- **Trilogies:** Publishers have been burned by fickle teen taste as some series get one or two books out, then disappear. Instead of using series writers or committees, publishers are getting "real" YA authors like Jean Thesman to write trilogies.
- **Cross genres:** Romance and mystery combined! Publishers are hedging their bets by putting out series that mix popular elements. Could a merger lead to *Sweet Valley Nancy Drew High's Files?*
- **The Venerables:** Will anyone ever graduate from *SVH?* The life of this series is amazing—too long to be just a fad. The publisher has been smart too, throwing in *Super Thrillers* and now *Superstars* to ever keep the series from getting too dull.

Boys series: Lots of publishers have tried, but with the exception of *Hardy Boys Case Files,* none of them has lasted long.

- **Sports:** Ballantine pushed a whole line of these recently (*Hoops, Rookies,* and *Blitz*) but they have ceased.
- **Adventure:** Boys who get hooked on *Choose Your Own Adventures* won't find much at the YA level except for the similar series *Time Machine.* A new series called *Escape from Lost Island* seems aimed directly at reluctant boy readers, which is a tough audience to get to check out books, let alone buy them.
- **Sci-fi/fantasy:** Adult series and trilogies are popular, but there's not much for younger YA boys (or girls).

Thriller series: This has been the real boom area and will remain so until publishers over-saturate the market. Mixing classic mystery techniques with a tip of the hat to horror (more in the titles and mood than actual events) these titles like *Fear Street* and *Horror High* have struck a nerve. Spurred on by the success of Christopher Pike, publishers have rushed to market with Scholastic and Archway leading.

BUYING SERIES

Getting information: You cannot count on the review media to publish data on series, even when a new series comes out. Instead, the monthly jobber catalogs *Hot Picks* by Baker & Taylor or *Paperback Advance* by Ingram will keep you current.

Keeping track: Now that there are fewer series, it is less of a problem, but you might want to keep a simple log using the form in Figure 3-3. This will tell you when you ordered each installment and how many copies. Later, update this log with circulation statistics to see how well the series is doing, and if you need to buy more/less.

Replacements: Series paperbacks have a short shelf life. Not just because of the poor quality of the binding, but also because most of them will get passed around a lot. It is important to keep a full run of the most popular series. Just because *SVH* is up to number 80 does not mean that someone isn't just starting the series who wants to read the first ten.

SHELVING SERIES

Chapter 7 covers merchandising more fully, but it should be noted here how to shelve series. While most YA paperbacks should be housed in some sort of face front unit, *SVH* and the like don't need that. In fact, normal library shelving adjusted to paperback size does just fine. There is no need for any signage or poster because a row of *SVH* with number 1 to 80 all lined up will attract attention and meet the series patron's need (the covers don't matter, it is all in the numbers).

Genres

A book's subject and/or its genre is one of the biggest selling points for a YA title. Many libraries shelve all paperbacks by genre rather than by author, or if not that extreme, then they provide extensive finding aids such as booklists or labels to help students locate certain types of fiction books. YALSA has gotten into the genre act by working with Baker & Taylor to produce genre book dumps based on the suggestions of YALSA genre committees. Like series,

FIGURE 3-3 SERIES LOG

SERIES NAME:_____

PUBLISHER: _____PRICE:_____

ORDER DATE	SERIES #	TITLE	# OF COPIES	CIRC STATS
_____	_____	_____	_____	_____
_____	_____	_____	_____	_____
_____	_____	_____	_____	_____
_____	_____	_____	_____	_____
_____	_____	_____	_____	_____
_____	_____	_____	_____	_____
_____	_____	_____	_____	_____
_____	_____	_____	_____	_____
_____	_____	_____	_____	_____
_____	_____	_____	_____	_____
_____	_____	_____	_____	_____
_____	_____	_____	_____	_____
_____	_____	_____	_____	_____
_____	_____	_____	_____	_____
_____	_____	_____	_____	_____
_____	_____	_____	_____	_____

genres change in popularity and sometimes some types of books will be more in demand than others, but here are the basic groups:

HORROR

YAs love scary movies and scary books, but unfortunately there are no YA horror writers. Pike, Stine, and Duncan write thrillers with some elements of horror, but they are not true horror. The most popular writers are adult authors like Stephen King. The YALSA genre committee on horror could not even find one YA novel to put on its list: the titles were either by adult authors or not scary (Mahy's *The Changeover* is supernatural, but there's no element of terror). A YA who has read *Carrie* is not going to settle for Duncan's *The Third Eye*. And if they've read all the King, finding other adult authors for YAs is not an easy task. Once you start looking at the use of language, sex, and violence in these other works, then King becomes mild.

REALISTIC FICTION (AKA THE PROBLEM NOVEL)

In the mid 1980s, *Booklist* did two lists called "teen traumas."[4] Sometimes there seems to be even more suicide, incest, and divorce in YA novels than in real life. This area peaked as new boundaries and taboos were first explored. The new trend is to combine problems. So now instead of a book about a teen alcoholic, the book might have a teen alcoholic with an anorexic sister who is having suicidal thoughts because their parents have just divorced. Despite the differences in subjects, the problem novel models are rather similar. A character has a problem or comes to that realization and then seeks to solve it. The one constant in almost all YA fiction is that the problem is solved, the protagonist grows and life is good.

Sex: If *Forever* is not the most read, then it contains the most read pages (p. 57 for example) of any YA novel. This book may not have the most circulations, but chances are it is the one that is most stolen, most beaten up, most often found anyplace but where it is supposed to be shelved, and most in need of replacement. This book won't ever be repeated and perhaps could not even get published today. Although there are certainly YA books with sexual themes, it seems the age of AIDS has elicited a more conservative approach from everyone: authors, publishers, and YA literature critics.

Substance abuse: More blatant "just say no" titles are coming out, and that message is being buried inside of other books as well.

Rather than the nightmare approach of a *Go Ask Alice,* this new breed contains more "normal" characters with less shocking abuses.

Headline books: As soon as some topics become "hot" you can count on a YA novel to follow. Nineties issues like steroids and date rape have already spawned YA fiction.

Physically challenged: A central theme in YA fiction is the overcoming of adversity. Books with YAs who are physically challenged thus will always have high appeal.

The gang novel: *The Outsiders* remains popular not just because of the violence, but because of the central theme of youth banding together without adult authority.

The secret: Christopher Pike's thrillers met success not just because of the suspense but because his early books were built around one teen character having a "dark secret past."

Violence: Another appealing aspect of *The Outsiders* is its violence. The media is overrun with violence and teens are finding their own environment—schools, homes, and relationships—increasingly violent. Thus, the popularity of these books, especially for boys.

Social issues: Issues like homelessness, sexism, and racism are showing up more often in novels which differ from the headline books in having a little more meat on the bone. As the environmental movement heats up more YA books will probably feature this as a theme.

Parent-teen relationships: The core conflict of adolescence is this relationship. The current literature puts less stress on the "parents are evil" message and attempts to show YAs the pressures and histories parents may have.

Death: Of a family member, of a friend, of a stranger, or self-inflicted. With YAs so full of life, the preoccupation with death is easy to explain and hard to ignore when choosing books. The success of Lurlene McDaniel's tear jerkers demonstrate this phenomenon.

Growing up: The biggest problem of all. Looking at the winners of the Delacorte Best First YA Novel award, most of the recent

ASSIGNMENT

To better understand what each of these "schools" is about read Lois Duncan's *I Know What You Did Last Summer* and Christopher Pike's *Chain Letter.* These two are similar in the basic situation, but different in their approach. After reading these two books (each should take less than two hours), compare the following points:

1. How is mystery set up?
2. Are characters likeable?
3. Does plot use red herrings? Cliffhangers?
4. Are there scary or gross events?
5. Which "letter" is more effective?
6. Is the ending believable? Shocking?
7. Which one did you like better?
8. Which one do you think YAs would like better?
9. Which one hangs together better?

ones have had no greater theme than this search for identity, independence, excitement, and acceptance.

MYSTERY/SUSPENSE

This has been a the hot area for the past few years. You could look at these as the big metaphor for YAs looking for clues to the mystery of their own identity, or flip 180 degrees and regard these books as providing great escapism from just those issues.

The Pike school: Fast read even though there are often a lot of characters. The "killer" sometimes steps in to narrate a chapter or two written in italics. The killer is usually one of the kids or sometimes an older sibling who is seeking revenge for some great wrong. Thus, the basic plot is revenge. Plenty of red herrings and the obligatory gross warning/prank: blood in the locker, prank phone calls, strange fires, etc. The books' covers are always well done with lots of dark colors and jacket blurbs that read like movie ad copy. The biggest complaints (by librarians, not YAs) against these books is that the characters are not likable.

The Duncan School: Usually a slower read with fewer characters, although most are likeable. Less reliance on the supernatural and more on detective work: Joan Nixon's books are typical of this category. These books are paperback reprints by award winning authors. Even though the times and YAs have changed, the basic "feel" of this book hasn't changed.

Nancy Drew school: Although Pike and Duncan's characters often "solve" the mystery, the main characters are not teen detectives. The Nancy Drew honored tradition of teen sleuths is still popular, and not just in series.

ROMANCE

Plenty of good romances come along which are of higher quality than those in a series. The main factor in a romance is the author's gender. Although some authors—such as Norma Klein—have written convincing first person male voice books, normally the gender of the author is the gender of the lead character.

Romance plus: Almost every YA book has a romance subplot of some sort. An award winner like *Saving Lenny* probably wouldn't be classified under any scheme as a romance, yet a boy-girl relationship is the central plot of the book. Interest in the opposite sex is certainly a main YA drive.

Boys romance: Although there are some boys who read series romances, they are not the main audience. Authors like Harry Mazer and Ron Koetge, however, write romances where it is the male character who does the pining and the chasing.

HISTORICAL FICTION

If teachers didn't assign it, surveys show few YAs would ever read it for pleasure. It's out there and it continues to be published but with a very limited audience.

HUMOR

Comics compilations: The latest compilation of Garfield comics will normally circulate more than just about any other item provided it stays in one piece. Comics by Simpson's creator Matt Groening are also hot. His *Life in Hell* series should remain popular despite what happens to the TV show. In addition, there are compilations for the younger YAs (*Peanuts, Hagar the Horrible, Mad,* etc.) and the older (*The Far Side, Calvin and Hobbes, Doonesbury,* etc.). All the most current ones will be listed in the monthly jobber catalogs.

Comic novels: *SLJ* ran an article about why a funny YA novel is better than a sitcom.[5] It's a nice thought, but probably is not shared by most YAs. Most would choose to watch a sitcom rather than read the latest YA fiction laugh riot.

Parodies: Usually a hit with older teens. Books like *Spy High* reach teens who are well past *Mad.* Although most are aimed at adults, the YA appeal is evident.

SCIENCE FICTION/FANTASY:

Many librarians who publish in the YA field are sci-fi and/or fantasy buffs. That means there is an inordinate amount of literature out there, with *VOYA's* annual "Best" list appearing in its April issue. Another reason this is such a big field is that, like horror, there is very little of this material written specifically for the YA market. Much of the YA sci-fi is read by older children because the YAs are already in to the latest 600-page trilogy by Brooks, Weis, or Donaldson. There is so much published in this field, anything here would be redundant.

TIE-INS

One of the "benefits" of the growing number of conglomerates in the entertainment industry is that every big movie is part of a package. The package also includes soundtracks, posters, t-shirts, and countless other merchandise. A popular movie will normally spawn tie-in books that are gobbled up by YAs—either to "relive" the movie experience, or because the movie is rated "R" and they didn't get in to see it. Most come with "eight pages of exciting photos" which will probably be torn out by the second circulation. There are also TV tie-ins, such as the books produced to go along with *The Simpsons* or *Late Night with David Letterman*. Stocking these items at the front of the YA area will attract attention fast.

OTHER GENRES

In addition to these categories, you can also find a limited number of original and reprint paperbacks on:

Sports: Two kinds of sports literature seems to be emerging. First there are the grown-up Matt Christopher types with lots of action and the game is the thing. Second are books like those of Chris Crutcher where sports is often the setting, but not really the most important thing in the book.

Adventure: YAs who like *Hatchet* or *My Side of the Mountain* will want YA outdoor yarns. Although there are not many currently being published, this genre (unlike problem novels) is timeless, so *Deathwatch* from the 1970s can still meet the need.

Short story collections: Donald Gallo has edited three excellent collections of stories by YA authors. They are good alternatives to Poe or De Maupassant when stories are assigned in English Class. Some YAs are "completists" who pride themselves on reading everything by a certain author. Collections of adult horror stories and annual best sci-fi/fantasy collections are also available in paperback.

Multicultural literature: See the fuller discussion of this subject in Chapter 8 of this book.

CLASSICS

The term classic means different things to different people. One definition is a book that is "never hot but never cold." Any book for which there is, and always will be, a demand is a classic. Under this definition then, *Moby Dick* and *Forever* stand side by side. For titles that fit this definition, make a list and check it periodically because they have a way of disappearing.

Another definition of a classic might be any book a YA would reasonably expect to find in any library—again that covers a lot of ground, but certainly includes Dickens, Bronte, Melville, etc. Often they are books written before any YAs' grandparents were even born. YALSA's *Outstanding Books for the College Bound* brochures and Arco's *Reading Lists for College Bound Students*[6] are excellent sources of classics. Two points: buy classics in perma-bound editions so you don't have to rebuy them constantly; second, the primary audience for classics knows what books they want—don't waste valuable display space, put them on a bottom shelf with a sign somewhere near the back of the YA area.

Best Books: In addition to the yearly lists, *Booklist* has published several lists created by YALSA:

- Nothin' but the Best (titles from YALSA's *Best Books for Young Adults*).[7]
- *Junior High Contemporary Classics*.[8]
- *Contemporary Classics for Young Adults*[9]

Summer reading lists: Most schools have summer reading lists filled with the books mentioned above. Because many schools rarely change their lists, there will always be a demand for certain titles.

Underground classics: *Grounding of Group Six, Night Shift, Go Ask Alice* and *Beginner's Love* are all pass-around books. They don't always make our lists, but they make several trips around a group of YAs with pages marked.

Cliff notes: These are the classics YAs love to read: brief synopses. For every copy of *Moby Dick,* you should probably have a Cliff Notes copy as well. Some libraries refuse to stock Cliff Notes. In that case, there are Baron's and Monarch's notes.

OTHER TYPES OF YA PAPERBACKS

Comic books: The argument for and against comic books in both libraries and classrooms is an old one. Cline and McBride provide an excellent analysis in their text *A Guide to Literature for Young Adults* including a section called "Comics as a Bridge to Further Reading." For many YAs, however, that is all they ever want to read. Fine: getting YAs in libraries to read is the goal. Comics are cheap, popular, take up little space and weed themselves. A good comics collection can attract reluctant and not so reluctant readers more than any star reviewed book in *Booklist* could ever hope to.

Graphic novels: A blending of the comics and the novel. A recent phenomenon born in the underground but now mainstream. A more sophisticated book aimed at the older YA who is willing to sit through the 200 pages of pictures and text. These are normally compilations of previously published individual comic books and more seem to be coming to market.

Trade paperbacks: The problem here is twofold: first, space in most YA areas is designed for the more popular mass market format. Even novels with YA appeal (*In Country,* for example) just don't fit anywhere except with the hardbacks. Second, the trade size is also used by children's publishers for not only series but most other releases as well.

This section on paperbacks gives a very broad overview of the various genres popular with YAs. Although the books most in demand will vary from library to library, the paperback format is consistently the most popular. The mass market YA paperback explosion began when publishers recognized that there was an untapped market with disposable income. Walden's and B. Dalton's YA sections have dramatically increased access to books for YAs, giving them a better idea of what is out there. Librarians must ask whether YAs can find "what's out there" in their library.

3.4 NONFICTION COLLECTIONS

YA nonfiction collections vary from library to library. Some libraries with YA areas don't buy nonfiction, instead it is purchased and shelved elsewhere. There are several basic configurations depending upon budget and shelving arrangements. There are four primary types of YA nonfiction:

1. Recreational
2. Informational
3. Educational
4. Reference

It is normally the first that would be housed in YA areas while others would be found in the general collection. When that is the case, the person responsible for YA collections must take care that many titles, especially those in series, don't get lost in the shuffle between adult and children's selectors—each thinking (or hoping) the other one will buy it. All four types of nonfiction are important. The recreational titles help YAs enjoy their lives, the educational and reference books help them do their job, and the informational titles just might save their lives.

To establish your priorities:

1. Leave your building. Investigate the strength of the school library collections. Look at:

   - the age of the books on the shelf (can you find a nonfiction title published after 1984?)
   - the reference collection (age of encyclopedias)
   - big ticket items (SIRS, Contemporary Authors, etc)
   - budget (if they'll tell you: Is it going up or down? Do they have one?)
   - mission and goals of school library

2. See if you can get a copy of the school's curriculum. Although not always followed to the letter, it might give you some idea of what YAs are studying.
3. Explore your library: is there duplication in current selection practices? Do the adult and children's selectors confer on buying YA titles? Or do they both buy/ignore them? When Gale publishes an expensive but essential reference tool, who picks up the tab?

TYPES OF NONFICTION

1. Recreational: Fiction is certainly not the only type of material which YAs read for fun. Part of being an adolescent is developing an intellectual curiosity and asking the question "why" a lot. YAs also develop special interests and will read for fun whatever they can lay their hands on about their own particular passion. Below are some areas of perpetual YA recreational interest. Many titles in all of these areas are available in mass market paperback. Again, look at jobber catalogs rather than review sources to find out about current releases. The problem with this area is that what is hot now is not tomorrow. You meet the demand for books about the *New Kids on the Block,* then a year later you have to throw most of them away. Some of the most popular recreational reading areas are:

- Trivia
- Parapsychology, especially "satanism," astrology, channeling, and Nostradamus.
- War and warfare
- Mythical beasts
- UFO's and unsolved mysteries
- Pets and animals
- Oversized car/motorcycle books
- Movie/TV/music star biographies
- Drawing and comic book collecting
- Sports card collecting
- Oversized film books, especially horror movies
- Sports: bios, trivia, and oversized team histories
- Nintendo (how-to books)
- True life adventure
- Holocaust accounts
- Vietnam accounts
- The 60s
- Music history, biography, and oversized criticism
- True crime, especially mass/serial murders
- "Courage" biographies
- Substance abuse first person accounts
- Joke books

2. Informational: YAs have many questions about their changing bodies and changing lives. Unfortunately, given their shyness, lack of confidence, and desire to achieve independence, they often allow these questions to go unanswered rather than confide in an adult. The library's nonfiction collection contains many of those answers. These books are often not checked out, but are read in the library either alone or in groups, then reshelved creatively. A trend in information books is to mirror the popularity of fiction series and create recognizable "products." There are many advantages to this approach. The YA learns to "trust" books in a particular series and, since all the books in the series are listed in each volume, a teen can find other titles of interest easily. Rosen's *Everything You Need To Know About* and *Coping* with series, although containing some flawed individual titles, are a breakthrough in providing information to YAs about the subjects that affect their daily lives. Shelving the series titles together rather than separately in call number order opens up access even more. Some popular informational/problem solving/ coping subject areas include:

- Self-esteem
- Teen-parent problems
- Sibling rivalry
- Sexual activity
- Sexual orientation
- Physical changes
- Dating and love
- Violence
- Eating disorders
- Substance abuse
- AIDS and other sexually transmitted diseaeses
- Depression
- Loneliness
- Suicide
- Adoption
- Death and illness
- Dysfunctional families
- Peer pressure
- Stress and anxiety
- Sexual and psychological abuse

3. Educational: Determining education trends is a big part of a YA librarian's job because YAs need current materials in order to do *their* job—going to school. New topics become "hot," others fade, and some remain "classics" because of their constant popularity. Collecting educational materials involves making choices about the collection's scope and balance. Given funds to purchase 10 books on abortion, for example, how is that money best spent? On 10 different titles or 10 copies of the same title? Each approach has problems. If there are 10 titles on a subject available, one YA could wipe out everything and no one else would be able to get a book. If you buy 10 copies of the same title, then 10 YAs each get a book, but only one book. Possible subject areas to collect in this area include:

- Abortion
- Capital punishment
- Environmental issues
- Substance abuse
- Family violence
- Homelessness and poverty
- Censorship
- Animal rights

- Euthanasia/living wills
- Genetic engineering
- AIDS
- Eating disorders
- Civil rights
- Gangs/cults
- Teen issues (pregnancy, parenthood, etc.)
- Sports issues (steroids, drugs, etc.)
- Suicide and murder

Papers about authors are also always popular. The same selection dilemma emerges: to buy 10 copies of the Twayne book on Poe or find 10 different titles? With the proliferation of reference books about authors, which provide students with other sources of information, the multiple copy approach of Twayne or Chelsea House's *Modern Critical Views* series makes good sense.

Another format for educational materials is the pamphlet. Purchasing pamphlets allows for the multiple copy approach and the short life of hot topics. You can buy 10 copies of an *Opposing Viewpoint* pamphlet much cheaper than most books, and they are easier to process/deprocess. Government pamphlets are sometimes free (or cheap), as are others to be found in the *Vertical File Index*. In the age of computers, the pamphlet file is a bit old fashioned, but it works. Materials here provide differing viewpoints and a wealth of information that can help YAs do their jobs.

4. Reference: Reference books are another area altogether. Each year all the major journals list the best of the year, and several guides to reference books aimed at YAs and/or children have been published. Careful selection is very important, and the choices can seem overwhelming as more and more titles (all of them expensive) come out on the market. No longer are they just in book format. Some are online, others are on CD-ROM. In ten years who knows what else will be available? Whereas ten years ago a student walking into a library might leave with the complaint, "I couldn't find enough stuff," now a YA might find "too much stuff" and not know what to do with it all. Technology changes so fast and time is so scarce that libraries often invest in some big ticket, high-tech reference items only to find they don't know what to do with them. There is so much in this field that it's impossible to list specific titles or even subjects, but following are the "types" of reference books most often used by students.

GUIDE TO YOUNG ADULT REFERENCE BOOKS

TITLE: *Best Science and Technology Reference Books for Young People*
SOURCE: Oryx Press

TITLE: *Guide to Reference Books for School Media Centers*
SOURCE: Libraries Unlimited

TITLE: *Recommended Reference Books for Small and Medium-Sized Libraries and Media Centers*
SOURCE: Libraries Unlimited

TITLE: *Reference Books for Children's Collections*
SOURCE: New York Public Library

TITLE: *Reference Books for Small and Medium-Sized Libraries*
SOURCE: American Library Association

TITLE: *Reference Books for Young Readers*
SOURCE: R.R. Bowker Co.

TITLE: *Best Books for Junior High Readers*
SOURCE: R.R. Bowker Co.

TITLE: *Best Books for Senior High Readers*
SOURCE: R.R. Bowker Co.

- Periodical indexes
- Full text services (SIRS)
- General encyclopedias
- Subject-specific encyclopedias
- Almanacs and yearbooks
- Biographical encyclopedias
- Literary criticism sources
- Atlases
- Document collections
- Dictionaries
- Sources for illustrations

NONFICTION COLLECTION ISSUES

Currency: No YA wants to be doing a report on the space program and find books on the shelf about how "one day man will go to the moon." Nonfiction collections must be constantly weeded as information is outdated. This is especially true in the hard sciences and health, where it is hard to find good material in the first place.

Organization: The more straightforward the better. Books that provide lists, charts, and graphs are popular with students because the information is easy to use. Students don't write reports by reading books; they write them by gathering information.

Format: Does it look like a children's book? Is it too big to fit on the shelf? Does the text have white space? Are illustrations and text mixed well? What a book looks like is important—even in nonfiction. If the format looks like a picture book and the text is dotted with illustrations of children, many YAs will pass on it, even for a book report, because it seems beneath them. Maybe librarians don't judge a book by its cover, but many YAs do.

Review: If the primary focus of your YA collection is popular materials (paperback fiction), then nonfiction choices become even harder, since less money has been allocated. As more reference books and services become available through CD-ROM and online sources, libraries may begin to think differently about nonfiction collections. If a library purchases a service that indexes current magazines and provides full text copies, will students still need to find five or six books on a topic? The days of a student coming to the library to do a term paper and using primarily books from the nonfiction collection are probably coming to a close.

3.5 PERIODICALS

Periodical collections also fall into the same four general categories of nonfiction:

- Recreational
- Informational
- Educational
- Reference

Periodicals for nonrecreational use are in a state of flux as new technology makes full text available online, on CD-ROM, and in microtext format, and begins to challenge traditional notions of magazine collections. Given these changes and the way periodical collections affect the entire library, this section will focus only on recreational magazines. Not all of these magazines are aimed specifically at the YA market. Nevertheless, magazine publishers know that many YAs have disposable income and will spend it on a magazine rather than a book.

1. WHY DO TEENS LIKE MAGAZINES?

Fads: *Bop, Sixteen,* and other fan magazines were on top of the New Kids on the Block before book publishers could rush out titles. Just the same, they drop fads just as fast. Old news is no news to many YAs, so the very nature of magazines makes them perfect YA reading.

Timing: One reason many YAs, especially boys, don't read books is simply physical: it means sitting still for too long. Magazines can be read quickly in between classes or under a teacher's glance.

Reading level: Many reluctant readers are not reluctant to read magazines. Readers who find books challenging will find in most YA magazines simple vocabulary, lots of pictures, and short articles.

Social aspects: Articles and pictures lead to discussions, sometimes heated ones.

Peer points: If a teenage boy gets "caught" with a book by his peers, he's thought of as a nerd in certain circles. The same kid seen with a magazine is asked to share it. There just isn't the same stigma attached to reading magazines as there is to reading books.

YA MAGAZINES

The following titles are grouped to provide an overview of the types of magazines available for YAs. Many of the ones listed are marketed for YAs only, while others are really adult magazines with high YA appeal. The 20 titles marked with an asterisk (*) might be considered first choices for a new YA magazine collection. Addresses for all these magazines can be found in the appendix.

GENERAL INTEREST

Boys Life
Sassy*
Seventeen*
Teen*
YM

MUSIC

Fan magazines
Bop*
Dream Guys
Hip Hop
Sixteen*
Splice
Super Teen
Teen Beat*
Teen Set
Tiger Beat

General
Creem
Rolling Stone*
Spin*

Metal
Circus*
Hit Parader
Metal Edge
Rip*
Rock Beat
Song Hits

Rap
Black Beat
Fresh
Full Effect
Rappin'
Right On
The Source*

Special interests: A YA interested in professional wrestling might be lucky to find one book in the library about this topic. But a library could meet this interest monthly with a magazine subscription. As YAs grow older, they begin to develop special interests to which magazines can respond better than books. The whole notion of magazines is to find a special interest group and provide a product for its members to buy.

More than recreation: Although titles like *Teen, Seventeen,* and *Sassy* are primarily recreational they are also a great source of information about all those teen issues discussed in the nonfiction section. The most current (and often the most readable) information available for teens on sex isn't in books, but in the pages of these magazines.

2. WHY SHOULD LIBRARIES BUY MORE YA MAGAZINES?

In addition to what your reader survey probably told you (that magazines are more popular than books among YAs), here are some other reasons to keep them coming:

Circulation: If you allow magazines to check out, they will check out over and over again until they fall apart or are stolen. A subscription to *Pro Wrestling Illustrated* ($18), for example, will circulate more than a similarly priced hardback fiction title.

Visibility: Magazine covers are bright, attractive, and attention-getting. If you put them in the sightline of your YA area, teens will be drawn in. Face-out shelving is essential.

Crowd control: Magazines can be a method of crowd control for the YAs who might otherwise do nothing but hang out. These YAs aren't disruptive; they're just bored. Magazines conquer boredom and keep them occupied, at least for a few minutes once a week (or month) when the new titles come in.

Excitement: It's not often that YAs run in and ask, "Are the new hardback fiction titles here?" They *will* ask when you expect the next issue of their favorite magazines. YA excitement for library materials is a thing to be savored and encouraged.

Public relations: As stated earlier, many boys consider reading a book a negative thing to do. If you push your magazine collection, then your public relations message is not only more positive, but taps a whole new audience who wouldn't read a book for anything.

Spice
Word Up*

Alternative
Alternative Press
Melody Maker
Option

SPORTS

General
Inside Sport
Sport*
Sports Illustrated
Sporting News

Big sports
Baseball Digest
Basketball Digest
Football Digest

Skating
Thrasher*
Transworld Skateboarding

Wrestling
Inside Wrestling
Pro Wrestling Illustrated
Sports Review Wrestling
The Wrestler
WWF Magazine*

Martial arts
Black Belt
Taekwondo Times

Boxing
The Ring
KO

Sports cards
Becket Baseball Card Monthly
Sports Card Trader

Bodybuilding
Bodybuilding Lifestyles
Joe Weider's Muscle and Fitness

Outdoor sports
Field and Stream
Outdoor Life
Skiing

TECHNOLOGY

Cars
Car and Driver
Hot Rod*

If you are trying to improve your library's image with YAs, adding titles like *Spin* or *Pro Wrestling Illustrated* will create a more positive image for you in the YA community than programs that might cost twice as much.

Free Posters: Most fan magazines contain posters. Rather than letting the YAs rip them out (which they will do), do it yourself first. You'll have a poster collection you can use to either decorate the area or give away as prizes.

Developmental tasks: Magazines help YAs do all the things they need to do to grow up. They provide them with an outlet for their excitement; they foster identity development as YAs find magazines to match their interests; they offer advice and self-help articles; and they are a mark of independence, helping YAs strike out on their own and develop their own tastes.

3. WHAT ARE THE DISADVANTAGES?

Problem: Headaches. Dealing with periodicals is a headache, from checking them in to claiming them to retrieving them.

Solution: If at all possible, don't use subscription agents (and lose your discount). Instead, work out something with your local news agent. This will allow for more flexibility in the titles and number of copies you can order.

Problem: High loss rate. Because magazines are so popular, they get stolen. This is almost unavoidable. If they are not stolen, then by the time they are read, passed around, thrown across the room, and clipped for photos, there is often nothing left.

Solutions: Accept these as disposable materials, designed to meet an immediate interest and not part of any sort of permanent collection. If you can get five circulations out of one issue of *Bop*, you have really achieved something. For many this is a real philosophical leap because we think of libraries as storehouses. That is not the purpose of this type of collection, however. If magazines are in good condition a year from when they come out, they probably aren't the right magazines. You need to communicate to YAs that it is their responsibility to monitor these magazines among their peers. Remind YAs that the magazines belong to them, not you.

Motor Trend
Road and Track

Cycles
Bicycling
BMX Action
Freestylin' BMX

Computers
Compute!
Game Players
Game Pro
Nintendo Power*

Movies
Cinefantisque
Fangoria
Gorezone
Starlog

HUMOR
Spy
National Lampoon
Cracked
Mad*

GAMES
Dragon (D & D)
Games

CURRENT AFFAIRS
News For You
Scholastic Update

ADULT MAGAZINES WITH HIGH TEEN APPEAL
Ebony
Elle
Entertainment Weekly
Essence
Glamour
Globe (tabloid)
In Fashion
Jet
Life
Mademoiselle
National Enquirer*
Newsweek
People
Premiere
Time
Us
USA Today (newspaper)
Vogue
Weekly World News*

Problem: Content. *Sassy* and *Rolling Stone* have both undergone intellectual freedom challenges. *Spin* magazine once put a condom in each issue, and many music/rap magazines reprint all the words to songs, including the ones you don't hear on the radio. *Fangoria* has close-ups of some of the goriest shots from horror films, and wrestling magazines have photos of wrestlers bleeding.

Solution: You should make sure your library's collection policy covers magazines, and that the titles you choose could be defended under this policy.

4. WHERE DO YOU FIND MAGAZINES?

Anywhere but in our professional literature. The library review media isn't very strong with magazines in general, and is practically nonexistent for YA titles. With few exceptions, it would be difficult to find library reviews of the magazines listed in this chapter. To locate magazines, you need to go to the source. Observe, ask, and survey YAs about the magazines they want. Most YAs don't subscribe to magazines; instead they pick them up at the newsstand or drugstore—which are probably the best places for you to get them, too. If you find them at the newsstand, then your local distributor can get them for you.

5. WHAT ARE THE BEST MAGAZINES FOR TEENAGERS?

This depends on where and when you are reading this. Community standards, likes and dislikes, and special interest will determine which magazines you will want to purchase. The rapidly changing magazine publishing industry, combined with the faddish world of teen culture, means that some of the titles listed may no longer be available.

Establishing a collection of recreational reading magazines will attract both users and nonusers. It will lead to an increase in circulation and traffic in the YA area. It will also create good public relations, a different image of the library in the YA community (and perhaps in the library), and even make some YAs excited about the library. Granted, magazines are expensive to purchase and maintain, but the number of YAs who can have a positive library experience make allocating funds for this purpose worth it.

3.6 NONPRINT

YAs are tuned in to media. The typical image of teenagers is not with their heads buried in books, but surrounded by headphones while watching something on a TV screen. It is no coincidence that as the amount of available media has increased, the amount of recreational reading done by YAs has decreased. Every time a new medium emerges—home video games, cable TV, compact disc players—it represents one more recreational option YAs can choose instead of reading. Libraries have attempted to "join 'em" (since we can't beat 'em) by purchasing heavily in nonprint areas. The first big breakthrough was in buying lots of educational nonprint materials, which has helped transform school libraries into library media centers. Now public libraries have joined in with the purchase of recreational media, including popular videotapes, to almost a staff-breaking point. Most public libraries have never met a technology or format they didn't like—YAs are the same. The nonprint YA collection, like the book and magazine collections, raises several important questions at the outset. Like the other collections, nonprint consists of materials that are:

- Educational
- Recreational
- Informational
- Reference

Again, librarians must make decisions and determine priorities in order to buy the best possible materials.

CHOICES AND PRIORITIES

Demand vs. quality: This is also known as the Two Live Crew question. You can't deny there is a demand for Two Live Crew or NWA rap tapes, but many would have a difficult time defending these materials by any standard. Librarians who would defend Judy Blume's *Forever* to the bitter end become strangely silent when discussion of NWA comes up.

Circulation vs. standards: Related, but with an important difference. Without the review media we have for books, how can anyone judge music releases? Professional standards don't exist in this area, and there is no way to determine how our peers would evaluate the "quality" of music. At one time *VOYA* had a music reviewer, but now only *Wilson Library Bulletin* provides any guidance for these.

Recreational vs. educational vs. informational: You have $40 to spend on a videotape. Do you purchase *Wrestlemania VII, SAT Review,* or an AIDS awareness tape? You have money for software. Do you buy a game or a learning tool?

Professional vs. careful: Anyone who wants to be careful selecting popular music for YAs in the 1990s had better hope for a Barry Manilow comeback. As rap, metal, and alternative music continue to solidify their positions, new "lines" will certainly be crossed as they were in the 1980s.

Demand vs. reality: Let's say you fall down heavily on the side of meeting demand and give 'em what they want. But you cannot afford it—nobody can. Even the hottest YA book will not have as many potential readers as a hot new tape/CD release will have listeners. YAs are not hearing excerpts from YA novels on the radio or seeing videos to promote them. Libraries face the same dilemma with bestsellers and with videos: there are never enough copies to meet the demand.

Scope vs. charts: Selecting music probably used to be a lot easier. There were no groups like the PMRC, there were fewer intellectual freedom issues to deal with, and music was more homogenized. The scope of music available today is very wide and getting wider. Some argue that, because you can never have enough copies of Madonna, you shouldn't even buy it. Perhaps you should acquire music that isn't at the top of the charts instead. Since YAs are more likely to buy their own music as opposed to their own books, you might consider having an eclectic music collection even if your book collection is demand-driven.

Listening vs. watching vs. participating: Nonprint is expensive and doesn't usually last long, so setting priorities is important. If you want a strong video collection, it might not be possible to buy any computer software. Your priorities will be determined by:

• Your vision
• Your library's AV purchasing policies

- Access to technology in the library
- Access to AV in the community
- Space consideration

As new technologies develop, such as digital audio tape (DAT) and video discs, libraries will face other choices: whether to get on the bandwagon and, if they do, what to abandon to make room for the new technology. YA nonprint collections are harder to develop than print not only because of these constant changes, but also because of YA awareness. More YAs will ask for the NWA tape than the latest Cynthia Voigt novel. That presents libraries with both a challenge and an opportunity.

Developing a listening collection for in-house use and checkout is difficult for many reasons. The high loss rate, the diverse range of YA musical interests, and the inability to ever get enough copies of the "hot stuff" pose significant challenges. Yet, music is essential to YA culture and offers a perfect opportunity for libraries to make connections with YAs. The importance of music in YA culture is related to some of the developmental tasks discussed earlier:

Identity: The idea that you are what you listen to is alive and well. The YAs who listen to punk/hardcore, for example, define themselves with that music and the accompanying fashion. When YAs fill out pen pal applications the type of music they listen to is almost always used as a factor to determine common interests.

Excitement: Listening is connected with action: dancing, concerts, driving, making out. Music creates and channels YAs' energy.

Acceptance: Since YAs establish identity through musical taste, it is not surprising that they also find acceptance in a peer group that way. For YAs, listening to music is often a social activity enjoyed by many at the same time. It brings young people together.

Independence: Music manifests YAs' independence in many ways. It can represent both means of acceptance in a peer group, and a rejection of the adult world. The rebellious aspect of rock music has existed from day one and continues (stronger than ever) to this day. Newer forms, especially rap, are reclaiming popular music as a form of expression for youth and youth alone. The advent of the "Walkman" allows YAs (and others) to tune out everyone else and create their own private world.

Now that we've examined why teenagers are so turned on to music, lets look at some of the different types of media they choose.

MUSICAL MEDIA

Records: Vinyl is history. Records are impossible to find and impossible to replace. Even the most die-hard LP listeners have begun to convert to compact discs. Libraries with huge record collections have to consider a similar conversion.

Cassette Tapes: This is still the most popular format, because they can be played in personal and car stereos. As compact disc playing technology advances and becomes less expensive, it will continue to impact on tape sales. The emergence of DAT, which has higher sound quality than traditional audiocassettes, will also affect sales. For libraries, tapes pose numerous problems that should be considered, if not solved, before a heavy investment is made in this area. These problems include:

- Security
- Damage from never-normal wear and tear
- Packaging (easy to steal)
- Display/access
- Warning labels

Compact discs: This is the format of the 1980s and probably the 1990s as well. Despite claims that CDs seem like a librarian's dream (that they can't be damaged), CDs can be ruined, although certainly not as easily as LPs. The plastic cases crack easily, and the long boxes they are sold in concern some environmentalists. Nonetheless, YAs will expect you to have compact discs, and lots of them. Because it is a new format, it will be necessary to order older titles. YAs will also want new titles and boxed sets—career retrospectives that usually include four CDs and a pamphlet. Boxed sets are a nightmare to shelve and a budget drainer at about $59.99 each.

CHOOSING MEDIA

There is no *VOYA* equivalent for music reviews. *Rolling Stone* and a few other magazines review new releases, but they are not aimed at the library audience. *Billboard* is a handy trade publication, but its reviews are always positive and therefore not revealing. Given this vacuum, you will need to use other evaluation methods.

Ask YAs: Set up a review committee of YAs to meet monthly and choose materials. Give the committee copies of *Billboard* or similar publications and some order slips and stay out of their way. You could also ask this group to review music and publish the reviews in a newsletter. Or you could set up a survey for distribution in the library and in schools each month. YAs are always more than happy to share their opinions about music.

Visit record stores: You really can't buy music sitting behind your desk. You need to get out and visit record stores, to see not only what's new, but also what is being pushed or hyped. If you can purchase music through a local record store, perhaps the manager can help you choose it, and give you various promotional goodies to use.

Use the charts: If you have access to *Billboard,* then you know the various charts can be very helpful. There are charts with the top pop, modern rock, rap, country, and rhythm and blues (r&b) releases. The charts indicate how long a release has been listed and how quickly it is moving toward the top.

MUSIC TYPES

Music fads come and go (remember disco?), so it is important for staff working with YAs to keep track of these trends. Just as there are popular standard YA fiction genres, pop music can also be divided into genres.

Pop: The music you hear on many radio stations—less influential among YAs than ever before. Example: Whitney Houston.

Bubblegum: Music aimed right at the heart of the younger YA girl. Example: New Kids on the Block.

Rock: Harder-edged than pop, but not quite heavy metal. (Older, more established groups fit well into this category.) Example: Bruce Springsteen.

Dance: Played on the radio, but more popular in clubs. Example: Paula Abdul.

Rap: The trend of music of the 1980s and probably of the 1990s. Rap has reached amazing levels of both mass acceptance and mass rejection. There are many different subgenres and more new ones are emerging constantly.

RAP SUBGENRES

- Filth rap (Example: Two Live Crew)
- Political rap (Example: Public Enemy)
- Gangster rap (Example: NWA)
- Top 40 rap (Example: Hammer)
- White rap (Example: Vanilla Ice)
- Comic rap (Example: Fat Boys)
- Psychedelic rap (Example: De La Soul)
- Fusion rap (Example: Nenah Cherry)

HEAVY METAL SUBGENRES

- Pop Metal (Example: Poison)
- Classic Metal (Example: Led Zepplin)
- Heavier Metal (Example: Guns N Roses)
- Black Metal (Example: old Black Sabbath)
- Christian metal (Example: Metal Church)
- Speed Metal (Example: DRI)

Heavy metal: The other real success story of the 1980s, also divided into many sub-genres.

Alternative: Used to be heard only on college radio, but there has been lots of crossover. (Encompasses what was once called "new wave.")

- *Geniuses:* Any group that might be considered "the greatest rock and roll band in the world" at a given time. Examples: REM and U2.
- *Old wave:* Artists that came out of the punk/new wave explosion of the 70s. Example: Elvis Costello.
- *Synth bands:* Music in which keyboards dominate. Example: Depeche Mode.
- *Industrial:* Hard to explain, harder to listen to. Example: Skinny Puppy.
- *Hardcore:* Songs usually under two minutes, with heavy emphasis on guitars, drums, and bass. Example: half of the YA bands in America.

Rhythm and blues: An old name for a number of musical styles such as soul and urban contemporary produced mainly by African American artists.

There are also many other styles of music YAs listen to, such as country & western and new age. The one constant in pop music—and in YAs' musical taste—is change. The more you can rely on YAs for assistance in developing listening collections, the better chance you have of changing with the changing times.

NON-MUSIC COLLECTIONS

Another potential collection development area is books on tape. Although nowhere as large as the market for children's or adult tapes, some YA fiction is available in the cassette format. Many classics on school reading lists are available on tape and will be requested by students. Study guides, languages courses, and other educational tools can be found in this format.

VIEWING COLLECTIONS

Videotapes have revolutionized how Americans spend their leisure time. They have boosted circulation levels beyond anyone's belief, but they have also given libraries another collection to purchase and maintain. Libraries can greatly improve service to YAs by creating or enhancing video collections for this audience. As with every other media, there are many decisions to be made:

How old? Many libraries who have adopted the Library Bill of Rights sometimes forget it when it comes to videos. The arguments against lending videos to those under 18 usually revolve around content and cost.

How many? Like music tapes, the demand for some videos will easily outstrip any library's ability to provide sufficient copies in a timely manner.

What types? Some libraries refuse to carry a lot of entertainment tapes; others seem more like a branch of Blockbuster than a public library. In planning a YA video collection, we find the same three types: recreational, informational, and educational.

RECREATIONAL

Movies: In addition to all the usual YA favorites, films made from YA books like *The Outsiders* should be purchased. Camp classics like *The Rocky Horror Picture Show* also have high YA appeal.

Music: There are three types of music videos: compilations of the videos shown on MTV; concert videos; and the new video magazines, which cover both rap and heavy metal.

Sports: Among the many different subgenres available are sports "bloopers," profiles and histories, "thrill sports" (skateboarding, surfing) videos, wrestling videos, and "greatest hits" compilations, showing greatest plays in a particular sport.

Television: Many YA cult shows like *Star Trek* and *The Adventures of Rocky and Bullwinkle* are now available on videotape.

INFORMATIONAL

Also known as "how-to" tapes, videos of this type are not as popular. Designed to provide factual data, these tapes are available about various YA topics. Since videos are not as private as a book, however, good informational videos on topics like AIDS are not checked out as often as one might hope.

EDUCATIONAL

Curriculum: Video companies are churning out tapes to help libraries and schools replace their 16mm, slide, and filmstrip collections.

Study aids: SAT, ACT, GED, etc. Tapes with an accompanying booklet are available on all the big tests.

SOFTWARE COLLECTIONS

Computer software is another area of collection development you must consider. Much has been written about the place of computer software in libraries and whether such material should be circulated or used exclusively in-house. What type of software you buy will hinge on what you are going to do with it and the equipment you have. With Apple and IBM now sharing technology, perhaps some of these decisions will be easier in the future.

The choice here is generally between "feeling the excitement of Nintendo" and educational programs. Educational software is reviewed in our professional journals, and the fun stuff is often requested by YA patrons. Before purchasing a lot of Nintendo cartridges, however, all the ramifications of that decision need to be examined. Once you purchase software, you create an expectation. The appeal of a "starter set" will wear thin after a while if nothing is added to the collection. If you can't support upgrades to a system next year, then you probably should think about not buying it this year.

REVIEW

Purchasing nonprint materials for YA collections is a challenge as patrons' expectations of what we should have smack up against both what we can afford and what we can keep up with technologically. The basic questions about the library's role once again play a part in this. If your library chooses the role of "popular materials center," that implies that you will buy multiple copies of Madonna tapes rather than having a more eclectic music collection or a wide selection of YA fiction on tape. The real difference with nonprint collections is this: libraries are usually not the only source YAs use. Yes, there are bookstores and other outlets for YA fiction, but school and public libraries are more likely places to find YAs looking for this material. On the other hand, go to any mall record store, video shop, or software center and see the place teeming with teens.

Nonprint makes the circulation numbers look good. Even with

the loss rate, "hot" tapes, disks, and videos will fly off the shelf faster than almost any YA book. Nonprint is good PR. You will win more friends at booktalks announcing that you just purchased *Wrestlemania VIII* than you will trumpeting the latest Cynthia Voigt opus in hardback. And you will certainly have more YAs looking for Nintendo than looking for educational programs. But is that what we do? If we are content to adopt a more bookstore-like attitude with our print collections, should we do the same with our nonprint collections?

3.7 INFORMATION SOURCES

Some of the review media for each format have already been mentioned. Despite the small size of the YA field, the list of sources is extensive.

BOOK REVIEW MEDIA

Jobber catalogs: Most YA paperbacks, particularly series books, don't get reviewed—and most don't really need it. Paperback originals usually get reviewed, but with some lag time. Jobbers like Baker & Taylor and Ingram all have monthly publications announcing new releases that include YA sections.

Publishers catalogs: To develop a retrospective collection, the best sources of information are publishers' catalogs. The appendix of this book lists the major YA fiction and nonfiction publishers and their addresses. Some publishers will also send you posters, teachers' guides, and other promotional goodies.

Professional periodicals: These can be subdivided according to the amount of space they dedicate to YA books. Addresses for all these publications are available in the appendix.

YA only
  Voice of Youth Advocates
  Kliatt Young Adult Paperback Book Guide
  ALAN Review
YA and children (school focus)
  Appraisal: Science Books for Young People
  Bulletin of the Center for Children's Books

ANNUAL LISTS

LIST: Best Books for Young Adults
SOURCE: Best Books Committee, YALSA
TO OBTAIN: Write to ALA (reprinted in *Booklist*)

LIST: Quick Picks
SOURCE: Reluctant Reader Committee, YALSA
TO OBTAIN: Write to ALA (reprinted in *Booklist*)

LIST: Books for Young Adults Poll
SOURCE: *English Journal*
TO OBTAIN: Appears in December issue

LIST: Best Books
SOURCE: *School Library Journal* editors
TO OBTAIN: Appears in December issue of *SLJ*

LIST: Easy-to-read Books for Teenagers
SOURCE: New York Public Library
TO OBTAIN: Write NYPL

LIST: Editor's Choice
SOURCE: *Booklist* editors
TO OBTAIN: Appears in January issue of *Booklist*

LIST: Best Science Fiction/Fantasy/Horror
SOURCE: *Voice of Youth Advocates* reviewers
TO OBTAIN: Appears in April issue of *VOYA*

LIST: Books for the Teenage
SOURCE: New York Public Library
TO OBTAIN: Write NYPL

LIST: Young Adult Book List
SOURCE: Los Angeles Public Library
TO OBTAIN: Write LAPL

LIST: Best Juvenile and Young Adult Books
SOURCE: Maryvale High School Media Center
TO OBTAIN: Write Nel Ward (3415 N. 59th Ave. Phoenix, AZ 85033)

Emergency Librarian
Horn Book
School Library Journal
Interracial Books for Children Bulletin
The Book Report
General media
 Booklist
 Kirkus Reviews
Keeping up with trends
 Most of the above and articles in:
 Wilson Library Bulletin ("The Young Adult Perplex" column)
 English Journal
 Journal of Youth Services
 School Library Media Quarterly

Annual lists A variety of organizations produce "best" lists that can be used for retrospective buying. Some of these lists are compiled annually and published in periodicals and/or in pamphlet form. Others are published less frequently but are still of great use. In addition to the lists, two prizes are awarded in the YA field. Avon gives out an award for best first novel by a YA, while Delacorte awards best first YA novels.

PERIODICAL REVIEW SOURCES:

Katz's Magazines for Libraries contains a few of the YA titles mentioned, but not many. There is no review source other than asking YAs, observing what they read, and hanging out at drug stores.

NONPRINT REVIEW SOURCES

Listening collections: In addition to the music magazines previously listed, a limited number of reviews of new releases can be found in *Billboard* and *Stereo Review*.

Viewing collections: The library review media aimed at schools covers educational and informational videos fairly well, as does *VOYA*.

Software collections: The library review media also cover educational and informational software fairly well. Reviews of entertainment programs can be found in magazines like *Nintendo Power*, *Game Pro*, and *Game Strategies*.

AUTHORS FOR RAMPANT READERS

Adams, Douglas
Andrews, V.C.
Angelou, Maya
Anthony, Piers
Asimov, Isaac
Atwood, Margaret
Auel, Jean

Baldwin, James
Bradbury, Ray
Bradley, Marion Zimmer
Brooks, Terry

Card, Orson Scott
Christie, Agatha
Clancy, Tom
Clark, Mary Higgins
Clarke, Arthur C.
Cook, Robin

Donaldson, Stephen

Edrich, Louise
Ellis, Bret Easton

Finney, Jack

Gardner, John (Bond)
Godden, Rumer
Greenberg, Jan
Guest, Judith

Hayden, Torey
Herbert, Frank
Hesse, Hermann
Hillerman, Tony

Irving, John

Jackson, Shirley
Johnston, Velda

Kesey, Ken
King, Stephen
Knowles, John
Koontz, Dean
Kozinski, Jerzy

L'Amour, Louie
LeGuin, Ursula

3.8 COLLECTION CONCERNS

As if building an active YA collection were not enough of a challenge, librarians also face a host of other related concerns.

Censorship: of books, videos, magazines, everything. YA materials are always the target of intellectual freedom challenges, with nonprint being the real battleground of the 1990s.

Illiteracy: Despite massive public awareness, school improvement campaigns, and other efforts, teen illiteracy is still with us.

Aliteracy: The ability to read but choosing not to. In some cases it becomes anti-literacy: an open loathing for reading.

Irrelevancy: YAs find much of the literature they're expected to read totally out of touch with real life. As long as schools avoid the YA titles that really can speak to teens, many YAs will see any reading as nothing more than a dreadful, boring task.

Escalators: In a time when it is a struggle just to get many YAs to read at all, many librarians, teachers, and parents would rather have them riding the reading escalator. This sends YAs up from *SVH* to Norma Mazer to Cynthia Voigt, then on to Jane Austen or the Brontes.

Rampant readers: Some YAs take the escalator on their own, which presents some special problems. The seventh graders who devoured, then got bored with *SVH* might be coming to you by eighth grade for more serious romances. Eventually by tenth or eleventh grade the materials in the YA section will no longer be of interest to them. Finding materials for this group is often difficult because although their reading tastes, interest, and abilities have matured, for many of them adult books might also be inappropriate. *School Library Journal* contains a section on adult books for YA readers, and *Booklist* also notes adult titles with YA interest. *Bookbait* by Walker[10] is aimed at finding adult titles for YA readers. A list of authors for rampant readers is provided in this chapter.

REACHING RELUCTANT READERS

YALSA's Books for the Reluctant Young Adult Reader Committee

AUTHORS FOR RAMPANT READERS (cont.)

Malamud, Bernard
Mason, Bobbie Ann
McCaffery, Anne
McCammon, Robert
McMurtry, Larry
Michaels, Barbara
Michener, James
Morrison, Toni

Neufield, John
Norton, Andre

O'Brien, Tim
Oke, Janette

Potok, Chaim
Pynchon, Thomas

Rand, Ayn
Rice, Anne
Robbins, Tom

Salinger, J.D.
Saul, John
Sheldon, Sidney
Spencer, Scott
Spiegelman, Art
Steel, Danielle
Stewart, Mary
Striber, Whitley

Terkel, Studs
Tolkien, J.R.R.
Tyler, Anne

Updike, John

Vonnegut, Kurt

Walker, Alice
Weis, Margaret
Weisel, Elie
Wharton, William
Wright, Richard

has developed a list of guidelines that will help you determine which books in your collection would meet this need. Arthea J.S. Reed, in her book *Comics to Classics: A Parents Guide to Books for Teens and Preteens*,[11] summarizes ten major reasons some YAs are reluctant readers.

1. They associate reading with school and/or failure.
2. They are not interested in ideas.
3. They are not capable of sitting still long enough.
4. Because of their egocentric natures, they are not interested in many of the books that are required reading.
5. Reading doesn't provide the level of entertainment they want.
6. It's "counterproductive" to read.
7. They grow up in nonreading environments.
8. Reading is a solitary task and is therefore considered antisocial.
9. Reading is considered an "adult thing" or "school thing" and is therefore rejected.
10. Reading is seen as difficult.

Reluctant readers are not stupid kids: they are just kids who do not choose to read. They need both encouragement and materials that will make reading a positive experience. Reaching the reluctant reader may require that you rethink some attitudes that the only real reading is book reading and come up with creative ways to reach this audience. Following are the ABCs of promoting materials to reluctant YA readers:

Advertise: In the school newspaper (promoting one or more books) or in the PTA/PTO newsletter (telling parents to contact the library for suggested titles).

Booktalk: Covered in detail in Chapter Four.

Contests: Run trivia contests about authors or subjects which connect YAs with your collection.

Dramatize: With a teacher's cooperation, lift dialogue sections out of YA novels and have a class act them out. This makes the action of the book seem more real.

Educate: Distribute classroom copies of *Quick Picks*, the booklist produced annually by the YALSA Recommended Books for the Reluctant Young Adult Reader Committee.

Find out more: Much of the best literature about reaching reluctant readers is not in our literature, but in the research on reading. Find out what teachers are doing and see how libraries can complement it.

Genres: Organize YA books by genre to match the way YAs think rather than how we think.

High visibility: Pull out the *Quick Picks* titles and others with high appeal and make them visible.

Incentives: Offer prizes if the library is running a reading program or work with schools to give extra credit for reading a certain number of books.

Joint ventures: Seek cooperation from principals, school libraries, teachers, and even sports coaches to see if there is something you can do together.

Knowledge: Many librarians working with YAs only know the name of Christopher Pike as the first captain of the Enterprise on *Star Trek*. Pike was publishing great reluctant readers books like *Slumber Party* that YAs knew about, but most librarians were clueless.

Lists: Take a piece of legal-size paper and cut it in thirds. Now you have a skinny piece of paper. Fill it with the author, title, and one word descriptions of books under 150 pages.

Magazines: Reluctant readers need items other than books.

Need: The time the reluctant reader will need you is the night before the book report is due. Work with the teachers so you can booktalk, arrange visits, or provide other help before that last night.

Out loud: It is not only small children who like to be read to. Schools doing read aloud programs can expand this to the upper grades. Often YAs will be moved by the sound of the words rather than their beauty.

Packages: Combine a book and the movie based on the book and put together a "package deal."

Quantity: Use bookdumps if you have multiple copies of some titles you think might catch on. The more YAs there are reading a book, the more "cool" it is to read that book.

Reach out: Some students are talking loudly about a subject. They seem quite interested in the subject but you also know they are reluctant readers. Slip away and find something: a magazine article, an entry in a reference book, anything about this subject. Bring it back and mention it casually. Demonstrate in small ways the value of reading for obtaining information.

Samples: Take a toothpick, a photocopy of an interesting page or photo from a book, attach an information tag on the page and leave these free samples out.

Trends: Follow trends, use them. The non-reading YA who is into Nintendo might be interested in any books or magazines you have to offer on the subject.

User (or non-user) survey: Find out for yourself why YAs don't read in your community.

Video reviews: Offer a YA a chance to be a video star by having him tell about a book or magazine article he's read on camera.

Writers: If a YA can see and talk to a real writer in person this makes reading his or her books a little more interesting.

X marks the spot: Using posters and other decorations make the YA area a comfortable, inviting place to be.

Yes: Find a way to say "yes" to most any request by a reluctant reader.

Zippy and Ziggy: Comic books also appeal to reluctant readers.

Reaching YA reluctant readers is not an easy task. There is, however, a good deal of literature and a YALSA committee out there to help. There is certainly a market as every YA librarian knows. Meeting this market means adopting strategies, changing assumptions, and thinking creatively about ways to promote library materials. YAs can't afford to have us fail.

ENDNOTES

1. Kenneth L. Donelson and Alleen Pace Nilsen, *Literature for Today's Young Adults,* 3rd ed, Glenview, IL: Scott, Foresman and Company, 1989.
2. Ruth Cline and William McBride, *A Guide to Literature for Young Adults,* Glenview, IL: Scott, Foresman and Company, 1983.
3. Patty Campbell, "Perplexing Young Adult Books: A Retrospective," *Wilson Library Bulletin* (April 1988): 20-26.
4. "Teenage Trauma: Realistic YA Fiction," *Booklist (July 15, 1980): 1525-1528. "Teenage Trauma: An Update on Realistic YA Fiction," Booklist* (December 1, 1983): 563-566.
5. Alleen Pace Nilsen, "Why A YA Novel is Better than a TV Sitcom," *School Library Journal* (March 1989): 120- 123.
6. Doug Estell, *Reading Lists for College Bound Students,* New York : Arco, 1990.
7. "Nothin' But the Best: Best of the Best Books for Young Adults," *Booklist* (October 15, 1988): 401-4.
8. "Junior High Contemporary Classics," *Booklist* (December 15, 1984).
9. "Contemporary Classics for Young Adults," *Booklist* (July 1985).
10. Elinor Walker, *Bookbait,* 4th ed. Chicago: American Library Association, 1988.
11. Aretha J.S. Reed, *Comics to Classics,* Newark, DE: International Reading Association, 1988.

4 YOUNG ADULT SERVICES

4.1 REFERENCE SERVICE

Most teenagers have a full-time job—going to school. To do that job well, they often need information and resources not available in the classroom. This is where reference service can be of invaluable help to YAs. First let's examine what we want reference service to YAs to accomplish by looking at some of the common questions or statements we hear from them over the desk—and formulating some possible responses.

"My paper is due tomorrow." The hectic nature of YAhood often flies smack in the face of good planning. YAs (like the rest of us) often put off unpleasant tasks until the last moment. Unfortunately, nothing is more unpleasant than writing a report or term paper under such circumstances.

When a student is feeling rushed, it is not the time to demonstrate how things work. Instead, try to find some useful information quickly. Walk over to the shelves, help the student find one or two sources, and try to help him or her relax if at all possible. No, you probably won't be able to find everything the YA could use for that paper, but don't let anyone leave empty handed.

"I have to do a paper on. . .". When most people come to the library looking for information, not only do they know *what* they are looking for but also *why* they need it. YAs are often different in that regard. Sure, they know why they need it (to complete the assignment), but many times they don't understand the context of the question they are asking. Nor do they even know how to phrase the question—resulting in the "garbled assignment" problem. Sometimes you can have several students all working on the same assignment and not realize it because each one has interpreted it so differently.

Whenever a student asks an assignment-related question, try to obtain a copy of the assignment sheet (if there is one). Some teachers actually put assignments in writing and—more amazingly—some students actually hang on to them. Copy these and organize a space at the reference desk to store them. Note on the copy the grade and class, if it's not already there, and when the assignment is due. You can also list possible reference books or search strategies on this sheet. Depending on the situation, you might be able to pull books from other locations in the library and set up a special collection.

"I want a book on. . ." Some YAs don't like anything you give them. The question they ask is probably their thesis statement, and they want you to find a single book that answers that question exactly (and has pictures). This is an opportunity to explain that what the student really needs is not *a book* but rather *information* which might be contained in several books or other sources.

"I can't use an encyclopedia." Actually this is more a teacher issue than a student one. Even if you suggest another reference source, the word "encyclopedia" in the title may make a student think it cannot be used. Normally teachers mean they don't want the *World Book* used. If you are unsure about what the teacher wants but know that, for example, the *New Catholic Encyclopedia* is the best source, encourage the student to use that source. Give a copy of your card to take to the teacher, or try to contact the teacher yourself. Unfortunately, libraries can spend thousands of dollars for reference books that many students think can't be used.

"Do you have any books on religion?" Beware of broad questions, for underneath lurks the real one. In this case, pointing to the 200s is, of course, not the answer. But asking "What do you *really* want?" may not be the best strategy either. Try providing the YA with several options. Sure, some YAs may ask directly if you have *The Satanic Bible,* but the "books on religion" question is more common. Don't invade a YA's privacy any more than you would an adult's.

"Do you have any books on health?" We certainly can't always assume that a YA asking a question is working on a paper; some may be working out a problem. Asking the student who wants books on AIDS when his or her paper is due, for example, can be embarrassing for both the YA and the librarian. Again, the YA's privacy is of utmost importance.

"My son has to do a paper on. . ." If there is one type of patron that all reference librarians try to avoid, it is the parent doing research for a child. This situation can present all sorts of problems, not the least of which are your own misgivings about the situation. Some parents conduct research for their children willingly, others do so out of desperation. In any case, helping them is always a challenge because you seldom can do a reference interview—they've already told you all they know about what they need. If you can't present them with options to narrow the search, you might want to broaden the search and give them lots of materials to take home. Then the YA can choose the best ones for the assignment.

In a related scenario, the parent comes in with the child, but the parent does all the talking. Focus your eyes on the student and ask him or her the follow-up questions that will help you complete the reference transaction. The key is to separate the YA from the parent whenever possible. If you don't, you will never learn what the student really needs, only what the parent thinks he or she needs.

"Everyone has to do a paper on. . ." A potential nightmare. Again, you want to try to obtain as much information as possible about the assignment from the students and try to contact the teacher, or at least the school librarian. Unfortunately, many teachers won't help librarians help their students by bringing us in on the planning process for research assignments—or at least letting us know what projects are coming up.

"Why don't you have any books on?. . ." YAs are easily frustrated. Despite how easy we say it is to use libraries, it isn't for YAs who don't want to do it but have to. Over the desk you'll be dealing with a lot of frazzled students who have looked in the card catalog under "Civil War" and found only one book in the whole library on that topic. How would they know the correct subject heading? The key to doing reference work with students is finding ways to reduce the frustration level.

"Where's the card catalog?" As libraries automate, this question comes from almost every young patron at one time or another. The special challenge with YAs, given their strong egos, is that most will tell you they know how to use the cataloging system even if they don't. If you don't have library instruction available, you need to do it on the fly with individual patrons. The same techniques apply here: go slow, keep it simple, and repeat everything.

"I couldn't find it on the shelf." It sometimes is tough because we are anchored at our desks, but walking to the shelf with a student is always a good idea. Not only does it greatly increase the chance that the student will find the material and have a positive library experience, but there are other benefits. First, they see you are a real person with legs and everything. Second, you are reinforcing the fact that you really do care that they find what they need, and you are debunking the myth that all librarians do is sit and point toward the stacks. Third, that walk to the shelf is a window of opportunity for making a connection with a student. Use it to find out a name, or at least a school.

"Why don't you have any books about Hemingway?" (Asked by a YA after looking in the fiction section.) It is clear to us how libraries are organized, but not to many YAs. "Shouldn't everything having to do with Hemingway be in the same place?" they wonder. To them, that makes perfect sense. You may need to take a few minutes to show your YA patrons how libraries are organized so that they don't waste their time (and yours) looking in all the wrong places.

"Why can't I find any magazine articles about him on Infotrac?" (Same student researching Hemingway) This is another situation in which the student has good intentions but just isn't using the right tools. Without going into great detail, you can explain the kinds of topics Infotrac and other systems cover, and those for which they should look elsewhere.

"How many books am I allowed to check out?" Sometimes you get this question from a student who is holding a stack of books but is only doing a three-page paper. You don't want to discourage an enthusiastic researcher, but you may want to lend some advice. The student may not realize that having the most books cited does not necessarily mean having the best paper, and that some of the books in the pile probably duplicate information.

"How do you do an outline?" You might find yourself helping with more than research if you're not careful. Often students will ask you to help them complete certain parts of a project or interpret what their teachers have asked them to do. This is a tough call: the student wants help, not for you to hand over a copy of the *MLA Handbook*. You are not the teacher, however, and you don't want to give out incorrect information. Your best bet is probably to ask a lot of questions to help students focus their thinking and talk through the problem at hand for themselves.

"I can never find anything here!" Maybe this is the truth, maybe it's an exaggeration. But even one bad library experience can be enough for some YAs. Reference service to YAs has to be positive. Always look for a way to say "yes," or at least a way to avoid saying "no." Of course, there are times when there seems to be no other answer ("Can I take this reference book home?"), but there usually are solutions to even the most problematic questions: "Let's see if we have a circulating one." "Lets make a photocopy." "The same information is available in this other book." "It will be here tomorrow when you come back." "Sure, but only for overnight."

Obviously, every question a YA may ask requires a different response, but following are five principles to apply whenever you provide reference service to YAs:

1. Help students find the information they need
2. Be friendly both verbally and nonverbally
3. Help them increase their "information independence"
4. Follow up
5. Try to reduce frustration when necessary

Sometimes these goals can be met by more training, more sensitivity to YA needs, or a more concentrated effort. Imagine how frustrating it must be for a student to walk into a library, ask a question, and not receive an answer he or she desperately needs. For us, that question is just one hash mark on a statistical sheet; for a YA it might be the most important thing in the world at that moment.

PROACTIVE REFERENCE

YAs who won't approach the reference desk at all are a problem. Some don't ask for help because they want do to it themselves; others think they should do it themselves and won't seek assistance for that reason. Then there is plain old fear. Unsure of what to ask for or whom to ask, some YAs don't bother because it seems easier than confronting the unknown. Whatever the reasons, there is a large percentage of YAs who use libraries without seeking assistance. Some don't need it, but most just don't know how to go about asking for help.

STRATEGIES

1. Proactive: If they won't come to you, you need to find them. They are easy to spot, either wandering in the stacks like lost tourists or anchored at a computer terminal. The approach must be careful. Rather than asking, "Do you need help?" you might ask, "Are you finding what you need?" It is a subtle but crucial difference—they can admit they are not finding something more easily than they can admit they need help.

User friendly: We try to make libraries into self-service centers, but it just doesn't always work. A step in this direction is the development of special collections that not only meet students' needs in terms of information but also in terms of approach. Chicago Public, Baltimore County and other library systems have developed such collections. The purpose of these collections and any other related services (tutors, peer assistance, homework hotlines, term paper workshops, etc.) is to meet the goals of YA reference service. Figure 4-1 is an outline for a homework center.

Pathfinders: It is often not possible to put together such collections, so the next best thing is to at least put them together on paper. That is, produce for distribution documents that will help students help themselves. Most pathfinders will:

- define the topic
- list subject headings in catalogs/indexes
- list special reference books
- list browsing call numbers
- list cross references, including names.

The pathfinder, Figure 4-2, is a shortcut for both the student, who either doesn't have time or chooses to seek assistance, and for the librarian, who can use it to access materials on the most requested topics. Sometimes these are called homework cards and kept in files for students to access themselves.

4.2 READERS ADVISORY SERVICES

As we learned earlier, librarians are often not where YAs turn to get advice on what to read. Because they don't ask, we don't always keep up on the literature. Also, because there are so few YA librarians, very few library staff on the whole are reading YA literature. As a result, many of us fall back on our own prejudices about what YAs should read as opposed to what they might want to read.

The goals of providing a YA readers advisory service are:

1. Match YA reading interest with the library collection.

2. Provide access to the library collection.
3. Learn the likes/dislikes of YA readers.
4. Promote reading through the use of documents.
5. Find the right book for the right YA at the right time for the right reason.

READERS ADVISORY STRATEGIES

Don't wait for them. Many YAs do want help but just won't ask for it because of bad experiences or just plain shyness. You need to find them when they are browsing in the stacks.

Ask questions. All of the obvious ones: not just what they have read but what they liked about it or didn't like.

Then, ask more questions. Often "I dunno" is the response to your perfectly asked, "What is the last book you enjoyed reading?" Ask about favorite movie or TV shows, places they like to go, music, anything that will give you an idea of a YA's fields of interest.

Develop your own core collection. Either on paper or in your mind, sit down and develop a core list of authors and/or titles. Learn the names of at least three mystery authors you can always recommend, three historical authors, etc. In the appendix of this book is a core collection list and a genre list to help you get started.

Narrow the list down. This involves asking more questions. Do they care if it's mostly about a boy or a girl? Younger or older characters? Scary or funny? Fat or thin? First person or third person? Classic or popular? Hardback or paperback? Rural or urban? New author or familiar, dependable author? Even if you can't recommend particular books, at least help the YA get a handle on his or her own interests.

Eliminate. A lot of YAs are inarticulate in telling you what books they like, but can easily list all the things they don't like in book. ("Long" and "boring" are the real chart toppers in this area.)

Use the books. If you discover something they've read (and liked), find the book and examine it. Most paperback publishers include "If you liked this book, then try. . ." ads right in their YA books. A related technique is to quickly scan book spines for books

FIGURE 4-1 HOMEWORK CENTER

A homework center is a separate collection of materials gathered in one area to assist students in completing common school assignments.

PURPOSE:

The purpose of a homework center is to make using the library a less frustrating experience for students by gathering materials in one easy-to-locate area, by providing multiple copies of materials, by providing special materials designed to meet students' needs, and by making items available to be retrieved independently and quickly. It is designed for the student who needs only a few resources to start on a paper and not more detailed instruction. It is designed as a self-service reference center.

A homework center is not a regular reference collection, a temporary reserve shelf, or an encylopedia set.

MATERIALS:

1. POP TOPS: Pop tops are a series of folders with information often requested by students for term papers and reports. The reason for pop tops is to see that student looking for information on topics for which all books may be checked out will not leave empty handed. These folders will not check out, but materials may be photocopied. Each folder will contain an "opposing viewpoint" pamphlet on the topic, five overview or "pro and con" type articles (either photocopied or purchased from the Social Issues Resource Series) and a ten item bibliography, which will be updated quarterly to provide access to articles that appear in general interest magazines held by the library. The purpose of this bibliography is not to replace periodical indexes, but to meet the expected demand for information on these topics.

2. CIRCULATING REFERENCE BOOKS: The center will contain multiple copies of various standard reference works available in paperback. These can be used either in the study center or to be taken home for overnight loan.

FIGURE 4-1   HOMEWORK CENTER, cont.

Works include:

*dictionary

*thesaurus

*foreign language dictionary

*almanacs

*medical dictionary

*Guinness Book of World Records

*mythology dictionary

*science/technology dictionary

*atlases

*geographical dictionary

*one volume biographical dictionary

*quotation dictionary

3. STUDENT HELPERS: The center will also contain multiple copies of various handbooks instructing students on:

    *how to write a term paper
    *how to write a book report
    *how to footnote correctly (MLA)
    *how to do a science project
    *how to use reference materials

4. OPPOSING VIEWPOINTS: The center will also have multiple copies of paperback editions of books in the Greenhaven Press series. Books will cover those topics in the Pop Tops folders and others. Books published in Watts' "impact series may also be considered for purchase.

FIGURE 4-2 PATHFINDER

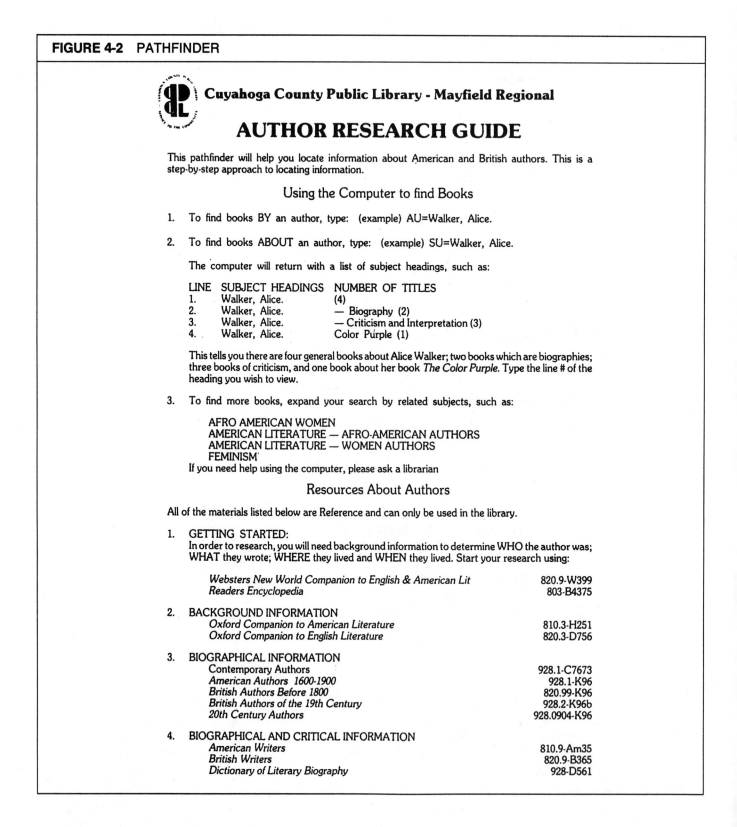

Cuyahoga County Public Library - Mayfield Regional

AUTHOR RESEARCH GUIDE

This pathfinder will help you locate information about American and British authors. This is a step-by-step approach to locating information.

Using the Computer to find Books

1. To find books BY an author, type: (example) AU=Walker, Alice.

2. To find books ABOUT an author, type: (example) SU=Walker, Alice.

    The computer will return with a list of subject headings, such as:

LINE	SUBJECT HEADINGS	NUMBER OF TITLES
1.	Walker, Alice.	(4)
2.	Walker, Alice.	— Biography (2)
3.	Walker, Alice.	— Criticism and Interpretation (3)
4.	Walker, Alice.	Color Purple (1)

    This tells you there are four general books about Alice Walker; two books which are biographies; three books of criticism, and one book about her book *The Color Purple*. Type the line # of the heading you wish to view.

3. To find more books, expand your search by related subjects, such as:

    AFRO AMERICAN WOMEN
    AMERICAN LITERATURE — AFRO-AMERICAN AUTHORS
    AMERICAN LITERATURE — WOMEN AUTHORS
    FEMINISM
    If you need help using the computer, please ask a librarian

Resources About Authors

All of the materials listed below are Reference and can only be used in the library.

1. GETTING STARTED:
    In order to research, you will need background information to determine WHO the author was; WHAT they wrote; WHERE they lived and WHEN they lived. Start your research using:

Websters New World Companion to English & American Lit	820.9-W399
Readers Encyclopedia	803-B4375

2. BACKGROUND INFORMATION
Oxford Companion to American Literature	810.3-H251
Oxford Companion to English Literature	820.3-D756

3. BIOGRAPHICAL INFORMATION
Contemporary Authors	928.1-C7673
American Authors 1600-1900	928.1-K96
British Authors Before 1800	820.99-K96
British Authors of the 19th Century	928.2-K96b
20th Century Authors	928.0904-K96

4. BIOGRAPHICAL AND CRITICAL INFORMATION
American Writers	810.9-Am35
British Writers	820.9-B365
Dictionary of Literary Biography	928-D561

FIGURE 4-2 PATHFINDER, cont.

5. CRITICAL INFORMATION BY LITERARY TYPE

Critical Survey of Poetry	809.1-C869
Critical Survey of Short Fiction	809.3-M272
Critical Survey of Long Fiction	809.3-C869
Critical Survey of Drama	822.009-C869

6. CRITICAL INFORMATION BY TIME PERIOD

Contemporary Literary Criticism	809-R34
19th Century Literary Criticism	809.034-N622
20th Century Literary Criticism	809.04-T918
Literary Criticism from 1400-1800	809.2-L712

7. CRITICAL INFORMATION BY NATIONALITY

Critical Temper (British & American)	820.9-C869
Modern American Literature	810.9005-Sch39m
Modern British Literature	820.90091-T247m
American Women Writers	016.81099287-Am35

8. CRITICAL INFORMATION/ PLOT SUMMARIES

Cliff Notes	pamphlet file
Masterplots	808-M272
Masterplots II (American fiction series)	809.3-M3931
Masterplots II (Short fiction series)	809.3-M3932
Masterplots II (British series)	823.0094-M393

9. INDEXES & BIBLIOGRAPHIES (list of other sources)

Drama Criticism Index	016.8092-B745
Literary Criticism Index	016.809-W431
Magills Bibliography of Literary Criticism	016.8-M272
Poetry Explication Index	016.821-K963
Short Story Explication Index	016.80931-W154

10. PERIODICAL INDEXES

    Unless you are researching a contemporary author, DO NOT USE InfoTrac.

Essay & General Literature Index	Index Table
Humanities Index	Index Table

11. SPECIALIZED REFERENCE BOOKS (examples:)

Arthurian encyclopedia (literary topic)	809.93351-A
McGraw-Hill Encyclopedia of Drama (literary genre)	809.2-M75
Modern Black Writers (ethnic literature)	809.8896-M72
Shakespeare Criticism (author reference book)	822.33 D Sh157

12. READY REFERENCE FILE

    The literature specialist at Cuyahoga County Public Library Mayfield Regional has compiled a handy file to provide quick access to hard-to-find resources. Please ask the librarian if you would like to see this file.

by the same publisher. It is not the most foolproof way to find a book for your YA patron, but you might stumble on the perfect title.

Be smart. If the person hasn't expressed a real interest in reading and has told you there is a book report due tomorrow, there is nothing wrong with setting *Moby Dick* aside and suggesting a "thin one."

Use the return cart. Everyone knows the best books are often the ones just returned. Bring over the items to be shelved and go through them together.

Be aware. You need to be very sensitive to how a young person is reacting to you. If the response is kind of quiet, for example, then you should stay low key to help the student feel comfortable.

Things not to say include:

"I loved (gush gush gush) this book."

"I loved this book in school."

"My teenage son/daughter loved this book."

"They use this book in many schools."

"Teachers often recommend this book."

"Everyone should read it."

Find a fit. Try to avoid outright stereotyping, but often a YA's clothes, hair, and manner say something about his or her identity, and possibly reading tastes. In other words, consider suggesting *Weetzie Bat* to anyone who wears a Mohawk.

Aim high rather than low. You will immediately lose whatever credibility you may have if you suggest a book that is below a YA's reading level or age group. As a rule, most YAs want to read about kids one to two years older than themselves. Thus, your high school juniors and seniors might want recommendations from the adult collection rather than the YA stacks, which they might consider "kid's stuff."

No advice can be the best advice. If you can't really peg the kid or if nothing comes to mind, just admit it. Remember, a lot of YAs get turned off because they get bad advice rather than no advice at all. The worst thing you can do is recommend the wrong book to the wrong person for the wrong reason.

Don't offer unsolicited recommendations. Sometimes a young person browsing is doing just that and doesn't want or need help—this time. But if you see he or she has tucked away a particular title (*The Outsiders,* for example), then jot down some possible titles for next time.

Offer recommendations "by special request." Offer a personal bibliography service for your avid readers. Have YAs fill out a card, Figure 4-3, and mail them the results of your search. Hang on to the cards, and notify them as new books come in that you think might interest them.

FIGURE 4-3 PERSONAL BIBLIOGRAPHY CARD

Want to find more good books to read? Here's an easy way. Just fill out this card and one of our librarians will mail you a list of recommend books based on what you told us about what you like and don't like. It should take about two weeks to compile your first list:

NAME:

ADDRESS:

SCHOOL:　　　　　GRADE:　　　　　AGE:

1. Name three of your favorite authors:

2. Please circle the kinds of books you like best:

HUMOR　MYSTERY　ROMANCE　NONFICTION　HORROR

FANTASY　SCIENCE FICTION　REALISTIC　THRILLERS

OTHER:

3. Which of these do you like the least?

4. Do you prefer books about:

YOUNGER TEENAGERS　YOUR OWN AGE　OLDER TEENAGERS

5. Do your prefer books:

UNDER 150 PAGES　UNDER 200 PAGES　DOESN'T MATTER

6. Anything else you can tell us that would help us find good books for you?

Prepare for parent visits. Many times it is Mom who has come in to pick up something for her non-reading son hoping (again) to find the one book that will hook him. For these occasions, every YA area should have copies of "Quick Picks," the list produced by YALSA for the reluctant teen reader. If the YA is there with a parent, you want to try to get the YA away from the parent long enough to gather information without commentary. The goal is to find out what the YA wants to read, not what the parent thinks he or she should read.

The big one. In addition to your core collection, you should also choose a personal favorite—the one "big book" you would recommend to almost any YA. This is especially necessary if all the other strategies fail and you need a rabbit to pull out of your hat.

SELF-HELP STRATEGIES

Some effective ways of helping YAs find books they'll enjoy involve letting them help themselves—and each other:

Card file: Since a friend's recommendation is the most common way YAs learn about books, you could sponsor that activity. Using a form like the one in Figure 4-4, ask YAs to write down what they liked about a book and file the comments by author, title, or even by "reviewer." This is a low-cost, low-maintenance activity that can be very helpful to young readers. You must make it very clear on the form, however, that the comments will be used in a public way or make use of reviewer's name optional.

Newsletters: You could take the same information and edit the best reviews in a newsletter. Better yet, try to recruit some YAs to do it. You could then post the newsletter in the YA area, distribute it to schools and school libraries, and send a copy to your local newspaper for use on the "teen pages."

"If You Like. . ." lists: Readers advisory is sometimes as simple as matching a book a person has liked with another one they will like. A series of prominently displayed "If You Like. . ." lists can work to that effect. Choose a very popular YA author or title and list books with a similar plot, theme, tone, or hook. You might even create a display on the shelf where the popular author's books are located. Just the exercise of doing such a list will expose staff to many YA authors. In addition to the lists in Figures 4-5 and 4-6, following are some recommendations you might make:

FIGURE 4-4 TALK BACK TO BOOKS FORM

TALK BACK TO BOOKS FORM

NAME_____ SCHOOL_____

ADDRESS_____ GRADE_____

AUTHOR_____ TITLE_____

In the space provided below , please describe this book and why you did or did not like it.

_____
_____
_____
_____
_____
_____
_____

THANKS ! Look for your review to appear in our newsletters.
Please return this form to the reference librarian.

FIGURE 4-5

If you liked

then you should try...

Bonham, Frank. *Durango Street*. A savage story of street gangs in the ghetto. Also by this author: *Viva Chicano*

Cormier, Robert. *Beyond the Chocolate War*. The boys who suffer at the hands of a gang leader band together

DeClements, Barthe. *I Never Asked You to Understand Me*. A group of unruly students land in an alternative school

Forshay-Lunsford, Cin. *Walk Through Cold Fire*. A young girl gets mixed up with a gang known as the Outlaws

- If you like Paula Danziger, then try: Ellen Conford, Nat Hentoff, Ron Koetge, Gordan Korman, Barbara Park, Marilyn Sachs, Jerry Spinelli, and Paul Zindel.
- If you like Stephen King, then try: Clive Barker, John Coyne, John Farris, Dean Koontz, Robert McCammon, John Saul, Peter Straub, and Whitley Strieber.
- If you like Gary Paulsen, then try: Michael French, Jean George, Felice Holman, James Houston, P.J. Petersen, Arthur Roth, Julian Thompson, and Robb White.
- If you like Christopher Pike, then try: Avi, A. Bates, Caroline Cooney, Richie Cusick, Lois Duncan, Diane Hoh, Joan Lowery Nixon, and R.L. Stine.
- If you like *Sweet Valley High,* then try: Cynthia Blair, Hila Colman, Caroline Cooney, Linda Cooney, Linda Lewis, Susan Pfeffer, Ann Reit, and Marjorie Sharmat.

FIGURE 4-6

If you liked

then you should try...

Betancourt, Jeanne. *Sweet Sixteen and Never*. A young woman's discovery of her mother's old diary helps her confront her sexuality and make a difficult decision

Bogard, Larry. *The Better Angel*. Three high school seniors cope with the changes happening in their lives

Filichia, Peter. *A Matter of Finding the Right Girl*. A high school senior has only two days to find "the sure thing"

Hart, Bruce. *Sooner or Later*. A thirteen year old girl's crush on a rock singer leads to a choice about growing up too fast

• If you like J.R.R. Tolkien, then try: Terry Brooks, Susan Cooper, Stephen Donaldson, Diana Wynne Jones, Ursula LeGuin, Anne McCaffrey, Robin McKinely, and Mary Stewart.

Leave out jobber catalogs: Rip out or copy the YA pages from Ingram and B & T monthly catalogs. These will tell YAs about upcoming releases and provide short descriptions.

Collect booklists: *VOYA, Booklist,* and other journals publish booklists constantly. Photocopy them, put them in a looseleaf binder, put subject headings on them, and put them on display for people to use. Put any of your own lists in here as well, or any lists you've collected from colleagues or conferences. A "list of book-lists" is included in the August issue of *Booklist*.

Collect reviews: In your peer review card file, you can also keep copies of reviews from professional journals. The best source is the *ALAN Review* because the reviews come ready to cut out as index cards, and because they cover both paper and hardback books.

Displays: Try doing catchy displays and changing them monthly. This is an excellent way to help YAs find materials.

Make your own booklists: In addition to an "If You Like. . ." series, you might want to put together some other lists. Although some studies indicate that lists are a tremendous waste of trees, others suggest they can be an effective tool for increasing patrons' awareness about titles. Before you begin putting together a list, however, there are some strategies to consider to make the list more effective.

BOOKLIST STRATEGIES

Decide on a format: You may want to use a form like the one in Figure 4-7 to help you organize your information. You also may want to decide on some basic style factors in advance such as:

In what tense will annotations be written?

How long will annotations be?

Are there any limits on how old or new the books listed will be?

What are your criteria in terms of in print status? number of pages?

FIGURE 4-7 BOOKLIST INFORMATION FORM

TITLE OF LIST:

AUDIENCE: CHILDREN   YOUNG ADULTS ADULTS

For each title on list please complete the following information:

AUTHOR: _____

TITLE: _____

CALL #: _____

PUBLISHER/YEAR:_____

ANNOTATION: (no more than three sentences; use
action verbs; end some with questions)

_____

_____

_____

_____

_____

Are multiple copies available? [ ]yes [ ]no

Is book in print in paperback? [ ]yes [ ]no

How should list be arranged? [circle one]

AUTHOR   TITLE   CALL NUMBER

NAME:_____ DATE:_____

Quick, not comprehensive: Maybe our dream is to find every book on the subject of our list, but a short list is better. It is less intimidating and easier for YAs to use. If you list everything, then you are not really using the list as a readers advisory tool (to recommend) but as a catalog of your collection.

Hooks, not books: Don't put any book titles on the front of the list. Instead, start the list with an intriguing question. For example, a booklist on teen stress might begin with the question, "Feeling stressed out?" Following are the "answers" to the question—the list of books you have gathered. The idea is to hook YAs on the idea of the list first.

Active, not passive: Direct mail marketing tells us that you should give the reader something to do—it increases interest in the piece. For the teen stress list, for example, you could add a stress test. At least part of a booklist should be interactive.

Pbk all the way: Why make 500 copies of a book list suggesting books of which there are only a limited number of hardback copies? Granted, even if every person who got the list wanted a paperback copy, you still would not be able to meet the demand, but you would meet it better than with one hardback copy. Also, if the list does generate real interest and you need to buy more copies, you can get paperbacks into patrons' hands more quickly and cheaply.

Create, don't copy: You don't need to do a book list on teen suicide: that is why you have a catalog. Rather than subject headings, use either broader themes (such as teen problems) or specific topics with limited subject access as your list topics. In the case of fiction, look not so much for common themes but for related emotions.

Copy, don't create: Write publishers and get permission to use their cover art as part of your booklist. If you use the recognizable cover of a popular book and put it on your list, the list is recognizable. Why use clip art when you could use the work of professional artists whose job it is to create interest in a book?

Excite don't annotate: An annotation only tells readers what a book is about. Your lists should tell YAs why they would want to read these books. Try a one-sentence catchy, tagline that defines the book. Like a short booktalk, it should excite the reader, not summarize the plot.

Borrow, don't write: Look at the back of some paperbacks and see how people whose job is it to write create interest in a book in just a few sentences. Borrow heavily from their ideas and words.

Display: Once your list is done, don't just leave it on a table somewhere. Gather books on the list and those related to them, enlarge a copy of the list to poster size, stuff each book with a list, and watch the books move.

Measure: Before you put your list out, log the status of the books on the list, then monitor all or selected titles. This will help you keep track of their availability and evaluate the success of your list.

Share: Depending on your relationship with local school librarians, you might want to work on the list together. If that is not possible, then ask the school librarian to look at the list and indicate which titles that library owns. You can then customize copies of the list and send them to the school with a * next to those titles. It is better to share the work and customize access than to just dump your leftover lists on schools as an afterthought.

Review and Revise: Once you develop a core group of lists, you should set up a revision schedule so lists are kept fresh and up-to-date.

Benefits: No list is going to quadruple YA circulation, but the time spent putting one together can have many other benefits. For the person compiling the list, the time spent wading through catalogs and other tools pays off in greater knowledge about the literature. If you have involved the school, then a bridge has been built with an important ally. Also, working on a list can involve other members of your staff, who might not otherwise have the experience, in the YA cause.

Tools: The best way to prepare yourself for recommending books is to read them all. Since that is not possible, you need to rely on the tools that are out there to help you. The tools for readers advisory are the same ones you would use for collection development — books like *Books for You* provide access by subject with descriptive annotations. Two other wonderful sources are the catalogs produced by Perma-Bound and Econo-Clad. These two companies' catalogs list scores of YA novels by subject and offer perhaps the best access of any tools in the field. In addition to the appendix of this book, there are numerous other sources listed in the bibliography that you can use to familiarize yourself with YA literature or for quick reference.

4.3 LIBRARY ORIENTATION

We know that 25 percent of public library patrons are YAs, but we don't know what percentage of YAs use libraries. Nevertheless, we can be sure that library instruction and orientation can increase that percentage dramatically.

Orientation means simply to orient YAs to their physical surroundings. It is not like being a teacher; it is more like being a tour guide. Depending on the amount of time available, a tour might cover only one section of a library or one department. You might show students the catalog so that they know where and what it is, but a tour is not the time to teach them how it works. Library instruction covers how things work and when they should be used. At the highest level, bibliographic instruction answers the "why" question and should be thorough enough to cover not just tools but also concepts of search strategy. Which type of activity a library offers depends a good deal on what the teachers are teaching and what they feel are the needs of students.

There is a body of literature about both library instruction and orientation available, but very little of it deals with public libraries. Nevertheless, the rationales provided to support this kind of instruction can be applied to public libraries. The public library can help bridge the gap between these two learning experiences, and the library itself can also benefit by providing such instruction.

WHY DO IT?

Efficiency: Instruction and orientation are efficient ways to reach YAs. Rather than explaining the same source over and over, a group instruction session lets you explain use of the source to several students at one time.

Fairness: The philosophy of public librarianship is that all patrons receive equal treatment, but the reality of busy reference desks often keeps this from happening. Sometimes students do not receive the help they need because they come in at a busy time, their questions are deemed to be less important than those of adults, or because some staff just aren't skilled at helping teenagers. In an instruction session, everyone gets equal treatment. Since for many students just getting to the library is a major accomplishment, an instruction session for YAs will give them another reason to visit the library.

Library literacy: Although schools are the primary providers of instruction to YAs, it is necessary for public libraries to augment this instruction. Because the public library is usually larger, many of the sources students need can be found there rather than in the school library. Some school libraries have flexible hours, but most are not open enough hours or at the right times (the night before the paper is due) for students to use them as much as they need to. In many communities the public library is more fully automated than the school library and provides the only exposure some students have to computer databases for information retrieval. Finally, all learning needs to be reinforced, and the public library can complement instruction already provided in the school library. All libraries need to be concerned that young people's information skills transfer: that the skills learned in a school library can be used in a public library, then in the college library setting, and throughout life.

Future users: Not all students go to college. Nonetheless, the skills developed to write a high school term paper can be used to retrieve other types of information that can benefit a student later in life.

Positive experience: For some YAs, their trip to the public library for an orientation or instruction session might be the only one they ever make. If the instruction session shows the library in a positive light, the students may choose to follow up and actually visit the public library to work on a paper. When they do, they are more likely to have a positive experience because they are not starting from scratch. Even if they don't remember (most won't) how a particular source works, they will at least know it exists and that they can use it. Instruction and orientation upfront helps decrease frustration and failure for the student later.

Community relations: But what does it do for the library? First, it is good public relations. Working with schools to bring in busloads of YAs makes a very positive impression. Second, it gets the face and name of the YA librarian known. This recognition factor is important in all phases of YA work. Third, it establishes a working relationship between the library and schools that can be helpful in many other ways. Finally, if you are bringing YAs in by the busload, signing them up for library cards, showing them materials and teaching them how to use various tools to find information, their use of the library is sure to increase.

Professional Responsibilities: By providing library instruction and orientation, we are meeting a professional obligation. The American Library Association states:

> In order to assist individuals in the independent information retrieval process basic to living in a democratic society, the American Library Association encourages all libraries to includes instruction in the use of libraries as one of the primary goals of service. Libraries of all types share the responsibility to educate users in successful information location, beginning with their childhood years and continuing the education process through their years of professional and personal growth.[1]

The advantages of library orientation and instruction are many for everyone involved. Although there has been some revisionist thought about the effectiveness of such programming, including an article in *Library Journal* called "User Instruction Does Not Work,"[2] a long history of success suggests that it does work. If libraries are in the information business, it seems the first step is to provide information to our users about how we store information and how they may retrieve it.

ORIENTATION: STRATEGIES AND DOCUMENTS

Planning: Almost every library conducts tours of some sort. But planning a successful tour is not as easy as it may seem. The first step is to organize your tour as a coordinated library program: something you can define, plan, implement, and evaluate (Figure 4-8). The better organized the tour, the more information you'll be able to collect and the more you'll be able to improve future tours. Organizing the overall tour program will help you expand your tour "client list" beyond the same teachers who contact the library each year. The rest of the library staff needs to know what you are doing, what their involvement will be and what you hope to accomplish.

Setting Objectives and Limits: Specific objectives should be

FIGURE 4-8   ORIENTATION PLANNING CHECKLIST

TASK	PERSON	DONE
1. Contact schools	_____	____
2. Develop planning documents		
a. Information sheet	_____	____
b. Set objectives	_____	____
c. Set policies	_____	____
3. Develop materials	_____	____
4. Recruit teachers	_____	____
5. Schedule tours		
a. Fill out form	_____	____
b. Check for conflicts	_____	____
c. Confirm date with teacher	_____	____
d. Mail out library card applications	_____	____
e. Mail out pre-test	_____	____
6. Conducting tours		
a. Gather materials	_____	____
b. Alert other departments	_____	____
c. Conduct tour	_____	____
d. Distribute library cards	_____	____
e. Distribute post test	_____	____
7. Evaluate tours		
a. Review student evaluations	_____	____
b. Review teacher evaluations	_____	____
c. Correct/evaluate pre and post tests	_____	____
d. Complete reporting form	_____	____
8. Evaluate program		
a. Review objectives	_____	____
b. Compile statistics/reporting forms	_____	____

flexible and, ideally, coordinated with teacher and school library practices, but your basic goals should always stay the same: to provide information literacy tools for every young person growing up in the community. The policies will determine what you will and will not do and must therefore be established up front.

Testing: Tours may not be instruction in themselves, but they can still be educational experiences. To learn how much students already know (as opposed as to what they claim to know), a short pre- and post-test such as the one in Figure 4-9, can be an effective tool. This could be done in the classroom or on the bus to and from the library. This is the only actual handout you will need for each group. Since the idea of a tour is to have students looking at what you are showing them, it is not really necessary to prepare other materials.

Planning the tour: Each library will have different highlights to

---

FIGURE 4-9   ORIENTATION: PRE- AND POST-ORIENTATION TESTS

1. What would you use in the library to find a magazine article about skateboarding?

_____

2. In what section of the library would you find music videos?

_____

3. Where would you look to find out if library owned any books about playing Nintendo?

_____

4. Library books can be checked out for _____ weeks.

5. Where is the library's Young Adult area located?

_____

cover on a tour, and each librarian will have a unique personal style. Any tour, however, can be broken up into the following components:

- *The Hook:* Lets assume most students are not going to be fired up about visiting the library. The first thing you need to do, then, is increase their level of interest. The tour should start with something that is attention getting: a section of YA movie tie-ins, videos, teen magazines or other popular items. You want your YAs excited right off the bat to get them interested in the tour, in the library, and in you. Explaining the card catalog first won't do this.
- *The Walk:* A major part of every tour is the guided walk —lots of walking and pointing. The tour route should be logical and follow the path the student is likely to follow in doing research. Be careful not to overload your guests with information. At each stopping point (e.g., the catalog), explain what it is, when it should be used, and where to go next. Use lots of examples and analogies, and reinforce points. Invite participation and interaction if possible.
- *The Grill:* You should let the students ask a lot of questions, and ask some yourself too. Sometimes a question can be used to begin a part of the tour ("What's the *Reader Guide?*"), or illustrate examples.
- *The Card:* As noted in the process section, you want to have cards ready to go at this point. Only students with specific problems need to interact with the desk staff, others can be given their new cards immediately. If you show students a lot of library materials, you need to offer them access to them.
- *The Search:* You want to reinforce what you have just shown. Leave time at the end for students to use the sources, visit the departments and examine the machines. You'll probably need to circulate among the students to answer questions. This can be either an organized activity (making up a list of things to find) or free time.

Captivate your audience. YAs are probably not the most willing audience you will find for a library tour, but here are a few strategies for catching their interest:

- *Start Young:* Whatever the youngest grade is in your library's YA scheme, that is the grade at which to start. Seventh graders are still open to new impressions, and you are laying important groundwork for library use throughout their remaining school years.

- *Keep Your Cool:* Since a tour is a group activity, you may run up against a peer leader who will want to challenge you. Refer back to the skills on dealing with YAs and take it with good humor. Just because that YA doesn't make a good first impression, you still have to.
- *Amaze Them:* There is so much technology out there that it is getting harder to "wow" YAs, but you still have to try. Use the machines you have, microfilm printers for example, and make a copy of something to put into somebody's hands. Let at least one person (maybe the leader mentioned above) walk away with something tangible.
- *Reinforce:* After you have visited each stop on the tour, reinforce either through statements or questions what has just been learned. Do a quick review at the end.
- *Say Yes:* During the tour YAs will ask questions, reference or otherwise. If you can't answer then, make sure to get names and follow up. For example, if a YA wants to know all the tapes you have by REM but your computer catalog doesn't have a printer, make a list if you can. It's a small thing, but it can make a big impression.
- *Keep It Simple:* Most of us want to share the many wonders of libraries, even with those who don't particularly want to hear about them. The goal with YAs is to make them feel comfortable about finding information, not to give them so much data that they feel overwhelmed.
- *Be Prepared:* In all the small ways. If you are going to demonstrate a microfilm copier, do you have the machine set up? Did you put an "out of order" sign on it about ten minutes before the tour to make sure it will be available? Do you have a dime that will work in the machine? Is there enough toner? All of these tiny things make a world of difference. By making the tour go smoothly, you are conveying an image of competence and confidence to your audience.
- *Listen To Yourself:* Every now and then tape yourself or ask another staff member to listen in on your presentation. Because tours are usually all the same, it is easy to fall into a rut doing them. If it seems boring to you, it may seem that way to your audience, too.

CONTACTING THE SCHOOLS

Although you can conduct tours for groups other than students, schools are your main contacts. At this point, you know what you want to do, why are you are doing it, and how you will do it. Working with the schools is the single most enjoyable and frustrating experience for most YA librarians. Connecting with schools is discussed further in Chapter Five, but here are a few strategies:

Start With Your Colleagues: If the school has a media specialist/librarian, that is probably the best place to start. This is not only because of professional courtesy, but also because the school librarian usually knows the most cooperative teachers in the building. Also, the librarian can help you through the maze of dealing with a school: in some schools you can call a teacher directly, in others regulations dictate that every outside contact start at the administrative level.

Meet Department Chairs: Have the school librarian introduce you to the various department chairs, especially English and Social Studies. Make yourself available to attend a department meeting and sell your program.

Success Breeds Success: If you are planning a major program, you'll want to start with a pilot effort. Use teachers you have worked with in the past and encourage them to enlist their colleagues' participation.

Best-Case Scenario: Much of this kind of thing is done on the fly. A more desirable approach however, would be to plan a program that encourages the involvement of all teachers. If you can set it up at the administrative level rather than with teachers and librarians, the principal is more likely to support expanding the program.

Scheduling: Once you have contacted teachers and/or developed your program, you are ready to schedule visits. Check your library's master calendar to make sure you are not conducting tours on the same days as other departments (unless it is a very big building), or when the library will be short-staffed. The tour has to be arranged not just to fit your schedule, but the whole library's plans for the day.

Evaluations: Ask both teachers and students to fill out short evaluation forms after the tour (Figures 4-10, 4-11). After collecting the evaluations and "grading" pre- and post-tour tests, you should analyze this information and report it. A reporting form (Figure 4-12) organizes all the information in one place and will come in handy when it's time to compile statistics for the whole program.

FIGURE 4-10 STUDENT EVALUATION FORM

SCHOOL: _____ DATE:_____

TEACHER:_____ GRADE:_____

All day long students ask librarians questions. Now it is our turn. Please tell us what you thought of your orientation so that we may improve our service.

Please check the most appropriate answer:

1. This presentation was:

[ ]organized [ ]somewhat organized [ ]disorganized

2. This presentation was:

[ ]interesting [ ]somewhat interesting [ ]boring

3. I already knew:

[ ]most of this   [ ]some   [ ]very little [ ]none

4. This information should be:

[ ]very valuable [ ]somewhat valuable [ ]of no value

5. I use the public library:

[ ]all the time [ ]often [ ]now and then [ ]never

The main thing I learned today was:

_____

_____

Other comments:

FIGURE 4-11 TEACHER EVALUATION FORM

ACTIVITY: Library Tour

Date: Time:

Teacher:

School:

# of Students: Grade: Class:

1. Did this presentation meet your objectives:

[ ]yes   [ ]no

2. This presentation was:

[ ]well organized [ ]somewhat organized [ ]disorganized

3. This presentation was:

[ ]interesting [ ]somewhat interesting [ ]boring

4. This information should be:

[ ]very valuable [ ]somewhat valuable [ ]of no value

5. Would you recommend this service to colleagues:

[ ]yes [ ]no

6. What did you like best about this presentation?

_____

7. What did you like least about this presentation?

_____

8. How could this presentation be improved?

_____

Other comments?

Please attach this to student evaluations and return to:

FIGURE 4-12 REPORTING FORM

Activity: Library Tour   DATE/TIME:

Teacher:

School:

# of students: Grade: Class:

Librarian:

Student evaluation totals:

1. [ ]well organized [ ]somewhat [ ]disorganized
2. [ ]interesting   [ ]somewhat [ ]boring
3. [ ]most of this [ ]some [ ]very little [ ]none
4. [ ]very valuable [ ]somewhat   [ ]of no value
5. [ ]all the time [ ]often [ ]now and then [ ]never

Test Results:

pre-test:	post-test:
5/5 [ ]	5/5 [ ]
4/5 [ ]	4/5 [ ]
3/5 [ ]	3/5 [ ]
2/5 [ ]	2/5 [ ]
1/5 [ ]	1/5 [ ]
0/5/ [ ]	0/4 [ ]

Teacher evaluations:

1. [ ]yes [ ]no
2. [ ]well organized [ ]somewhat [ ]disorganized
3. [ ]interesting   [ ]somewhat [ ]boring
4. [ ]very valuable [ ]some value [ ]no value
5. [ ]yes [ ]no

The library orientation program is an important first step in establishing YA services. It creates good will with schools, it brings YAs into the library, it puts your face in front of your target group and it exposes the rest of the library staff to YAs. The purpose of the forms given here is to provide a useful structure for services you may wish to initiate or improve upon in your library.

Conducting a tour seems like an easy thing, but it really isn't. Too often it is seen as an inconvenience. In fact, for many YAs the tour is the first time they've been in your library or at least the first time they've been there without their parents. The tour is your chance to make a good impression and wipe out some of the negative stereotypes YAs may have about your library. Finally, the tour is your chance to make the connection. You will meet YAs who will come visit you that very same day. Others will see you on the street or at their school and remember you. The key to making the *connection* is making an *impression*.

4.4 LIBRARY INSTRUCTION

Library instruction is the next step. You might give a thorough instruction session to the same group of YAs later in the year, perhaps when they have a specific assignment. Most likely, however, you'll find yourself helping high school students when they are deep in the term paper bog. There are primarily two kinds of instruction: the general "how to do any term paper" type and the more detailed, focused instruction on certain types of sources. Both kinds of instruction operate on the same principle. Teaching not just what tools to use, but also how to use them and why.

STRATEGIES AND DOCUMENTS:
Use the following questions to guide your planning and prepare you for potential obstacles.

What are teachers doing and saying? Sometimes quite a lot, sometimes nothing at all. Sometimes a school library is not strong or teachers in the school don't think students need it. Selling some teachers on the importance of library instruction can be the hardest instruction of all.

What are school librarians doing and saying? Co-operation with the school library is essential for a variety of reasons. First, you want to build upon what students have already been taught and not dwell on things they already know. Also, as stated in the section on tours, a school librarian can be a valuable source of contacts. Unfortunately, a strong public library instruction program is sometimes seen as a turf invasion rather than as a collaborative effort to provide students with the information they need to be library-literate. Settling the turf issue is important because a good program gives students a better understanding of how all libraries work.

What is being done in your own library? A related turf issue might exist in your own library. Maybe each department does its own instruction and thinks it should stay that way. To be most effective, however, instruction should be coordinated by one department or individual who can involve other staff as needed. You may need to provide a justification for library instruction (as stated earlier) to convince a library director that it is worth the effort. Given our diminished resources, it seems any program that organizes resources better, creates more knowledgeable and independent users, better utilizes available resources, and eliminates duplication of staff effort is worth pursuing.

What will library instruction entail? Library instruction is more time consuming than orientation tours. Although you can develop general materials, teachers may want sessions tailored to their specific needs. Even if you can give the general term paper talk, you might have to add (or subtract) certain sources given the nature of the assignment. Teachers and your own staff need to know how your user instruction program is different from what is already being done.

What will instruction accomplish? The objectives of library instruction are similar to those already outlined for orientation, but there are important differences. Although orientation is educational, all you really want students to leave with is some information and positive feelings about the library. Instruction, however, is educational—the result should be learned skills. You need to establish learning objectives for the student and, because instruction is time-consuming to organize, give everyone involved (librarians and teachers) a clear understanding of what they will get out of it. Pre- and post-tests (like the ones used in orientation) can be modified to reflect the content of the instruction session.

How is instruction arranged? After initial contacts have been made with schools, it is time to contact individual teachers and the school librarian regarding scheduling of sessions. Because each teacher will want to focus on different sources, you will need to obtain more information from them than you did when scheduling the orientation tour. Once a teacher contacts you, you will want to book the date on the calendar, but also send out a form for the teacher to return so you can be prepared (Figure 4-13). Even better, try to meet with the teachers at the library. Chances are the teachers are not aware of many of the things you know students need to learn. Again, educating teachers about libraries often has to come first. The school librarian looks at this day in and day out and should be able to provide many insights.

What needs to be learned? Even though you've asked teachers to help tailor each session, you will still need to have a couple of set teaching outlines (Figure 4-14). These outlines will help you organize your thoughts and are valuable in case you want to involve others in the process. You will need an outline for the general "any topic" term paper. You will also want to develop a general one for American history, literature and whatever subject specialty your library offers. As with a tour, it is important not to introduce the card catalog too early in the session. You need to "win them over" and get their attention. Tell them something like, "If you give me your attention for the next 20 minutes, it will probably save you hours of frustration." Or ask how many of them want to spend extra hours doing research instead of the hundreds of fun things they would rather be doing. For each source you need to explain:

- What it is
- When to use it (and when not to use it)
- How to use it
- How to find the materials
- Where to find the materials.

The inner workings of each source and machine would be nice to cover, but there is not enough time, and most students won't remember a lot of details. Along the way, reinforce each point with questions and restatements.

For most students a research paper is a nightmare. Library instruction doesn't make the nightmare a dream, but it can help. I tell YAs to take their wonderfully crafted thesis statements and turn them into questions for their own use. Then, when they do

---

FIGURE 4-13 STUDENT LEARNING OBJECTIVES

Teacher:

School:

# of students:　　**Grade:**　　**Class:**

Day/time/length of visit:

Assignment:

Please check the types of sources you would like to be covered during your library instruction session:

[ ] Catalog

[ ] General periodical indexes

[ ] Newspaper indexes

[ ] Clipping services (SIRS/vertical file)

[ ] Subject periodical indexes:
　　[ ] General Science Index
　　[ ] Humanities Index
　　[ ] Business Periodicals Index
　　[ ] Social Science Index

[ ] Reference materials:
　　[ ] General encyclopedias/almanacs
　　[ ] Literature
　　[ ] Social sciences
　　[ ] Current events
　　[ ] Business
　　[ ] History
　　[ ] Biography

[ ] Other sources:

Would you like to discuss...
　　[ ] Choosing a topic?
　　[ ] Narrowing a topic?
　　[ ] Search strategy?
　　[ ] Footnotes/bibliography?
　　[ ] Other?

[ ] Will you want to schedule a second session for students just to work in the library?

Comments (materials? services? instruction tips?):

Please return this survey with pre-tests and completed library card applications at least one week before your visit. Thank you.

research they can concentrate on the materials that will answer these questions. That is what instruction does—help people answer questions. The only difference is that you're doing it for 20 students at one time rather than 20 times for one student. Throughout the instruction session, urge students to ask questions about everything—from how to find something to how a machine works. They need to know what we already know: the most valuable resource in the library is the staff.

This entire teaching outline can be covered in under thirty minutes. If at all possible, you want students to be able to take what they have learned and apply it immediately. Instruction sessions shouldn't last longer then 90 minutes total. More than sixty minutes of application won't work—YAs will begin to wander off to McDonald's. If you find most students are not using this time, you can either eliminate it from the schedule or work more closely with teachers to monitor students. You can eliminate the problem of 30 students crowded around the same machine if you work with the teacher to set objectives for each visit. Divide classes into groups with some working on books, others on magazines, etc. It will not only create less confusion, but it might make students use their time more effectively.

Handouts can be another way to help students do their work at the end of the session and when they return to the library on their own. LOEX (Library Orientation Exchange service in Ypsilanti, Michigan) is a clearing house for these instruction tools, which they collect from member libraries. Unfortunately, most public and school libraries don't belong to LOEX, and each library invents its own wheel.

There are other types of instruction aids you might develop: pathfinders and booklists were discussed earlier. You could develop handouts on specific tools (for example, how to use Infotrac), which could be distributed or left near the machine for "point of use" instruction. Or, you could develop a term paper kit to be used in conjunction with instruction as well as independently by students.

How is instruction evaluated? The evaluation tools used for tours can be used for instruction as well. The reporting form can also be used to collect all evaluation information. To round out the evaluation process, staff needs to observe the following:

- Do students seem to work more independently?
- Are questions more sophisticated? (Are they asking about a

FIGURE 4-14 TEACHING OUTLINE: INSTRUCTION

1. **Introduction**

   a. Introduce self and library
   b. Define purpose of visit
   c. Define your expectations of class

2. **Recognition of needs**

   a. Survey about current library use
   b. Survey about need to use for this paper
   c. Explain this session will save them time

3. **Reinforcement**

   a. All students have had library instruction
   b. All student know how to use school library
   c. All libraries work the same way (review concepts)
   d. Thus, students know how use public library
   e. What are differences and special sources?

4. **Defining topic**

   a. Topics to avoid
   b. Finding topic not too broad or narrow
   c. Turn thesis statement into question--all research should answer that question.

5. **Search strategy**

   a. Step-by-step approach
   b. Learn what source is, when to use, and how to use it
   c. Logical pattern to finding information

6. **Using catalog**

   a. Access points
   b. Problems with subject headings
   c. Finding bibliographic information
   d. Finding location of book in library
   e. Requesting/reserving materials not on shelf
   f. Problems with books (too big, too old)

FIGURE 4-14   TEACHING OUTLINE INSTRUCTION, cont.

7. Using periodical indexes

   a. Access points
   b. Problems with subject headings
   c. Finding bibliographic information
   d. Finding location of magazines
   e. Variety of formats/making copies
   f. Other indexes available

8. Using newspaper indexes

   a. Access points
   b. Problems with subject headings
   c. Finding bibliographic information
   d. Finding location of newspaper
   e. Variety of formats/making copies

9. Vertical file/clipping services

   a. Access points
   b. Using materials

10. Reference books

   a. When to use
   b. Different types (statistical, biographical)
   c. How to find

11. Review

   a. Search strategy
   b. Subject access
   c. What you use to find what

12. Conclusion

   a. Pass out test
   b. Pass out evaluations
   c. Collect forms
   d. Answer questions

particular magazine citation as opposed to asking how to find the magazines?).
- Are the reference materials mentioned in instruction used more and without as much difficulty?
- Is time being saved?

You will also want to follow up with teachers to get answers to the following questions:

- Were term papers better overall?
- Did students list more types of sources in their bibliographies?
- Did students comment positively on the experience?

By teaching, not only are you helping students achieve independence, but you are using all of your staff and material resources better. Staff is asked more sophisticated questions rather than having to start from scratch with each student. Students become aware of more sources. In other words, students have more information about finding information.

4.5 BOOKTALKING

If orientation introduces students to the physical layout of the library and instruction teaches them how to use the materials, then booktalking excites them about using the library—in particular, about reading YA literature. Booktalking is often easier to arrange than orientation or instruction because it involves one librarian going out to a school rather than bringing busloads of students into the library. If instruction connects YAs with library resources, then booktalking connects them with library treasures.

The definitive text on booktalking was written in 1980 by Dr. Joni Bodart. *Booktalk! Young Adult Booktalking and School Visiting*[3] covers all the mechanics of booktalking and contains hundreds of talks. Two subsequent editions have included more talks, and Bodart's newsletter, *The Booktalker* included in *Wilson Library Bulletin,* keeps those in the field up-to-date with talks on current books.

STRATEGIES AND DOCUMENTS:

Look at booktalking not as a sometime activity but as a regular part of a larger service program. Like the other activities, booktalking requires the same planning steps, but compared with instruction and orientation, much more preparation time is involved. Just as everyone can't be a successful instructor or tour guide, it takes some special talents to be a good booktalker. Nevertheless, these talents can be learned and perfected.

For most libraries, it is hard to find enough bodies to cover the desk. Bringing in tours is traditional, and at least no one has to leave the building all day. Booktalking is different—it is outreach. You have to leave the building to plan with teachers, and to do the actual talks. When staff is short, how can you be spared? And why? Because:

1. Booktalking increases circulation.
2. Booktalking promotes the library as a place for recreational use by YAs.
3. Booktalking allows the YA librarian to work with schools and be seen by students.
4. Booktalking is an efficient way to promote YA collections.
5. Booktalking provides YA librarians with an opportunity to use their creative talents for the good of the library.
6. You will reach more YAs in one day of booktalking than you will probably see over a week's time in the library.
7. Booktalking is one of the few library activities for which the primary audience is nonusers. There are two ways to increase circulation: get current users to check out more and create new users. Booktalking can accomplish both tasks.
8. Booktalking presents the library as an active force promoting reading in the community rather than just a warehouse of books.
9. Booktalking increases the audience's awareness of the library. The first step toward getting people to take action is to increase their awareness.
10. Booktalking is good PR—in schools, in the community, and personally for the successful booktalker.

If you can sell your boss on it, then selling it to teachers should be no problem. First, you'll need to increase their awareness, because chances are many teachers have never seen anyone booktalk. Although some school librarians are involved in this kind of activity, most can not offer this service. Booktalking is a kind of win-win proposition, benefiting both the students and the library. Most teachers want to accomplish the same thing you do—getting students to read more.

OBJECTIVES:

The objectives of booktalking are the same as those of the library's public relations department: to increase awareness and to increase use. The books you use may change, but the objective does not.

You might wish to set a policy on how many talks you will do in one day. Some people don't mind doing one in each of all six or seven class periods of a day, others do. It is also best, as suggested by the policy, not to combine classes. If you do, then the excitement of getting together becomes the center of attention, not the booktalk. Also, combining classes might mean mixing different reading levels. The best setting is the single classroom, with the librarian "taking over" the class from the teacher for that period.

SCHEDULING:

Scheduling booktalks takes a lot of work. You need to conduct a thorough interview with any teachers who are using your service for the first time. If you don't have any background about the class, you will probably not do well. The time of day must also be considered. Since booktalking requires a lot of energy from you and the class, the end of the week is generally not a good time, nor are classes first thing in the morning or late in the afternoon. Classes right after lunch are the most fun and challenging as the "Twinkie rush" kicks in during the middle of your presentation. The last trick of scheduling: book yourself for the entire class period. Darting in and out of rooms for part of a period is confusing for the teachers, provides for little interaction with YAs, and makes it too difficult for you to get into a good pace. You also need to allow time at the end of the sessions for YAs to choose among the books you've "talked".

ASSUMPTIONS:

Once you've scheduled the session and the teacher is expecting you, you have a big job: develop a fifty minute presentation which will excite teenagers about reading. Let's look at some of the assumptions about booktalking you should consider before your first booktalk.

Students won't be thrilled to see you: You may find it hard to believe that teenagers wouldn't be thrilled by someone from the library coming to talk about books. They may not be hostile, but don't expect an immediately warm reception. Assume that you have to win them over—and fast.

You are a performer: It's hard for some people, but that's the reality of the situation. You will be standing in front of a room as though on a stage. The YAs will be at their desks like an audience, and (like an audience) they will have a certain set of expectations.

You are a salesperson: Although it is called booktalking, you really are selling reading as an activity. You are trying to persuade, convince, even manipulate this audience to buy your "product." Look at what other "performers" and "sales people" do with their audiences. Here are some examples to watch for:

Movie previews: Watch how they are put together. They are designed to do exactly the same thing as a booktalk: create an interest in a product by telling just enough about it to make listeners want it all.

Pop Music: Tune in your radio and listen. Which song captures your attention? Think about what makes that song inviting. Most great songs have what are known as "hooks" that generate interest. The hook could be anything: the beat, the chorus, the instrumentation, a sing-along part—anything that creates interest and makes the song memorable.

Stand-up comics: Not that you should tell jokes, but look at the construction of a stand-up comic's act. Jokes usually have a tried-and-true opening line ("A funny thing happened. . ." or "This guy walks into a bar. . ."). They develop using limited detail and some characterization, then end with a punchline. A booktalk can be put together in much the same way.

Storytellers: Many children's librarians recognize the performance aspect of their job. They sell stories through characterization, sound effects, the use of props, or in a variety of other ways. They go beyond the text by making the story come alive, and they know that they are giving a performance. Librarians giving booktalks must have a similar mindset. They must realize it is show time.

WRITING

After examining your assumptions about what booktalking is and what it can be, you are ready to write some talks. At this point, it really becomes a matter of individual choice. Sometimes the teacher will give you a reading list and ask that you booktalk titles from that list only. Some people write booktalks as new titles cross their desk, while others take home stacks of paperbacks at a time. In *Booktalk,* Bodart describes the variations of writing the booktalk. Some people never write them down at all—everything is stored in their memory. Sometimes after reading a book, you just can't figure out what to say about it. Fortunately, there are several sources of published booktalks from which you can either lift ideas verbatim or adapt them to suit your needs:

Bodart, Joni, *Booktalk* (NY: Wilson, 1980).

Booktalk 2 (NY: Wilson, 1985).

Booktalk 3 (NY: Wilson, 1988).

Booktalker newsletter, Wilson Library Bulletin, 1989-.

Gillespie, John, *Junior Plots 3* (NY: Bowker, 1987).

Senior Plots (NY: Bowker, 1989).

Rochman, Hazel, *Tales of Love and Terror* (Chicago: American Library Association, 1987).

Spencer, Pam, "Easy Talking," *Voice of Youth Advocates,* 1988-.

Walker, Elinor. *Bookbait,* 4th ed. (Chicago: American Library Association, 1988).

If you are just starting, you will probably want to write your booktalks down. A booktalk card, shown in Figure 4-15, is a good way to organize your thoughts for the first time you do the talk and retain ideas for later talks. You'll want to have these cards handy when you are reading. Get down all the important points, such as character names and plots immediately so you don't have to dig for them again. From this working rough draft, you can begin to build the booktalk. Once you have completed these cards, file them for ready access. Although the actual talk will probably differ somewhat from what you write, the card charts your approach to the material and can give you a sense of security.

Bodart describes four common approaches to writing a booktalk based on four different structures.

1. *Plot summary:* Summarize the plot to a certain point, then stop. Obviously, this cliffhanger approach works well with suspense books and mysteries, but it also works for other genres. How much of a summary you should provide depends on how long the book goes on before something "big" happens. For some books, that can happen on page 100, for others it is on page two. Plot summary is probably the easiest of the four approaches because it is the one most people are accustomed to using when talking about a book.

2. *Character-based:* The thing that most attracts YAs to YA literature is that the main characters are their own age. Natural-

---

FIGURE 4-15 BOOKTALK CARD

Author:

Title:

[ ] fiction   [ ] nonfiction

Subjects:

Main characters:

Summary of plot:

"Hook":

Possible approaches:

[ ]plot based   [ ]character based/which one:

[ ]scene based/what page: [ ]mood based/what page:

Booktalk (write on back)

---

ly, YAs can relate best to YA characters. Sometimes, the most interesting thing about a book is one particular character. You can describe that character as you booktalk or even speak as that character. If there are several characters of special interest, you should tell a little bit about each one.

3. *Mood-based:* This often evolves from picking up on the author's use of language to create a certain mood. Mood can also be conveyed by your tone of voice, choice of words, and emphasis. This type of talk works very well with scary stories.

4. *Scene-based:* If there's one gripping scene that really hits you when you read a book, that's the one to pull out for your booktalk. Rather than telling the whole plot or even a portion of it, talk only about this scene and the things that make it dramatic, funny, or memorable.

You can use these approaches individually or combine them.

FIGURE 4-16:

DO'S AND DON'TS OF BOOKTALKING

DO...

1. Have copies of the books with you.
2. Have talk memorized so you're not reading.
3. Vary the types and themes of your talks.
4. Keep a record of which groups have heard which books.
5. Alternate booktalks of different lengths.
6. Start strong; end strong.
7. Talk books which you have multiple copies of only.
8. Relax.
9. Have fun.
10. Be yourself.

DON'T...

1. Booktalk books you have not read.
2. Booktalk books you don't like.
3. Gush over a book. The fact you are talking about it tells your audience you would recommend it.
4. Give away the ending.
5. Give literary criticism.
6. Say who would want to read the book: "This is really a boys' book."
7. Oversell a book.
8. Read unless there's no other way to get your point across.
9. Talk about controversial subjects (such as sex) without talking it over with a teacher first.
10. Be boring.

Sometimes the mood of a scene hits you and you want to read it. Maybe a character sets an interesting mood. The key is to write booktalks in each style. You might even try the same book several different ways. As you read, you'll probably see into which of these categories the talk would "fit" best. There is no wrong or best way, but there are a few do's and don'ts to remember (see Figure 4-16).

Your first sentence is your most important. It must get people's attention right away. As with the four approaches, there are several different types of first lines to consider. Which kind you use really depends on what you want to have happen in this talk.

1. *A character:* In your first sentence use a quote or description to give the audience a good (or bad, if appropriate) first impression of a character. If you use a quote, try to do it with a character voice. This gets attention and announces that something is different about this book.
2. *An emotion:* Use your first sentence to set the emotional mood. If you are talking about *When the Phone Rang* for example, the sentence might convey loss or grief.
3. *An action:* Start with something somebody does that is dramatic and attention grabbing: an act of aggression, daring—even stupidity.
4. *A shared experience:* Highlight something from the book that most of your listeners have probably felt, done, or said. For example, if booktalking *The Pigman,* the first line of your talk could be, "Have you ever made a prank phone call?" Right away, audience members focus on something either they or someone they know has done.
5. *A shocker:* It's a cheap way to get attention, but it works. Shocking things happen in many YA books. Rather than using these events to build up to, use them to leap off from.

There are, of course, as many variations on the first line as there are talks, but these five are standards. Another standard item is the ending. Many booktalks end with the title of the book as a "punchline." The idea is that the last line should be memorable— and what is the one thing you want YAs to remember? The ending variations are similar to those for the first sentence.

The middle of a booktalk is the hardest part to create. Many people, in fact, write the first and last sentence before anything else. The middle will vary depending on which booktalk model you have built upon and the length of your talk. In this middle section you want to:

1. *Keep it simple.* Use mostly short declarative sentences.
2. *Follow a narrative.* Go from point to point without detours.
3. *Keep to a few characters.* Your audience can get confused by too many.
4. *Repeat things.* In instruction you always repeat what you want people to remember, and the same goes for booktalking. Work in the book's key phrases, title, or any "taglines" at least a few times.
5. *Avoid "big" words.* A booktalk is not the time for a vocabulary lesson. Make sure the words, images, and allusions are appropriate for the grade to which you are speaking.
6. *Read sparingly.* Your task is to sell the book, not recite it. Reading takes your eyes off your audience and your audience's eyes off you.
7. *Stick to a reasonable time frame.* You don't want to cover a three-year period in one booktalk. Tell about the book's time span, but events you choose to relate shouldn't happen too far apart chronologically.
8. *Choose a mood and stick to it.* Unless you have something tricky in mind, you shouldn't alter the mood of your talk midstream.
9. *Watch your watch.* Movie trailers and pop songs (two booktalk models) last about four minutes. Anything over a four-minute booktalk should be a special case. Remember, the person who wrote the blurb on the paperback book jacket gets it down to less than a minute's worth of reading.
10. *If in doubt,* leave it out.

Using hooks: A hook is whatever immediately catches your attention and holds your interest. Paperback publishers are experts at using hooks—the taglines you see in big letters on the back of books—to pique reader interest. A successful hook answers the question, "Why would I want to read this book?" Booktalks for YAs can use hooks in exactly the same way. Just as a hook is what makes each book different and memorable, each booktalk can have a different spin. All of the models we examined used hooks. Sometimes the hook will come naturally out of the book; other times it will have to be developed. This will take time. At first, booktalkers are so concerned with getting all of the characters' names correct that they don't want to think about adding anything extra to the talk. After a while, especially when doing the same booktalk for a different audience, you'll notice what works and what doesn't.

Audience participation: Get the audience to repeat the title of the book or a tagline several times during the booktalk. You may need to be direct and ask them to repeat it, but sometimes they might just catch on by themselves.

Boring, but. . .: Start with a rather dull beginning to lull your audience into thinking the story will be boring, then quickly introduce a dramatic turn of events that changes the whole story at the last moment.

Cliffhanger: The most basic booktalk technique. Summarize the plot until the audience is indeed on the edge of their seats—then stop abruptly and leave them wanting more.

Definitions: Start the booktalk by asking the audience to define key words in the book's plot. Write them on the board and go back to them at the end of the booktalk.

Empathy: Ask questions at the beginning that put the audience "in the same shoes" as the character. For example, if the theme is loneliness, use rhetorical and "how does it feel?" questions to get them thinking about feeling alone.

First Sentence: The Kafka approach. Sometimes the first sentence of a book is all you need to sell it.

Gross out: Describe the grossest, goriest, bloodiest scene in a book. Works best after lunch.

Headlines: Relate the book to a news story or current event topic.

Interactive: Often books have funny sections of dialogue. Retype them in play format and ask the natural hams in the class to assist you.

Jump Cut: *The Perils of Pauline* begins with a shot of her tied on the railroad tracks, then jumps to a shot of the oncoming train. Do the same with a book, stopping at the point just before the two scenes converge.

Know a Secret: Talk about it, around it, hint at it, and make the audience crazy—but don't dare tell it.

Linking: Link a book with a movie or book with a similar theme or setting.

Mystery: Turn the book into a game of *Clue*. Introduce the suspects, their motives, their opportunities, and ask audience to write down "who done it." (You won't tell them if they are right, of course.)

Next Line: Find a good action scene in a book and read it aloud right up to the point where something pivotal happens. Then, literally stop in mid-sentence.

O. Henry: Similar to the "Boring, but. . ." technique but rather than using surprise, introduce a twist in the plot.

Props: Like a storyteller, use props to help you act out the story.

Questions: Begin your talk with a series of questions to set the mood or arouse interest. For example, start your booktalk on *I Know What You Did Last Summer* by asking YAs how they feel when they get special mail.

Repetition: Repeat the same words or tagline phrase over and over.

Sounds: Use sound effects to set the mood, as storytellers do.

Themes: Discuss several books based on a common theme of interest to YAs. Start with a well-known title if possible.

Unexpected: Toy with your audience's expectations. Keep them off balance by creating one set of expectations, then changing them, then changing them back again.

Violence Works: If you are trying to reach males, reading or describing a scene of violence will make an impression.

X-Rated: Just read the "warning" for Strasser's *A Very Touchy Subject*.

You: Go beyond just putting the audience in a character's shoes. Make them face the same choice facing the book's protagonist.

Zonk: If all else fails, there is *Killing Mr. Griffin,* which can't.

Adding hooks to your booktalk means you care about more

than just telling the story—you're also concerned with how you tell the story. Hooks are more than a matter of style. They are tools of the trade, a means librarians can use to improve their booktalks.

After accepting that booktalking, like storytelling, is a performance and admitting that you want to influence your audience, you'll begin to handle your booktalks differently. You'll learn to perform rather than recite, and you'll acquire your own performance style. If you arouse the audience's curiosity with sound, movement, repetition, and other hooks, create empathy for characters, and evoke emotions while entertaining your audience with a lively presentation, you will succeed.

Booktalk presentations: Booktalks come in all different shapes and sizes. Some are long; others are just one sentence. After you have written your individual booktalks, you need to structure them into a presentation. The elements of your presentation will depend on the class you are visiting. If you've seen the group before, either for booktalks or for a tour, you don't need to go through the whole "introduction"—you can jump right in. If it is your first time with the group, however, an introduction may be necessary. In general, you should know ahead of time what you want to cover.

Being organized, however, is not enough. You need to decide how many titles you will talk about in the time you have. Which ones will you do first? Last? When a band puts a concert together, the unit they work with is called a set. Within that set, they order the songs to create a particular effect. Lots of bands begin with an "old favorite" to get immediate recognition, then they play new material, followed by an encore of more old favorites. That's a good model to keep in mind when putting together booktalking presentations. Here are some other ideas:

Don't start with books: As we learned in Chapter 3, this is not the format of choice. Introduce your presentation by discussing something students already like, such as magazine titles or audiovisual materials.

Movies: If you have videos, show some examples. Give away movie posters if you have them on hand.

Movie tie-ins: A good choice for a first booktalk is a title they recognize—perhaps a book on which a movie was based. You can either choose something current or discuss a classic like *The Outsiders*.

Use a known author: Even in your second booktalk, you are still establishing credibility and making them listen to you. Doing a Stephen King book here further establishes the common ground between their interest and your resources. You don't need to sell Stephen King, but you do need to sell the idea that your library has "good stuff".

Series: By the same token, you can also mention the various series books, especially to younger YAs.

Use questions: One good transition technique for going from booktalk to booktalk is asking questions. A lot of hooks can be introduced with questions.

Relate personal experiences: Don't bore them with the story of your high school prom, but you probably can dig into your personal experience and find something they'll be able to relate to. A personal anecdote makes you more of a whole person to them and speaks to common YA emotions.

Relate inside information: If you can relate any personal information about the author, it makes the book more real.

Set the mood: Not just by reading, but by altering the room. Shut drapes and dim lights if you discuss a scary story—it's not subtle, but it is effective.

Use themes: As you prepare booktalks, note the subjects or themes of your selected titles. You can then arrange them into a special presentation for teachers. You'll make an expecially good connection if any of your theme presentations relate to a unit a teacher is working on.

Booktalk in teams: This not only means that each person has to prepare less material, but there are other advantages. People on a booktalk team can work from their strengths and keep a higher energy level. Teams also provide an opportunity to learn new techniques and even borrow other people's material. Finally, you can have a lot of fun playing off each other.

Take requests: Once you've been booktalking for a while, you can put together a list of books you can do easily. You can then pass out the list and ask the audience to tell you based on the title and a one sentence tagline which book they want to hear about.

Give something away: End the booktalk presentation by putting something in their hands. It could be a list of the books or a flyer about upcoming programs. You also can give away posters from magazines.

Use your captive audience: While you've got their attention, why not give them a short survey? You can use one from this book about library use or reading interests or design one of your own to find out whatever might help you plan better services. You might ask them about their music or programming interests. If you're trying to form or maintain a YA advisory group, this also is a good opportunity to get names and phone numbers.

Be organized: Have all books ready to go in the order in which you will present them. Have whatever notes you need handy or clipped to each book.

End with a bang: You should save your best talk for last. Be careful of the timing, though. You don't want your best talk cut off by the bell.

Pace yourself: After the introduction, do a couple of short talks, then build to a longer one. In a normal fifty minute period you should be able to cover from eight to twelve titles.

Transitions: The transitions between your talks should be smooth to give the impression of an "act," rather than just a random selection of books. For example, you might try making the last word of one booktalk the first word of the next. Or, if doing horror stories, a good transition would be, "If you thought that one was scary, . . ."

Talk with the teachers first: Not only do they need to introduce you, but they can help you set the mood for the class. If you want YAs to be excited and even talkative, tell the teacher. If not, you may be trying to "get them up" while the teacher is working at cross purposes to settle them down.

Find a friendly face: Try to identify one student who appears to be very attentive. Making eye contact with that student will help you evaluate how certain things are working.

Find an unfriendly face: In the same way, find someone who is not responding, someone who seems bored or disinterested and "play" to that person. If you get such a student turned on, you know you've accomplished something.

Find the leader: Watch the dynamics of the class before you start and try to identify who the "leader" in this group is. This is another person to play to. If you are doing any sort of interaction, try to get that person involved. If he or she participates, that adds legitimacy to what you are doing because the leader has sanctioned it.

Always prepare more than you need: You don't want to run through all of your titles in twenty minutes and utter the inevitable "any questions?" Have both long and short version of booktalks ready so that you can stretch/shorten depending on time and on the reaction a book seems to be getting.

Keep notes handy: Some people actually bring a written booktalk with them; others operate entirely from memory. A good compromise is a cheat sheet—an index card you can stick on the back cover of a book so that you can look at it as you hold the book up the audience. List the names of the major characters and a few one or two word reminders so that you can get from point a to point b even if your memory goes blank.

Consider using AV: Some people use slide shows along with the book jackets: some school librarians do booktalks over the PA system. Regardless of how you use it, AV materials are always a good complement to a booktalk.

Check out books for an immediate payoff: If at all possible, bring multiple copies of titles with you for checkout in the classroom. It will answer the immediate enthusiasm a YA may have for the book, which might cool before he or she can get to the library. Sure, you may lose some the titles, but the teacher or school librarian could assist you in keeping track of who took what. Or you could write down patron barcodes and book barcodes and enter them into the computer when you get back. The important thing is to get books into the YAs' hands. Think of all the YAs who got a book HOT and NOW. If you can't bring books with you, you can at least take names and put requested titles on hold (most YAs will come get them).

Bring your calendar: If you've only arranged to visit one teacher, ask that teacher to invite others to your booktalk. Chances are you'll land some more engagements.

Evaluating: After each booktalking session, you'll want to evaluate how well you did. You'll ask both students and teachers to do this (see Figures 4-17 and 18) and you'll do a self-evaluation. Some people like to tape themselves on audiocassette or videotape, while others find that becoming aware of their "tics" inhibits them. You can't always judge your delivery by the reaction you are receiving from the audience. Remember, no one will earn "peer points" from reacting to you, at least not at first. Also, depending on the teacher, you might find that the class is just dead. Perhaps the teacher has told them to "be quiet," and there's nothing you can do to break the mood. Anytime you try out new talks, you might be met with stony silence until you get down the hooks and the delivery. But after a while, each booktalk will become more finely tuned.

You'll be surprised by the responses you receive on the evaluations. The talk you thought just died might have been the most popular, or vice-versa. If one talk keeps coming up in the "worst" section but happens to be your favorite, it is time to look for a new hook or drop it from the act. The most concrete measure of success is circulation of the books themselves. Your best booktalk might be for a book no one finds interesting, or your worst sales job might be on a book which needs very little selling.

You'll want to record information on a reporting form (see Figure 4-19), similar to ones used for instruction and tours. Since you will probably see the same students again next year, you'll want to keep accurate records so that you don't repeat yourself. The best safeguard against repetition is to do certain books for certain grades. You can add books, but don't shift them between grades. If you're not careful, you could find yourself in the middle of a booktalk with someone telling the ending or moaning loudly "We've heard this one before!" On the other hand, you may be asked to repeat certain talks if they are particularly popular.

It seems simple enough: read a book and tell someone about it. But booktalking also involves a lot of planning, preparing, and evaluating. Because booktalking is a performing art, the main thing that makes you a better booktalker is doing it often. You can practice, write talks down, and try them out on your friends, but eventually it is getting in front of a classroom of YAs that makes you better. The communication you establish in telling YAs about books written for and about them is one of your best opportunities to link libraries and young adults.

There are certainly plenty of sources available for sample booktalks. Starting with someone else's talks is perfectly acceptable provided you've read the book. Or, you might use someone

FIGURE 4-17   STUDENT EVALUATION FORM: BOOKTALKING

SCHOOL: GRADE:

TEACHER: CLASS:

Please answer these questions, it will help us improve our services to you.

1. This presentation was:

    [ ]very interesting [ ]somewhat interesting [ ]boring

2. I already knew about:

    [ ]all of these books [ ]some   [ ]a few   [ ]none

3. The things I liked best about this presentation was:

4. The thing I liked least about it was:

5. The best booktalk was:

6. The worst booktalk was:

OTHER COMMENTS:

FIGURE 4-18 TEACHER EVALUATION FORM: BOOKTALKING

TEACHER: GRADE(S):

SCHOOL: CLASS(ES):

DATE: TIME: # OF STUDENTS:

Please answer the following questions:

1. This presentation was
    [ ] interesting [ ] somewhat interesting [ ] boring

2. Did this presentation meet your expectations?
    [ ] yes [ ] somewhat [ ] no

3. Would you recommend this service to your colleagues?
    [ ] yes [ ] no

4. Did the librarian hold the students' interest?
    [ ] yes [ ] no

5. Did the librarian adequately involve the students?
    [ ] yes [ ] no

6. Were the books appropriate in terms of content?
    [ ] yes [ ] no

7. Were the book appropriate for reading level?
    [ ] yes [ ] no

8. What did you like most about this presentation?

9. What did you like least about this presentation?

10. This presentation could be improved by:

Thank you

FIGURE 4-19 REPORTING FORM: BOOKTALKING

Activity: Booktalks

TEACHER:

SCHOOL:

OF STUDENTS: GRADES: CLASSES:

DATE/TIMES:

LIBRARIAN:

STUDENT EVALUATION SUMMARIES:

1. [   ] interesting [   ] somewhat interesting [   ] boring

2. [   ] all [   ] some [   ] few [   ] none

3. liked best:

4. liked least:

TEACHER EVALUATION FORM (ATTACH)

LIBRARIAN EVALUATION:

1. Problems:

2. Plusses:

3. Changes:

Increase in circulation of talked titles for month:

Overall increase in YA circulation for month:

else's talk as a starting point—to show you what to focus on or what the "hook" is. Then you can develop your own talk from there. Following are a few samples:

HOOK: EMPATHY

***Year Without Michael* by Susan Beth Pfeffer:** Waiting. Waiting fills you with such a sense of utter hopelessness. Remember waiting for the school bus on a cold winter morning. The longer you waited the colder it became. And you'd take a step out (mimic) and look down the street (mimic), somehow thinking that would make the bus arrive faster. But you can't rush waiting. Or how about waiting to get back an exam or a paper from a teacher? Each day you go into class thinking today will be the day. Or waiting for your report card to come in the mail. Just looking at the mailbox and waiting. But you can't rush waiting. Or if you've applied for a job, waiting to hear something—anything—even if the letter in the mail says "We are very sorry but. . . ." Or waiting for the phone ring. That is worse. You're waiting for some important phone call from some important person in your life about some important event, and you sit there and you stare at the phone and you wait. But you can't rush waiting. And now waiting for so many things: waiting to be old enough to drive or graduate or drink or be married or anything else, but the wait seems so long. So, so long.

A couple of weeks ago one of my cats ran away. If any of you have had this happen, you know that sick feeling you get in your stomach. I'd left the door open and she got out and I was in shock. After the shock, there's a desperation that sets in. So there I am sitting on the porch, opening cans of cat food, calling out her name, and making "lost cat" signs. And as I'm sitting in the silence of the night hoping just to hear her meow, I swear I hear my heart beat so loud, just like a big bass drum. BOOM BOOM BOOM. And I wait, and wait, and wait, and wait. And all the while I am waiting, I am worrying: Is she okay? Is she coming back safe? Is she lost? Is she afraid? Is she even alive? Waiting just to know, and I swear time freezes still just like when I was waiting for the bus on that cold morning. Just waiting. But you can't rush waiting.

Michael disappeared on his way from his home to a softball game. The night passes and morning comes and he has not arrived home or even called. The police are called in, but there's nothing they can do. Michael's parents are worried and upset and totally helpless to do anything. His younger sister Kay grows frantic while his older sister Jody assumes the family's burden. And they all wait. And to Jody, it feels like a weight—because it is heavy and a burden and it seems endless. The police continue to search, but nothing changes. A detective is hired, but nothing happens. Flyers are posted and neighbors contacted and advertisements run and pleas made, but nothing, just nothing happens, nothing but the waiting. But you can't rush waiting.

So I want you to imagine the scene. It's been a few days and Jody is sitting all alone. Imagine how she feels each time she hears a car door slam (He's home!) or hears a child laugh (It's him!) or hears the phone ring (Is it really you?). Imagine her sitting all alone in the silence and listening to her heart beating BOOM BOOM BOOM, and she wonders and she waits. She wonders, "Will Michael come back? Is he safe? Is he afraid? Is he lost? Is he even still alive?" And as she walks through his room, she sees all his things waiting, just waiting for Michael to come home. Imagine spending your life doing nothing but waiting. Every second of every minute of every hour of every day of every week of every passing month—just spent waiting. You can't rush waiting, and Jody and her family spend a *Year Without Michael*.

HOOK: REPETITION

***Izzy, Willy-Nilly* by Cynthia Voigt:** You don't get up one morning and decide who you are going to be for the rest of your life. It is not like all one big decision. Instead, a life is made up of a series of small, even trivial, decisions which, when they are added up, make a difference. The small decision you made today might just change the rest of your life. Tenth grader Isabelle (nicknamed Izzy) *decided* to become a cheerleader—that was her choice. And when a football player asked her out, *Izzy decided* to go out with him. And even though Marco was older than Izzy—a senior—*Izzy decided* to go out with him. Even though she didn't know him real well, she agreed to go to a party with him—that was her choice. And when her parents objected, that was when *Izzy decided* how important it was for her to go, so despite her parents, *Izzy decided* to go. And at the party, when Marco deserted her, *Izzy decided* to stay. And when she asked Marco to take her home and he just laughed at her, *Izzy decided* to stay. And when her friend Tony offered her a ride home, Izzy thought it wouldn't look right, so *Izzy decided* to stay. So *Izzy decided* to get into the car with Marco even though he was drunk. So *Izzy decided* to let Marco drive her home even though he was drunk. And when he drove to fast, *Izzy decided* not to say anything. And when he drove carelessly, *Izzy decided* not to say anything. But after the accident, it would not be for Izzy to decide. As she lay in bed—her body hurt, her leg mangled from the accident, it would not be her decision at all. This time *Izzy wouldn't decide,* the doctor would decide. And it was the doctor who decided looking at her mangled leg that "it will have to come off." Now Izzy has to decide how she will live the rest of her life.

HOOK: UNEXPECTED

***Crazy Horse Electric Game* by Chris Crutcher:** I want you to think about the scariest movie that you ever saw. For me, it was the movie *Alien*. Why? What could be scarier than being trapped in a place with a monster. But instead of a haunted house, how about being trapped in a spaceship in the middle of the universe with no escape possible. And if you think about a lot of the great scary movies, aren't they all about being trapped one way or another by a monster from which you cannot escape? Now let me tell you about the scariest book I've ever read. It is called *The Crazy Horse Electric Game,* and it is about baseball.

The book's main character is Willie Weaver. More than anything else in the world, Willie Weaver wants to be a hero. Not only does he dream about it, he actually feels that it is meant to be. And even though he's always done well in sports, he has never really had a chance at that one moment in sports which can make someone a heroe. Remember Kirk Gibson hitting that home run on his bad leg in the World Series a few years ago? That is the kind of moment Willie Weaver is searching for. Here comes his chance, as his team plays three-years-running baseball champions Crazy Horse Electric. This is Willie's moment of truth. As he goes out to pitch, he feels that his destiny has arrived. Watching him from the stand is his Dad, Big Will, probably the town's biggest sports hero ever. And watching from the stands is Jenny, probably the town's prettiest girl. So when Willie walks to the mound that day, he doesn't walk alone, and he walks tall. Crazy Horse can't touch him—Willie is firing seeds. Except for a long foul ball to Whitworth, nobody's hit him hard. Willie's had the hardest hit of the day, a triple which drove in his team's only run. Now as each inning goes by, Willie knows he is closer to the end of the game and the start of his destiny.

It's the ninth inning now and it's all down to one inning. One out later, and Willie can taste it. Then, it happens. Up to the plate comes Crazy Horse slugger Whitworth. The count is worked to three and two. Willie's destiny is not down to one game or even one inning or even one out, but one pitch. The distance between everything Willie Weaver is and everything he wants to be is sixty feet, six inches—the distance from the mound to home plate.

There's the set and the pitch, but at the top of his windup something goes wrong. It's as if he was so high he had to come down, and the ball slips out his hand and he loses his balance. Instead of a fastball, he throws a floater into Whitworth, and he falls out of fielding position, his back almost to the plate. SLAM— line drive, and as it screams off the bat toward Willie and center field, it seems as if it is all over—inning, game, career, dreams all gone. But at the last split second, Willie Weaver leaps up and catches the ball behind his back to save the game. A quick toss for the double play and Willie Weaver is the hero he always dreamed he would be. All summer everyone wants to talk about the Crazy Horse Electric Game, and all Willie wants to do is remember that game forever. Cut now to a couple of months later. Same situation, but different sport. With his father and Jenny, now his girlfriend, Willie is going to become the big hero waterskier. Off they go, and then it happens—just like on the mound, when he is trying so hard he loses his balance, SLAM—the ski bounces off the wave and hits Willie Weaver right in the forehead. Okay, now you are thinking: "Wait, this is supposed to be scary, not sad." Listen to this: This part of Willie's brain, the side that remembers the Crazy Horse Electric Game and being a hero is fine. This part of his brain, the side that dreams of being a hero once again, is fine too. But this part, the part that controls Willie's speech, his legs, and his arms, doesn't work so good anymore. Willie Weaver is trapped, trapped inside something worse than any haunted house—he is trapped in the one thing he can't escape from: his own body. And he is haunted, haunted by the memory of *The Crazy Horse Electric Game*.

ENDNOTES

1. American Library Association, *American Library Association Handbook of Organization,* Chicago: American Library Association, 1990.
2. Tom Eadie, "User Education Does Not Work" *Library Journal* (October 15, 1990), 42-45.
3. Joni Bodart, *Booktalk!* New York: H.W. Wilson, 1980.

5 MAKING CONNECTIONS

5.1 CONNECTING WITH SCHOOLS

One of the keys to providing quality YA services in the public library is to develop a quality working relationship with schools. For schools, the advantages of working with the public library are numerous. Connecting with libraries helps schools:

- Complement their own educational resources
- Share resources in a time of diminishing budgets
- Develop innovative programs and activities
- Broaden students' access to information and materials
- Increase students' information literacy
- Network within the community.

For libraries, there are even more advantages. Connecting with schools helps libraries:

- Increase students' library awareness and information literacy
- Provide better service to students, since they have more information about YA needs
- Gain captive audiences
- Share resources in a time of diminishing budgets
- Develop innovative programs and activities
- Utilize the library's resources more fully
- Fulfill an educational mission
- Network within the community
- Eliminate misunderstandings.

The student, however, gains the most when schools and libraries work together. Students will find that cooperation might lead to:

- Reduced frustration in using libraries
- Increased access to information
- Ability to obtain materials easily
- Library staff having a better understanding of their needs
- Innovative programs to meet their needs
- Clearer assignments
- Reduced time spent in library after school
- Increased access to recreational reading
- Increased access to information technology

• Better instruction in use of libraries.

So, if it is such a wonderful thing where everybody wins, why are there sometimes cooperation problems? From the school's point of view, some reasons might be:

• Lack of time to establish contacts
• Lack of understanding of library's potential role
• Past unsuccessful contacts
• Lack of administrative support
• Lack of time to dedicate to outside activities outside of the classroom
• Feelings of being self sufficient
• Separate agendas
• Lack of perceived need
• Lack of information about library's resources
• Lack of planning.

Libraries are often unsuccessful in working with schools for a variety of reasons, which include:

• Failure to communicate through proper channels
• Past unsuccessful contacts
• Lack of time to establish contacts
• Arrogance ("They need us")
• Separate agendas
• Lack of administrative support
• Inability to influence decision makers
• Lack of time to plan or implement programs
• Lack of resources to meet school's needs
• Unwillingness to dedicate staff to this role
• Interdepartmental rivalries
• Lack of innovate programs to offer schools.

Each library and school might experience its own specific barriers to cooperation as well. Sometimes it is something as absurd as the person in charge (principal or director) just not caring enough. Looking at these common problems and barriers, it is apparent that the relationship needs to be developed along these lines:

1. Initial communication at any level
2. Followup communication at decision making level in each agency

3. Recognition of strengths and weaknesses
4. Discussion of shared needs and goals
5. Development of a shared agenda
6. Establishment of contacts and other avenues for ongoing communication.

When schools and libraries don't work together, students—clients for both agencies—suffer. Reference requests in particular often lead to frustration for both students and the library staff under these circumstances. Following is a list of sample reference requests and some strategies for making school/library connections that enhance the learning process:

"Everyone in my class has to read. . ."

1. Schools could send the library a list of books that will be required during the school year, or the library could survey teachers for titles.
2. Schools could send the library individual titles before they are assigned so that the library could purchase extra copies and/or gather all copies in library system.
3. Together, the school and the library could investigate grantors or other outside agencies that might fund a cooperative supplemental reading collection.
4. For a public library serving many schools, the library could explore developing a special collection of the most requested supplemental books in response to the "literature based" curriculum movement.

"I have to do a scrapbook on. . ."

1. The library needs to communicate directly with teachers giving such assignments to avoid the problem of students cutting up library periodicals.
2. The library could offer vouchers for free photocopies.
3. Magazine discards could be saved and routed to teachers for their use.

"My whole class is researching. . ."

1. Teachers could be surveyed about each term's research projects.
2. Library instruction sessions can be scheduled.

3. Collection development could be focused accordingly.
4. "Temporary reference" collections could be established.
5. Pathfinders could be developed and mailed to each teacher.
6. Since many teachers don't change assignments from year to year, the library could document which assignments can be expected.
7. The library could distribute mail-back postcards to teachers at the beginning of each term. (See Figure 5-1.)
8. If assignments are on paper, the library could photocopy them and post them at the reference desk listing possible sources and strategies.
9. "Assignment Alert" sheets could be distributed to school libraries so they can notify the public library when assignments might be coming their way. (See Figure 5-2.)
10. Problem assignments need to be identified. If possible, staff

---

FIGURE 5-1 TEACHER POSTCARD

TEACHERS NAME:_____

SCHOOL:_____ GRADE:_____

CLASS: _____ # OF STUDENTS:_____

Help us help your students by alerting us to assignments that might require your students to use our library. Thank you for your cooperation.

ASSIGNMENT: DATE:

1._____ _____

2._____ _____

3._____ _____

4._____ _____

5._____ _____

FIGURE 5-2 ASSIGNMENT ALERT FORM

Dear Media Specialist:

As you know, often students will use the public library to find resources to complete assignments. Help us help them by alerting us to assignments that require library use when you find out about them. Together, we can help students find the materials they need.

MEDIA SPECIALIST:_____ DATE:_____

SCHOOL:_____ TEACHER:_____

GRADE:_____ CLASS:_____ # OF STUDENTS:_____

ASSIGNMENT:_____

_____

_____

SPECIAL REQUIREMENTS (# OF SOURCES, LIMITS, ETC.):

_____

_____

_____

SPECIFIC STUDENT TOPICS IF KNOWN (LIST ON BACK)

ASSIGNMENT DUE:_____

DID STUDENTS RECEIVE LIBRARY INSTRUCTION? [ ]YES [ ]NO

COMMENTS:

should find out from students which teacher gave the assignment and contact that teacher for more information.

11. School librarians and public librarians need to work together on educating teachers. Together, they could host a workshop, sponsor a lunch, prepare publications and documents, reward teachers who cooperate and troubleshoot problem areas.

12. Libraries can communicate back to teachers through students about frustrations students encounter and reasons they are not able to complete their assignments. (See Figure 5-3.)

"My teachers said you would have . . . here."

1. Teachers cannot make assumptions about what libraries do and do not have.

2. Libraries could contact schools' human resources/staff development departments about being part of any new teacher orientation or staff development program.

FIGURE 5-3   MATERIALS UNAVAILABLE CARD

LIBRARY: _____   DATE: _____

Dear Teacher:

(Student's name) came to the library today to find materials on

_____.

We are sorry, but we were unable to help your student because:

[ ] All materials were checked out.

[ ] A reasonable search failed to find materials.

[ ] Materials are for "in library" use only.

[ ] Clarification of request is needed

[ ] Library does not own enough copies of material
    to meet research needs of entire class.

[ ] Other:_____

If you have any questions, please contact me. Often we can help students and reduce their frustration in using libraries when we are notified in advance about school assignments like this one. We can provide instruction, gather materials, and offer other services to benefit all of your students.

LIBRARIAN: _____   PHONE #:_____

3. Libraries could put together annual teacher appreciation days, which would recognize teachers who cooperate and encourage others to do so.
4. Libraries could offer refresher courses to schools as part of their in-service program.

"My teacher said I can't use an encyclopedia."

1. Help educate student to differentiate between a reference book and an encyclopedia.
2. For example, if a student is researching a history topic, send the teacher a list of core reference books you would suggest be used in place of an encyclopedia.
3. Teach students they can still use an encyclopedia as a first (but not the only) step in their research.

"I need a fiction book on. . ."

1. Send the teacher any prepared lists the library or ALA has created.
2. Work with school librarians to develop lists that highlight materials in both collections.
3. Share resources like *Fiction Catalog* and *Books for You* with teachers.
4. Give students a copy of your card when you recommend books.
5. Call teachers and offer to booktalk for their classes.
6. Set up special collections of books which meet assignment criteria.
7. Share any teachers' guides sent to you by publishers.

"I need a filmstrip on. . ."

1. Share with teachers any library produced AV catalogs through either the department chair or the school library.
2. Send each teacher a list of media available (and not available) complete with rules and procedures for using/booking.
3. Ask school librarians to add to their lists of new media titles/ sets you have acquired.

"How do you do a bibliography card?"

1. Request from each school librarian the style sheet that teachers use and keep it posted at the reference desk or keep a copy of

whatever source the required style was derived from, *e.g., The Chicago Manual of Style.*

2. With schools, put together a term paper kit as mentioned in the section on library instruction.

"I need to read. . .this summer."

1. Contact the school librarian in early spring about the school's summer reading list.
2. Lobby for inclusion of YA titles. (Most lists won't have them.)
3. Buy extra copies of Cliff Notes and list titles. Audiocassette versions can be purchased if money is available.
4. Offer to booktalk titles from the list.
5. Post and file all lists where your staff can find them.
6. Buy titles on more than one list in permabound editions.
7. Scour book donations for these titles—students who did buy the book will sometimes donate it to the library.
8. Provide feedback to schools on the number of copies in your system and in-print status.
9. With the school librarian, gather information packets on authors from standard sources to post for students and/or give to teachers.
10. Reach out to a local bookstore as an ally if there is a problem—they'll have just as many YAs coming in looking for a title as you will.

Most teachers feel they have too much work and too few resources. Libraries need to reach out to teachers and help them understand how the library can operate as a resource for them and their students. Some teachers are very good about working with libraries, both in their schools and the public library; others seem hopeless. But as with YAs, there is a vast "silent majority" of teachers who have some awareness, even willingness, to cooperate but have not been moved to action.

METHODS FOR CONTACTING TEACHERS

You might first consider calling on a colleague. Start with the librarian in the school or library media coordinator for the school system. This seems easy enough, but even with this first simple step, there are many problems:

• Some school librarians have absolutely no power, influence, or even knowledge of what is going on. They can't help you because they can't help themselves. They are all alone in the building and often treated like outsiders. They have either given up or have never fought for recognition to begin with. Finally, they don't command respect from teachers, so having them help you is really very little help at all.

- Many schools don't hire MLS-degreed librarians for their school libraries. If you have your MLS and come on strong, you can seriously intimidate the nonprofessional school librarian and damage the relationship from the start.
- School librarians are like most teachers in that they feel they have too little time and resources. Work around their schedules and share resources like professional magazines with them. The message you want to send is "we can help each other." Sometimes, however, that is interpreted as a turf invasion, so be sure to incoporate words like "complement" and "supplement" into your vocabulary.
- School librarians have their own problems, even if they are also yours. They know all about teachers not notifying them about assignments and they will be amazed that you would expect a teacher to call you or write you a letter about the assignment. Since their problems are also your problems, you can help each other find solutions.
- Be sensitive to the school librarian's concerns. If you work with a teacher and offer booktalks or library instruction, the school librarian might fear criticism because these services aren't offered at the school. You should conduct all activities with the full knowledge of the school librarian and offer him or her the chance to participate (or decline participation) in all aspects.
- School librarians can also feel underappreciated. Look for ways to provide them with recognition, because chances are they are not getting much in their schools. Thank you notes and complimentary letters to the principal are always welcome. You also can invite them to join in any professional activities or associations in which you participate.
- Many school librarians feel poor compared to public librarians without sufficient funds to buy even the essentials, let alone anything extra. Give them your discards, ALA freebies, or any other resources you can share. The public library may get more professional magazines, so put your school libraries on the route list.
- Because they feel so overwhelmed, school librarians may think that cooperation with public librarians is too time consuming, especially if you are eager and have a lot of ideas. Instead of presenting a laundry list of cooperation opportunities, try start-

ing with one small project the two of you can work on together. It could be a union list or reference book rotation plan—maybe even customizing some of the documents in this manual. Choose one project that needs both librarians working on it. Once a start is made, larger projects involving more cooperative planning may seem more feasible.

- Some school librarians may not be willing to share. They may feel they have absolutely nothing to gain by working with you—they know their teachers and what they need. You have to find what you have to "exchange" in order to get the school librarian to help you. It really can become a win-win situation. Sometimes you just have to figure out, "Now, what can I do to help?"

Navigating the school maze: Despite all these potential obstacles to overcome, the school librarian must be your first contact. Chances are, he or she knows the ropes and can help you speak with the right people. Every school's protocol is different. Sometimes the first "official" contact needs to be made on the administrative level, with a library director contacting a school superintendent or individual school principals. This contact is necessary because to distribute anything you often need approval at that level. In the best case scenario, your director writes the superintendent, explains your ideas for working with the schools, and asks for permission to make contacts.

Who your next contact will be depends on the school system. You might have to work through another supervisory layer and work with a library media supervisor, a curriculum supervisor, or department head. After that, you might be able to move to the individual school level and contact the principal. The thing to remember about school principals is that they have 1,000 other things to do. Keep whatever you have to say short and let them ask the questions. If you can get the principal's blessing, then you can operate in the school.

Depending upon the size of the school, you can either contact teachers directly or work though a department chair. The ultimate goal is meeting teachers. If you can invite yourself, or better yet get invited, to a department meeting, you have finally reached your target audience. Now you can begin making individual contacts.

Who you contact depends not only on the culture of the school and library, but also on what your first objectives are. If you want to publish and distribute a newsletter for teachers, that will be an administrative decision for sure. If you want to begin booktalking, then perhaps a teacher is your best contact. In any case, you'll want to develop a log sheet so you can keep track of all your school contacts.

Documents: A document to assist you in obtaining and organizing information about schools is the school planning form, shown in Figure 5-4. When completed, it can be used both as a planning tool and as a way to evaluate cooperative activities at the end of year. The document takes you step-by-step through the kinds of information you will need to work with schools. You also can use it (and other materials like teacher and club lists) to put together a mailing list.

To gather information for the form, either stop by the school or call and speak to the school secretary. Be sure to call during what would be a slow period for the school office, when someone will have time to talk with you. Explain who you are, what you are doing, and why. The secretary may either give you the information or refer you to someone who can. If it is the school secretary who helps you, get that person's name and immediately send a thank you note. As in most institutions, the secretary is often the "gate-keeper" and can be a valuable ally.

Once you have your list of contacts, you can invite teachers to contact you. Send teachers a list of the services you offer, such as the one in Figure 5-5. Highlight your collections, especially special collections, on the list. Poster size copies of this document should also be distributed to the school library and to administrators. Another variation: shrink the services section onto a blank, pre-addressed postcard and print one for each teacher.

Another way of keeping teachers informed of what the library has to offer them is an educator newsletter. This too has many variations: it could be put together by YAs as a program; it could be done in cooperation with the schools; the public library could "tell its story" on one side of the page, and the school library could use the other. If it is not possible to produce a newsletter, then send press releases on programs and services to the school for distribution to teachers.

Still another handy communication vehicle is the cooperation guide (Figure 5-6), pointing out how schools and libraries can better work together. This kind of flyer is only a tool—it cannot replace making contacts or following up with teachers. It should accentuate the positive, highlighting all the good things that come out of cooperation rather than just listing problem areas.

Like so much about young adult services, school-library cooperation presents a contradiction. Nothing would help YAs more

FIGURE 5-4 SCHOOL PLANNING FORM

(Complete one for each school in service area)

SCHOOL:_____

ADDRESS:_____

PHONE#:_____

PRINCIPAL:_____

LIBRARIAN:_____

SCHOOL SECRETARY:_____

ENGLISH DEPT CHAIR:_____

READING DEPT CHAIR:_____

SCIENCE DEPT CHAIR:_____

SOC SCI DEPT CHAIR:_____

GUIDANCE DEPT CHAIR:_____

CONTACT PERSON:_____

OTHER KEY PERSONNEL:_____

1. Created mailing labels? [ ]yes [ ]no

2. Obtain school calendar? [ ]yes [ ]no

3. Obtain school handbook? [ ]yes [ ]no

4. Obtain list of teachers? [ ]yes [ ]no

5. Obtain bell schedule?   [ ]yes [ ]no

6. Obtain list of clubs?   [ ]yes [ ]no

7. Obtain info on PTA/PTO? [ ]yes [ ]no

8. Obtain copy of school newsletter? [ ]yes [ ]no

9. Obtain copy of PTA/PTO newsletter? [ ]yes [ ]no

10. Obtain copy of school newspaper? [ ]yes [ ]no

11. New teachers invited to orientation? [ ]yes [ ]no

12. Library card applications included in any packet prepared for new students? [ ]yes [ ]no

13. "Welcome" letters sent at start of school year to all contacts? [ ]yes [ ]no

14. Regular meetings scheduled with school librarian? [ ]yes [ ]no

FIGURE 5-4 SCHOOL PLANNING FORM, cont.

15. Tours arranged for ___ grade(s) [ ]yes [ ]no

GRADE:___ DATE:_____ # OF STUDENTS:_____ TEACHER:_____

GRADE:___ DATE:_____ # OF STUDENTS:_____ TEACHER:_____

GRADE:___ DATE:_____ # OF STUDENTS:_____ TEACHER:_____

16. Library instruction for ___ grade? [ ]yes [ ]no

GRADE:___ DATE:_____ # OF STUDENTS:_____ TEACHER:_____

GRADE:___ DATE:_____ # OF STUDENTS:_____ TEACHER:_____

GRADE:___ DATE:_____ # OF STUDENTS:_____ TEACHER:_____

17. Booktalks for ___ grade(s)?   [ ]yes [ ]no

GRADE:___ DATE:_____ # OF STUDENTS:_____ TEACHER:_____

GRADE:___ DATE:_____ # OF STUDENTS:_____ TEACHER:_____

GRADE:___ DATE:_____ # OF STUDENTS:_____ TEACHER:_____

18. Summer reading in __ grades(s)?   [ ]yes [ ]no

GRADE:___ DATE:_____ # OF STUDENTS:_____ TEACHER:_____

GRADE:___ DATE:_____ # OF STUDENTS:_____ TEACHER:_____

GRADE:___ DATE:_____ # OF STUDENTS:_____ TEACHER:_____

19. Attend dept meeting(s)

DEPT:_____ DATE:_____ TEACHER:_____

DEPT:_____ DATE:_____ TEACHER:_____

DEPT:_____ DATE:_____ TEACHER:_____

20. Contact for Banned Books Week?   [ ]yes [ ]no

21. Contact for National Library Week? [ ]yes [ ]no

22. Obtain summer reading lists? [ ]yes [ ]no

23. Obtain yearbook?   [ ]yes [ ]no

24. Obtain exam schedule?   [ ]yes [ ]no

25. Thank-you notes to all contacts? [ ]yes [ ]no

On back, list all contacts made during year - include teacher's name, date and reason.

FIGURE 5-5 SAMPLE SERVICES MENU

CONTACT THE SPRINGFIELD CITY LIBRARY

The public library now has a wide variety of services available to teachers. How can we help you?

_____ **Booktalk in your school**

_____ **Tour of the Central Library**

_____ **Tour of art and music room at Central Library**

_____ **Tour of the _____ branch library**

_____ **Library instruction in your classroom**

_____ **Library instruction in the library**

_____ **Reserve collections for specific assignments**

_____ **Puppet shows**

_____ **Booklists or pathfinders**

_____ **AND MUCH MORE**

FIGURE 5-6

LET'S ALL WORK TOGETHER

Cooperation between schools and the public library can help enhance the learning experience for students. Cuyahoga County Public Library would like to share some observations with you.

Problem: Reading lists or assignments are given for which the library cannot supply the required materials.
Solution: Cuyahoga County Public Library librarians are willing to advise you on the availability of materials and to suggest alternatives if necessary.

Problem: Mass assignments on a specific subject result in the first few students borrowing all the available material.
Solution: Provide your County Library branch with assignments. If necessary resources can be supplemented with materials from other branches. Also, some books can be set aside as a temporary reference resource.

Problem: An assignment given orally frequently becomes garbled by the time it reaches a librarian.
Solution: Give assignments involving library use in writing and provide your local branch with a copy in advance.

Problem: An assignment requiring illustration(s) has tempted students to cut up library material.
Solution: Encourage original illustrations and save old magazines for classroom use.

We encourage you to visit your local branch of Cuyahoga County Public Library to become more familiar with our resources. We want to work with students.

CUYAHOGA COUNTY PUBLIC LIBRARY

than for these two institutions, which both strive to meet their needs, to really work together. Yet for many reasons, it seems nothing is harder to do. Perhaps one of the benefits of smaller budgets will be that schools and libraries will help each other. This cooperation will benefit both institutions, and students most of all.

5.2 CONNECTING WITH AGENCIES

Other potential allies in serving YAs are community agencies. Although each community is different, there are usually many others out there trying to reach and help YAs that are facing many of the same problems. By making connections and working with these agencies, problems can be solved jointly, programs planned cooperatively, information and resources shared, and bridges built to create a better quality of life for YAs. Like schools, community agencies are often "tough to crack" for many of the same reasons, including lack of time and protection of turf. The strategies used in working with schools can be used with other organizations as well. The planning process is also much the same.

STRATEGIES AND DOCUMENTS

The first step is to identify agencies that you might be able to work with. The directory of community agencies, published by your local United Way chapter, is your primary resource. If this is not available, The United Way should have an information and referral file or service to link individuals with human services agencies. This should provide you with contact information for larger groups and government agencies. The directory will have the primary agencies you might be interested in networking with, listed under some of the headings on the following page.

Some communities also publish directories of clubs (more social than social service organizations, but still helpful) and of education resources. Although these publications contain directory-style information, you will want to tailor the information to meet your specific needs. For some organizations you can just transfer the information from the directories, for others you will need to make a phone call. As with schools, explain who you are and what you are trying to do. If they can't answer your questions over the phone, mail or drop off a card for them to fill out (Figure 5-7). Finally, watch the newspaper for new groups forming or groups

COMMUNITY AGENCY HEADINGS

- After-school care for children
- AIDS
- Birth control
- Boys' organizations
- Camps
- Children's homes
- Christian youth activities (and those of other religions)
- Clinics
- Community centers
- Counseling
- Crisis counseling
- Day camps
- Education
- Employment
- Financial aid/scholarships
- Gay/lesbian resources
- Girls organizations
- health
- Hispanic services (and other minority services)
- Hotlines
- Illiteracy
- Information & referral
- Juvenile delinquency
- Medical care
- Mental health
- Neighborhood centers
- Recreation centers
- Scouts
- Sex education
- Youth services

you might have missed. This information gathering process will take a long time upfront, but once the information is compiled it will be well worth the effort.

After you have your list of agencies, scan it for the ones that might be most helpful to you. You might want to follow up with an initial mailing to these key contacts describing the types of services you offer to YAs (Figure 5-8). Invite them to respond. For the agencies you are most interested in working with, follow up with a phone call and try to arrange a meeting. At this meeting, you want to find areas of possible cooperation. Ask your agency contacts:

- Other than the usual (time, money, staff), what are their primary barriers to serving youth?
- What steps could be taken to overcome these barriers?
- What is their mission statement? What are their goals for the year? the next two years?
- What types of programs would they like to do but can't because they lack the resources?

FIGURE 5-7 AGENCY INFORMATION CARD

AGENCY NAME: _____

ADDRESS: _____

PHONE: _____

CONTACT PERSON: _____

AGENCY MANAGER: _____

AGENCY PROFILE (SERVICES, PROGRAMS, ETC;):

_____

_____

_____

AGES SERVED: _____

SERVED: _____

Agency on mailing list?   [ ]yes [ ]no

Contacted by mail for meeting? [ ]yes [ ]no

Follow up phone call?   [ ]yes [ ]no

On back, put notes from meeting and other comments.

FIGURE 5-8 SERVICES MENU: AGENCIES

The public library offers a wide variety of services and resources now available to youth serving agencies. How can we help you? What's it to you?

[ ] tour of the library

[ ] recreational afterschool programs

[ ] educational afterschool programs

[ ] cultural afterschool programs

[ ] books, magazines, tapes and CDs to loan out

[ ] films and videos for showing

[ ] library cards available to all

[ ] collection of library materials in your agency

[ ] reading promotion programs in your agency

[ ] booklists available upon request

[ ] meeting rooms

[ ] speakers to discuss libraries and youth

[ ] information on grant writing

CONTACT:

PHONE:

Together, the library and your agency can better serve the youth of this community. Thank you.

- What do they see as the problems facing youth in the community?
- What networks are in place for youth-serving organizations?
- Do they need assistance in planning and producing programs?
- Would they be interested in arranging group activities, either at the library or in their agency, cosponsored by the library?
- Which of their programs overlap with library programs?
- Which agency can best provide this service?
- Do they have any speakers available?
- How do they publicize their programs?
- What programs and services work best and why?
- What programs and services have failed and why?
- How can you best keep them informed of the library's programs?
- How can they keep you informed of their programs?
- What is their relationship with local schools?
- Do they have a youth volunteer program?
- What is their relationship with other youth organizations?
- Is there one small, short-term project the library and the agency could work together on to benefit youth in the community? As with schools, agencies are just as overworked and will be just as overwhelmed by your little speech on "how much we can do for each other." Again, choosing a small project—an afterschool program, a deposit collection, etc.—will help you establish a working relationship you can build on later.

The library has to decide what its role will be in making community contacts. It can assume a leadership role if the library administration is willing to support this arrangement, the advantages of which are numerous:

- The library enjoys a high profile within the community.
- Organizing information is what libraries do best.
- Public libraries are "neutral" agencies in a way that Planned Parenthood and Dignity are not.
- Public libraries can provide meeting space and other valuable resources.
- Libraries are already seen in many communities as a central community information agency.
- Youth benefit through cooperation.
- Networking might bring the library additional funding sources.
- Programs can either be planned cooperatively or eliminated if other agencies meet the needs.

On the national level, YALSA's National Organizations Serving the Young Adult Liaison Committee provides a shining example of interagency networking and cooperation. If YALSA can make contacts with organizations like the Boy Scouts and 4H on the national level, then libraries have a model for doing so in their own communities. What kinds of problems can be solved through interagency cooperation?

1. Information and referral: Information is our business, yet while we might have twenty YA books on a topic such as dating violence—and all these nifty computers to access magazine articles—do we know in our own community where to refer YAs with this specific need? Many libraries keep information and referral files, and many YA departments publish "Teen Yellow Pages" that list all the important agencies for teens to know about in their community, as well as national 800 numbers. Our role is not that of the social worker, but it is that of an information professional who can direct YAs to the proper agencies, either through referral or by providing access to this information.

2. "The Crowd": This might be a group of YAs who "invade" the library because they have nothing better to do. Sometimes it is because the school has abandoned them by not meeting their needs for afterschool programming. Maybe they are latchkey kids, or maybe they just don't want to go home. Libraries can plan afterschool programs, but many agencies already do this as their primary activity. You don't want to remove these kids from the library (although some of your staff might rejoice in that), but you do want to make them aware of other resources. If there are no other resources, then it is not just a library problem, it is a community problem. If it is a community problem, then it is one that several community agencies can work together to solve.

3. Babysitting clinics: Is there any group serving teenage girls that doesn't offer this service? In some communities the problem isn't too little programming, but too much. Your resources are precious, so if someone else is running a program you might help them, but don't duplicate their efforts. On the other hand, when learning about other agencies' programs, glaring needs will become clear. These perhaps might make a better focus for cooperative ventures.

4. Sharing speakers: Normally, each agency has someone assigned as its resident expert and public speaker. This person could be the focus of a program. You may not even have to pay for the appearance. Chances are, this official also could put you in contact with other local, state, or even national speakers for possible engagements. You can offer to speak at their programs if you want to reciprocate for their cooperation.

5. Money: Since no one has enough money and everyone seems to be getting less every year, many agencies have to pursue—or at least consider—outside funding. Some foundations and other sources are more receptive to cooperatively planned programs than to unilateral ones. Also, while some libraries are leery of writing grants for fear that their governing body might subtract any money they get from the normal budget, cooperative grantsmanship might eliminate that possibility. Finally, when agencies are financially bound, the commitment to work together is strengthened.

6. No surprises: You want to get agencies in the same habit as teachers—making contact before making a visit. If you have successfully networked with the Boy Scouts, you probably have diminished the possibility of 35 blue uniforms showing up unannounced to use the microfilm printers.

7. Increased program attendance: For many programs you might do, an agency can provide a built-in audience. For example, you might be doing a martial arts demonstration and, even though the local Boys Club didn't choose to co-sponsor it with you, they still might be interested in attending the program by the vanload.

8. YA advocacy: As stated in point 2, one of the possible benefits of networking is to encourage the various youth-serving agencies to speak with one voice. The solidarity that networking can bring will help change everyone's role from that of youth agencies to youth advocates.

9. Staff training: One of the agencies you connect with might have a speaker who can assist you in conducting a staff training program serving young adults, or at least provide you with some training tools.

10. Increased access: Many YAs who don't visit libraries do visit community centers. Deposit collections or bookmobile stops could be made here so these YAs can find reading materials more readily. Library card sign-up campaigns are another way to reach out to YAs at these centers. Teens in temporary housing situations such as runaway shelters also might benefit from having access to library materials, as well as those YAs in detention centers, hospitals or other places outside the home.

11. Volunteerism: YAs make up a large segment of the volunteer force. Networking might assist you in placing YAs with other agencies, or vice versa. Getting to know the people in the Voluntary Action Center or a similar agency is an invaluable contact. If you can give them ideas of projects for which you could use YA volunteers, they can help you recruit, and sometimes train, these teenagers.

12. Respect: Despite what we think or hope, to many we're still "the book people." By working with other agencies successfully, that image begins to be replaced by an image of a more active, involved institution meeting needs of youth, not just putting date-due cards in books.

Most of the success stories resulting from agency connections are about not just the agencies, but the YAs involved as well. By reaching out and working with other agencies, we gain more access to more YAs than any single library program could hope to achieve. If we want to create more YA library users, we need to find them on their own turf. If we want to serve YAs better, we need to communicate better with those who share our concerns. And if we really want to connect with YAs, we need to connect with schools and agencies, which can help us break down all the barriers.

6 PROGRAMMING

Programming, like many other aspects of YA services already discussed, presents another contradiction. The goal of programming is to get YAs excited about the library, but the library is far down on the list of exciting places to go for most YAs, if included at all.

Nevertheless, it has been done, and done well for years. *Top of the News* (now the *Journal of Youth Services in Libraries*) published two "Program Roundup" articles in the late 1970s. The amazing thing about these articles today is how many of the programs listed are still staples of the YA programming diet. The "disco dance" demonstration of the 1970s gave way to the "break dancing" workshop of the 1980s, which steps aside for the rap contest of the 1990s. Other programs like literary magazines and college nights are still around. Only that 1970s sure bet—film nights—has given way to the influence of both cable and video. The purpose of programming then was the same as it is today: to produce activities that connect young adults and libraries.

6.1 PLANNING

Several writers in the library literature have been negative about the idea of programming of any kind. They argue that programming is not cost-effective and that it doesn't achieve its stated objectives of increasing use or circulation. Stated plainly, it doesn't work and is a waste of resources. As the financial constraints of the 1990s affect priorities, activities like programming are seen as "extras" and are considered for elimination. Given the difficulty of planning some YA programs, they are often the first to go.

PURPOSES
But YA programs do serve a purpose. The purpose isn't reflected in attendance but in other outcomes. More than just providing entertainment, programs help YAs get through the process of being a YA.

- Group programs support YAs in their quest for identity and help them feel that they belong.
- Programs provide a structure in which YAs can socialize and work together.
- Informational programs on topics like drug abuse or sex education fill a void in the community.

• Programs give YAs a chance to participate in library decision making and assume responsibilities.

The fact that YA programs are given low priority is both an obstacle and an opportunity. Because nobody cares, there is a chance to be experimental. Innovative programs come out of YA services because they have to. Also, librarians serving YAs need to do things that get YAs' positive attributes noticed. Most staff only notice the rowdy YAs because YA staff isn't able to offer anything that shows YAs in a better light.

Yes, many YA programs are underattended. A cost-benefit analysis would wipe them all out (and many other library programs as well). YAs are already in libraries, so programming simply attempts to redirect them. On occasion, programming may turn a non-library-user into a user, but its primary purpose is to help YAs make the connection between their world and ours.

PROCESS

The planning process for programing is a series of choices and steps. It normally starts with one bright idea that is carried through a process and nurtured. Many YA programs fail because the idea was sound but the execution was faulty. There are no guarantees that even a perfectly planned program will be a huge success, and sometimes a thrown-together, last-minute job will succeed. Following are some questions to help guide your planning.

1. Why? Is the program to meet a specific objective? To meet a specific need of the service population? Or is it because it is part of a job description? A clear objective and answer to the "why" question is a good thing to have on paper in case your library director asks or you ask yourself in the middle of the process.

2. What (type)? Not the topic, but the type. Some possible types include:

Educational: Designed to further a YA's general education, either independently or related to a school curriculum (example: SAT workshop).

Cultural: Allows YAs to pursue artistic or intellectual pursuits. YALSA made a big push recently to have more of this type of humanities programming in libraries (example: art show).

Informational: Speaks directly to YAs' need to obtain important information about matters that concern them. Might be about social, health, or economic issues (example: career program).

Recreational: They might learn something, but the goal is to teach YAs that fun and libraries are not at opposite ends of the spectrum (examples: Wrestlemania contest or Dungeons and Dragons tournament).

3. Who does it?

Passive: YAs are audience members only. The staff does not take an active role on the day of the program, either (example: any program with a guest speaker).

Participatory: Engages YAs in some sort of activity (examples: tie-dye workshop or baseball card swap).

4. How often?

Permanent: This type of program is planned to reappear on a regular basis. Although there has to be a first time, the idea is to package the program so it can be repeated (example: babysitting class).

One-shot: Big event like an author visit. This type of program needs lots of promotion because it doesn't have a history.

5. What format?

Program: A program is normally defined as a library-sponsored or co-sponsored event that appeals to a group rather than an individual. The key concepts are "event" and "group."

Activity: An activity meets adolescent needs, but in the context of the reality of YA life. With more teens holding jobs, being involved in other activities, and having more recreational choices, it becomes harder to get together a group for an event. An activity is still an event, but one that doesn't require coming together as a group. These activities speak to YA needs, but also recognize that group activities are not always possible. A summer reading program or contest is an example of such an activity—YAs "do" the program independently when they have time and at their own pace.

6. Who plans?

Cooperative: A program that the library plans, promotes, funds, and produces with one or more agencies outside the library. Figuring out where the library can connect with other groups (see Figure 6-1) is the first step toward cooperative planning.

Solo: You do it.

Cosponsored: Maybe outside agencies can't help you plan it, but they might "bless" it. By co-sponsoring, they are putting their name on it, helping with the promotion, and putting people in the seats.

Intergenerational: Working with juvenile and adult departments leads to intergenerational programming, providing an event or events of interest to all members of a family. More and more emphasis is being given to programs involving YAs with elders. The drawback is related to YA life: doing things with Mom and Dad is often a low YA priority.

7. What topic? At this stage of the planning process, you have almost all the major decisions made except for what your program is actually going to be. For some the topic is the first thought; for others it comes last because ideas are so hard to think of.

Ask YAs: Don't guess or count on professional judgment—just ask. The best YA programs come from listening, not thinking.

Involve YAs: If you can organize a small group of YAs to help you through the process of generating ideas, planning, and promoting, then your chances for success increase dramatically. Not only have members of this group related to you topics of interest to their peers, but they have a stake in the program and will work to see that it succeeds. More on this later.

Polls: Any sort of organized classroom visit or library tour provides the opportunity to hand out a short survey listing possible program ideas and to ask for other ideas and volunteers.

Patrons: Ask for ideas in the stacks, over the reference or checkout desk, or as you are escorting noisy YAs out of the library.

Pulse: In addition to *VOYA,* the other required reading for staff

FIGURE 6-1 POTENTIAL PARTNERS FOR COOPERATIVE PROGRAMMING

SCHOOL RELATED

student council
class council
social club
academic club
political club
cultural club
academic departments
parent organizations
academic advising department
counseling services
media services
school library

YOUTH SERVICES AGENCIES

group homes
boys/girls clubs
YMCA/YWCA
Junior Achievement
youth counseling services
substance abuse prevention
free clinic or health service
scholarship service
employment service
legal service
adolescent psychologists
social services

YOUTH RELATED BUSINESSES

exercise studios
gyms
bike shops
skateboard shops
hair salons
clothing stores
model shops
sporting goods stores
cable tv
radio
fast food/teen employers
martial arts
sports card stores
comic book stores
amusement parks

CULTURAL AGENCIES

museum
theatrical groups
music groups
film groups
zoo and/or park dept.
colleges/universities
dance groups
photography studio
storytellers guild
writers workshops
artists groups
gaming groups

WITHIN THE LIBRARY

children's department
reference/adult dept.
AV dept.
Library Friends
homebound services
subject specialists
other branch/libraries
consortium
special services
nationwide programs
volunteer program
colleagues

BIG BUSINESS

publishers/author visit
national programs
magazine contests
foundations
national associations
game companies
software companies
chain bookstores
chain computer stores

COMMUNITY

neighborhood centers
Red Cross
city services

serving YAs is *Teen*. By looking at YA magazines and the collection you can get some of idea of "what's hot and what's not." You don't want to waste time planning programs about fads that are already history.

Reality check: If you are generating program ideas on your own, you need to do a reality check of some kind. A reality check means asking yourself, "If I were a YA (now, not when you were), would I choose this program over the other demands on my time?"

Brainstorm: If not with YAs, then with parents, teachers, or other staff. One good technique is to use a structure that is already in place as a starting point. For example, look at one range of Dewey numbers and develop a program in each area, or brainstorm using broader terms.

Avoid traps: Avoid at all costs YA programs for which the rationale begins with the following statements:

1. My kids would just love this.
2. When I was a kid I would have loved this.
3. I have a friend kids would just love.

Steal ideas: As there is no national YA program clearinghouse, look to the literature for program ideas and reports (Figure 6-2).

8. What will it cost and who will pay for it?

If you are bringing in a speaker, you need to have a check on program day. You also need to ask yourself if that money would be better spent enhancing the YA collection.

9. Will it work?

Place: Suppose you are planning a battle of garage bands. Where will you hold it? What about security? Are there enough electrical outlets for all of the equipment? What if it rains? The two things you most need to know you won't know until it's too late: the number of people attending and the weather.

Time: When will the program fit into the library's calendar? What about the school's calendar? Look for a time when there is a lull in both.

FIGURE 6-2 PROGRAM ROUNDUPS

Barnett, A. "Illinois Idea-rama for YA Programming," *Illinois Libraries* (Sept. 1983): 431-7.

Boylan, P. "Programs at Prices You Can Afford," *American Libraries* (July - August 1982): 482-3.

Brady, J. "Programming for Young Adults," in *Meeting the Challenge: Library Service to Young Adults*. Edited by Andre & Ann Gagnon. Ottawa, Canada: Canadian Library Association, 1985: 147-152.

Chelton, M. "YA Programming Roundup," *Top of the News* (November 1975): 43-50.

Gomberg, K. *Books Appeal: Get Teenagers into the School Library*. Jefferson, NC: McFarland, 1987.

Gomberg, K. *More Books Appeal: Keep Young Teens in the Library*. Jefferson, NC: McFarland, 1990.

Hammond, C. "A Decade of YA Programing," in *Libraries and Young Adults*. Edited by JoAnn Rogers. Littleton, CO: Libraries Unlimited, 1979: 75-89.

Lefstein, L. *3:00 to 6:00 PM: Programs for Young Adolescents*. Chapel Hill, NC: Center for Early Adolescence, 1983.

Maryland Library Assn. *Gambit*. Baltimore: Maryland Library Assn., 1975-.

Meyers, D. "YA Programming Roundup II," *Top of the News* (Fall 1978): 81-88.

Michigan Library Assn. *Library Program Sourcebook*. Lansing, MI: Michigan Library Assn, 1978.

New York Library Assn. *Second Young Adult Program Guidebook*. New York: New York Library Assn., 1987.

Steinfest, Susan. "Programming for Young Adults," in *Reaching Young People Through Media*. Edited by Nancy Pillon. Littleton, CO: Libraries Unlimited, 1983: 123-150.

"Young Adult Library Services," in *American Library Association Yearbook*. Chicago: ALA (annual).

People: Who is going to be there? YAs, of course, but which ones? Can you visualize the audience on program day? Define a certain market for each program and focus on that segment in your promotion effort.

Measures: The classic programming evaluation, "The three people who were here enjoyed it," is not good enough. State a performance measure up front and measure your results against it after the program.

Answering all these questions is part of the planning process for YA programs. If you have not yet involved any YAs in the process, you have one more chance to do so. Form a focus group and get their reactions to each idea. If you didn't take time to give yourself a reality check, this group will do it for you.

Once you have decided on a program, start documenting your work using the form in Figure 6-3. This documentation can then be used to transmit information to other staff and to colleagues in other libraries. This is your preview, your coming attraction. You've planned, now you need to plot.

10. How will it get done?: Plotting the program means detailing each step and determining who will take it and when. You can use the Program Planning Worksheet at the end of this chapter to help you with this task. This type of plotting is essential to organizing a successful YA program, especially "big events," where so many other duties can interfere.

Costing: You have already figured the base cost: whatever fees you are paying. The real cost of the program, however, is much greater. Although it is difficult to track each minute spent, keeping track of costs (Figure 6-4) shows just how expensive programming can be.

Detailing: Even a simple program like a chess tournament can involve many small details. Avoid problems before they happen by covering all bases and making sure you have someone to complete each task.

Timelining: Every task has a deadline. List each task, who is going to complete it, and by when. Send copies to all persons involved, highlighting their names and tasks.

Confirmation: If your program involves a speaker, you need to confirm everything in writing (Figure 6-5). The speaker needs to understand exactly what is expected, how to get to the library, and other details. Almost anyone who has planned a YA program can tell horror stories about speakers who don't show up or don't have what they need.

The planning worksheet covers almost everything you have to do before the program. Now, all you have left to do is get people to attend.

6.2 PROMOTING

Promotion moves people to action. It means getting flyers into people's hands and your program into their awareness. Programs need to be promoted both within the library and outside it.

CREATING DOCUMENTS

Flyers and posters are a requirement. The quality of your flyers really hinges on what tools you have available. Libraries with desktop publishing capability can produce better materials than someone with clip art and some glue. You should try to make your materials different from any others being produced by the library: a different paper stock, different colors—you might even add a special YA logo. There is plenty of information available about designing p.r. pieces for the library. Following are just a few strategies you might try:

- Use an eye-catching graphic and typeface as in Figure 6-6
- Use graphics with high YA appeal
- Use a book jacket graphic and style as in Figure 6-7
- Use a customized lettering style that can then be used on all subsequent pieces

ESTABLISHING CONTACTS

Even if a program is not cooperatively planned, you can still promote it to other groups. Many of the groups you have in your file might be interested in having YAs attend a library program. But unless you contact them early, they won't be able to arrange transportation. Send them the p.r. materials with a personal invitation, then follow up with a phone call.

FIGURE 6-3 PROGRAM INFORMATION SHEET

LIBRARY: **LIBRARIAN:**

PROGRAM TITLE: _____

DATE: **DAY:**   **TIME:**   **TO**

LOCATION:

SPEAKER NAME:

  ADDRESS:

  HOME PHONE: **WORK PHONE:**

PURPOSE OF PROGRAM:

AGENDA/DESCRIPTION:

MATERIALS/SUPPLIES:

EQUIPMENT:

ROOM SET UP:

APPROX. COST: _____   **SOURCE:** _____

AUDIENCE: [ ] children [ ] YA [ ] adult [ ] all

EXPECTED ATTENDANCE: _____

FIGURE 6-4   COSTING FORMULA

1. Speaker costs:
    fee
    travel
    meals
    other:

    TOTAL _____

2. Supplies cost:
    materials bought
    materials rented
    other materials

    TOTAL _____

3. Staff time:
    Programmer hours x wage
    P.R. dept hours x wage
    Other staff hours x wage

    TOTAL _____

4. Public relations:
    Flyers [   ] x [   ] per
    Posters [   ] x [   ] per
    Bookmarks [   ] x [   ] per
    Other [   ] x [   ] per
    Releases [   ] x [   ] per
    Misc.

    TOTAL _____

5. Other costs:
    Books for display
    Refreshments
    Follow up mailings
    Misc.

    TOTAL _____

TOTAL PROGRAM COSTS: _____

FIGURE 6-5 SPEAKER CONFIRMATION FORM

_____ has been contracted by the
_____ library to appear on _____ from _____ to
_____ to present a program on _____.

The library will pay the speaker a fee of _____. The speaker agrees to
arrive _____ minutes before the program begins and stay _____ minutes after to
answer questions.

This program is intended for an audience of _____ with an expected
attendance of _____.

Please describe the following requirements:

1. Room set up: (how many tables? chairs? etc?)

_____

_____

2. Audio visual equipment needed (including mic.)?

_____

_____

3. Any supplies/materials to be provided by library?

_____

_____

4. Please list information for your introduction:

_____

_____

SIGNATURES: _____ LIBRARY

_____ SPEAKER

ENCLOSED: Map to library; diagram of program area; brochure; SASE; other:

FIGURES 6 AND 7 SAMPLE FLYERS

The epidemic of teen suicide will be discussed Feb. 26 at 6 p.m. at the Pine Point branch of the Springfield City Library, 204 Boston Road. Cheryl Clark, a doctoral student at American International College who specializes in suicide prevention will lead the program. Suicide causes and prevention will be covered and a booklist will be distributed. The program is open to junior high age on up to adults. Register by calling the branch at 782-2335.

"PROMOTING FROM WITHIN"

Everyone in the building working with YAs needs to know what, when, and where this program is taking place if they are going to help promote it. Even if they can't or won't promote it, by informing them you might stop them from "unpromoting" it. That is, if a YA has heard something about a program and asks a staff member who replies, "I don't know anything about that," you might lose a potential participant. You probably can't make the whole staff share your excitement for the program, but you certainly don't want them to dampen the enthusiasm of YAs.

INFORMATION DISTRIBUTION STRATEGIES

1. Post flyers/posters in the YA area, school library, neighborhood centers, and anywhere else the YAs roam.
2. Write public service announcements (PSAs) for radio and television.
3. Write press releases for newspapers—local, weekly, school, and PTO/PTA newsletters.
4. Mail flyers to YAs on any established mailing list.
5. Give your phone over to YA volunteers who can call friends and peers about the program.
6. Write PSAs for daily school announcements.
7. Make commercials for the local cable access station.
8. Approach teachers about program attendance for extra credit.
9. Approach school groups and clubs.
10. Print your program calendar on the back of report cards or another such document.

CREATING HYPE

Promotion alone won't do for big events like author visits: those require hype. Make the program seem like a "can't miss" event. Demand preregistration, even issue "tickets" (about which you could say, "Supplies are limited."). Have buttons made up with the program or author's name and nothing else—or maybe just the date of the program. Create bookmarks and get them stuffed into every stack of books checked out by YAs. Create not just awareness, but curiosity. The only thing better than telling a YA about a great program is having them ask you.

DISPLAYING MATERIALS

Create a display of books and other items about the topic. Use props, magazines, posters, and anything else that works.

CREATE REPEAT BUSINESS

The most effective selling point of all is a track record of good YA programming. You can publicize, promote, even hype your program, but ultimately it needs to deliver. Then you've started to earn a reputation for interesting activities.

6.3 SHOWTIME

If a hundred things have not already gone wrong, the day of the program offers many more opportunities. By now all the tasks on your timeline are checked off. You just need to await the arrival of your speaker and your audience and attend to a few last minute details:

The day before the program:

1. Contact the speaker to confirm.
2. Call local media to cover the program.
3. Make sure you are not scheduled on the desk.
4. Remind all staff with a note in the staff room.
5. Have the speaker's check prepared.

The day of the program:

1. Organize any materials needed.
2. Set up the meeting room or program area.
3. Set up and test any AV or other equipment.
4. Get someone to photograph and/or videotape the event.
5. Have someone to greet speaker at the door.
6. Have someone to introduce the program or speaker.
7. Have water, coffee, soda for the speaker.
8. Set out evaluation forms (Figure 6-8) and pencils.
9. Have library card applications ready for distribution.
10. Bring books from display into the program area.
11. Check people in if preregistration was required.
12. Have refreshments ready.
13. Make sure you have copies of your business card.
14. Set out any flyers about upcoming programs.
15. Line someone up to clean up.

FIGURE 6-8 PROGRAM EVALUATION FORM

DATE:_____ DAY:_____ LIBRARY:_____

PROGRAM:_____

1. Have you ever attended a program at this library before?

    [ ]yes [ ]no

2. This was program was interesting:

    [ ]yes [ ]somewhat [ ]no

3. This program met my expectations:

    [ ]yes [ ]somewhat [ ]no

4. I will attend more programs:

    [ ]yes [ ]maybe   [ ]no

5. How did you learn about this program?

    [ ] flyer/poster   [ ]radio   [ ]from librarian
    [ ] television   [ ]school   [ ]from a friend
    [ ] newspaper   [ ]parents   [ ]other:

6. What other types of programs would you attend?

    [ ] educational   [ ] recreational
    [ ] informational   [ ] social

7. What other topics of programs would you attend?

    [ ] college info   [ ] game tournaments
    [ ] music   [ ] computers
    [ ] creative writing   [ ] other:

8. What is the best time for you to attend?

    [ ] after school   [ ] nights   [ ] weekends

9. Age:_____ Grade:_____ School:_____

If you would like to help us plan programs for people your age, please tell us:

Name:_____ Phone:_____

Address:_____

The day after the program

1. Send a thank-you letter to the speaker.
2. Send a thank-you letter to any groups that attended.
3. File program information sheet, planning sheet, and one copy of various p.r. materials (flyers, posters, PSA, etc).
4. Review program evaluations.
5. Complete program reporting form (Figure 6-9).
6. Speak with YAs who attended.

EVALUATION

The early stages of planning required that you think realistically about your market and how you would measure success. After the program, you should evaluate it in light of what you set out to accomplish. Evaluate all aspects of the process: from idea to planning, plotting, and promotion. To determine what worked, what didn't work, and why, answer the following questions.

1. Did you have the right topic?
2. Did you schedule the program at the right time?
3. Did you promote it properly?
4. Did you overestimate the popularity of the topic?
5. Did you involve YAs or other target groups sufficiently?
6. Was the program really necessary?
7. Did you interact enough with YAs to invite them?
8. Did you give YAs a good reason to attend?

The best promotion strategy for YA programs is making sure the YA librarian knows the YAs in the community and vice versa. Knowing means speaking and listening to YAs and, whenever possible, involving them in the planning process.

6.4 SPECIFIC PROGRAMS

There are several types of YA programs that might be considered classics. Following are some guidelines for doing four very specific and very popular YA programs. While all the planning steps previously outlined still need to be taken, these guidelines provide additional information about how to produce one of these programs at your library.

FIGURE 6-9 REPORTING FORM

ACTIVITY: Program

DATE:

EVALUATION TOTALS

1. Have you ever attended a program at this library before?

    [   ] yes [   ] no

2. This was program was interesting:

    [   ] yes [   ] somewhat [   ] no

3. This program met my expectations:

    [   ] yes [   ] somewhat [   ] no

4. I will attend more programs:

    [ ] yes [   ] maybe   [   ] no

5. How did you learn about this program?

    [   ] flyer/poster   [   ] radio   [   ] from librarian
    [   ] television   [   ] school   [   ] from a friend
    [   ] newspaper   [   ] parents   [   ] other:

6. What other types of programs would you attend?

    [   ] educational   [   ] recreational
    [   ] informational   [   ] social

7. What other topics of programs would you attend?

    [   ] college info   [   ] game tournaments
    [   ] music   [   ] computers
    [   ] creative writing [   ] other:

8. What is the best time for you to attend?

    [   ] after school   [   ] nights   [   ] weekends

9. Ages, grades, schools, comments (on back)

PERFORMANCE MEASURE:

1. Expected attendance   _____
2. Total attendance   _____
3. Total cost   _____
4. Cost per person   _____

YOUNG ADULT ADVISORY GROUPS

1. Recruiting:

Regulars: Start with the YAs you know. Almost every library has a group of YAs who congregate there on a regular basis. Get names to go with the faces and learn their interests. Find materials that speak to their interests so they know you are there to help them. Use a soft sell—don't come on too strong. Just let it be known that you and the library would like to do something for them and that you need their help. If they seem responsive, begin talking about the kind of group you are interested in forming. See if you can get a commitment to attend at least one meeting. Making contact with just a few YAs this way will lead to other contacts.

Schools: Distribute surveys to classes and leave a place for volunteers to list their names. Approach all the schools in your service area, not just the closest one. One of the selling points of your group is that it can be a chance to interact with students from other schools. Also contact school club advisors. See if groups like the National Honor Society would place a representative on your advisory group. You don't want to rely too much on existing groups, however, because the YAs you are primarily looking for may not be members. Seek out the ones who haven't broken into a "social circle" in school and give them a chance to belong and make a difference.

Library friends: Your Friends group might give you start-up money if your group will be one of student Friends. For better or worse, this might mean recruiting some of the children of your Friends of the Library members.

Follow-up: Did your children's department do a summer reading club? If so, do you have the names and grades of those who participated? Use these lists to contact the just-turned 7th graders who have demonstrated interest in library activities.

The Challenge: If you hear a YA complaining about how boring school, the library, and western civilization are in general, challenge that YA to make a difference by joining your group.

2. Organization

First Meeting: Get a commitment to attend one meeting. This is difficult for younger YAs because of transportation problems. There is also the problem of finding time between school and other activities. Send everyone who expressed an interest a personal invitation to attend the first meeting at the best time you can manage.

Define goals and roles: You'll need to lay out your goals for the group, which could be varied. The normal role of an advisory group is to help plan programs. Define your role as being like that of a class or club advisor. You will advise and try to get funds, but you will not decide, plan, or organize: that is the group's job.

Be patient: All groups take time to jell. The turnout for the first meeting may be abysmal, or interest may wane before the next meeting. No matter what, don't pressure kids. Start with small goals and small projects to establish a group identity and, after the first meeting, put them in charge of recruiting more members.

3. Doing:

Activities: For some libraries, recruiting YAs is no problem; finding something for them to do is the real challenge. At first, they may be unsure of what to do, so you may need to lead them a little. Ultimately, the group must work toward developing projects that will give YAs positive library experiences.

4. Problems/solutions:

Retention: YAs will drop in and out as their interests and time commitments change. You have a better chance of retaining them if you give them something they can accomplish and chances to be recognized, succeed, and feel good about themselves. Recognition can come from within the group or in letters to parents, teachers, or the YAs themselves.

Consensus: The only thing people in the group may have in common is the fact that you recruited them. At first, achieve a consensus by taking an active broker role in discussions. Help set priorities and guide discussion on topics. The group needs limits and direction. Achieve consensus by working out compromises through negotiation and exchanges.

Manipulation: You recruited YAs into the group to help you do your job, not to do it for you. The purpose of the group is for YAs to have a positive library experience, not to do grunge work like dusting shelves. It needs to be clear from the start that the group does not do library work unless they choose to do so.

YOUNG ADULT BOOK DISCUSSION GROUPS

A book discussion group can either be general in nature or have a specific focus, such as a genre, theme, author, or school-related topic. The interest level in this kind of group must remain high, since it requires YAs not only to show up on a certain day and time, but also to read a particular book.

1. Recruiting:

Regulars: Start taking notes about which YAs read which types of books. As with the advisory group, probe interest and get at least a few YAs committed before venturing on. If your library's children's room ever did a program like this, see if they still have the list of participants.

Schools: Most teachers can tell you who the class readers are and which students like to talk a lot about the books they've read.

Promote: Use the share-a-book form mentioned in the readers advisory section to develop a file of names of YAs who read and like to express their opinions about books. Develop a flyer and put it on display in all the usual places. Announce a time and date for the first meeting, which will be organizational in nature.

2. Organizing:

Choosing books: You can do this yourself or let the group do it. There are advantages to both approaches. If possible, letting the group choose is preferable, but you'll have to tell them which titles are available in multiple copies. If you decide to choose the books, be sure to throw in some sure winners like *Carrie* and *The Chocolate War*. Either way, you will need access to multiple copies of paperbacks. In addition to the obvious genre, author, and theme discussion groups, consider:

- ALA's "Best of the Best" book list
- Books that became movies—read the book one week, watch the video the next, and discuss the differences
- "College bound" titles, using ALA brochures or lists produced by local colleges.

3. Doing:

Being a discussion leader: You may want to delegate this after a while, but at first you'll have to lead the way. A discussion leader needs to:

- Keep the discussion moving by asking open-ended questions rather than making statements
- Include everyone and not allow one person to dominate
- Discover the level of the group and what aspects, characters, or themes most interest them
- Keep the conversation on track and keep digressions to a minimum
- Concentrate on the positive aspects of the book as well as what people didn't like
- Capture YAs' imaginations by having them cast the book as a movie or suggest alternative endings.

Other possible activities: You might try writing to authors whose books the group is reading and asking them to send autographed copies. Or, you could videotape your discussions and make the tape available to schools, for checkout, or to your local cable access channel.

4. Problems/solutions: The challenges involved in planning a book discussion group are in many ways similar to those of the advisory group. A problem specific to this kind of group, however, may be differing reading interests. To please everyone, you need to choose a wide spectrum of books. Some YAs won't show up if the book being discussed is not "their kind of book." Impress upon the group the need for fairness, compromise, and respect for each other's opinions and tastes.

SUMMER READING PROGRAM

Almost every library has a summer reading club for children. Kids from preschool through sixth grade are brought to the public library, expensive and elaborate graphics are created, games and activities are designed, and a lot of money is spent on prizes and parties. Then children hit grade seven, when decisions about reading or not reading are being made, and everything stops. These young people are either not allowed to participate in the summer reading club or they choose not to for obvious reasons.

These kids are being "lost"—lost for the summer and maybe even lost from the idea of recreational reading altogether. Some libraries have combatted this problem by designing YA summer reading programs. Most are based on the children's model: read so many books and win a prize. Some are very staff-intensive, with lots of programming, activities, and interaction. Others let YAs complete the program independently. YA summer reading programs themselves are in a form of adolescence, looking for an identity away from the children's model yet still serving the function of encouraging recreational reading.

1. Planning:

Funding: You already have an idea; now you need cash to cover your promotion expenses: printing, buttons, t-shirts and whatever else you decide to use. Sometimes you can get a local print shop to donate some goods or give you a discount rate—the same with buttons and t-shirts. Still, like the children's reading club, it can't really be done on the cheap. If your library is unable to come up with funding, you need to look for outside sources. Look to foundations of course, but also to local businesses that tend to serve a lot of YAs. Fast food restaurants, pizza shops, and record stores want to attract teen customers. You might offer to put their logo on your materials in exchange for a little bit of funding.

Developing a theme: All reading programs have some sort of theme. The right theme can turn kids on to a program, and the wrong one can turn them off. Your theme should be short and to the point, like a slogan. It can play off some aspect of pop culture or fads. The theme should stress fun and should *never* include the world "club." A club is for children, and that is not how YAs see themselves.

Developing a look: Your logo should be consistent with your theme. It can be a graphic or a stylized print of the theme and should be on all program materials.

2. Promoting:

Focus: Don't try to visit every single class. Instead, focus your attention on the students most likely to join: the younger readers.

Send a Message: You want YAs to know that this is not the same kiddie reading program they've been in for years. Stress how it will be different and what types of prizes will be offered. Also, be sure they know that it is an independent experience. No one will tell them what to read or not read, no one will quiz them on titles, and they can read as many or as few books as they choose.

3. Running the Program: Most YA summer reading programs require little staff involvement once the planning and promoting are finished. You will certainly want to interact with as many of the YAs participating as possible, but you don't want to make that a forced encounter.

How it works:

- YAs read books of their own choice, fill out an entry form for each book, and place the forms in a clearly marked container.
- The honor system must be applied here. You should not monitor what participants claim to read. On the other hand, if you are suspicious of someone filling out 50 forms a day for books by Tolstoy, you might need to remind that YA of the purpose of the program.
- Each day, week, or month (depending on the number of prizes you have available), draw out names. Then call or write to the winners and post their names (if they agree) so everyone can see who won prizes.
- At the end of the program, have a prize for everyone who participated or met some stated criteria. You might give away one big prize (like a portable CD player) as the incentive or buy lots of small prizes.
- Throw a party at the end of the program and invite everyone who participated. Give them refreshments, entertain them, and talk with them about what they read and what they thought of the program. This is not only a chance for you to meet YAs—it can also be a great photo opportunity.

4. Problems/solutions:

Lack of interest: Many kids stop participating in summer reading programs well before seventh grade. Work with children's librarians to develop programs for fifth and sixth graders so that they are still interested by the time you get to them.

Waning interest: You might get YAs excited at the start of your program, but as the summer goes on interest often wanes. Innovative programming or a constant stream of prizes and activities can help keep interest high.

Low response: Something like this probably isn't going to set the world on fire its first year. It will take a couple of years to develop, work out the kinks, and establish an identity. It needs to become something that children doing a children's program will look forward to.

LITERARY MAGAZINES

A YA literary magazine combines the best of all possible worlds. It gives YAs chances to show off their talents, to search for identity through writing, to gain a sense of accomplishment, and to learn decision making and teamwork. For the library, it provides an opportunity to work closely with young people and "show off" what good can come from the connection between libraries and young adults.

1. Planning:

Funding: This can be an expensive project if you have to go to outside printers. If you do it in-house, your graphics department needs lots of warning and plenty of paper. Again, you will want to look for outside funding, if not for the printing expense, then to donate prizes for the best writing in various categories.

Recruiting: You need a core group to serve as an editorial board. The library is the publisher, but the editorial board are the editors. Recruit from the usual sources, but make it clear this requires a substantial time commitment.

Defining a mission: What are you doing and why? The mission statement of your magazine should contain:

- Title of the magazine
- Ages of students whose work will be published
- Geographical area represented
- Statement of purpose.

Setting editorial guidelines: Like any magazine, you need to decide what you will and will not publish based on some pre-established criteria. Some examples:

- *Categories:* Poetry and short stories are givens, but what about essays, song lyrics, raps, comics, plays, or diary entries?
- *Length:* How many pages?
- *Submissions:* How many will you accept from each YA? How many per category?
- *Acceptance:* Do you accept and print everything given to you, or are there certain standards?
- *Language/concept:* If this magazine will go to schools, will you publish works with four letter words? Racist, sexist, or homophobic

remarks? Works that "slander" teachers? Are there other controversial subjects you will accept or not accept?

- *Manuscripts:* Are they returned? Do they have to be prepared in a certain way?
- *Deadlines and timelines:* When are submissions due? When will the magazine be laid out? When will it go to the printer? When is it available to the public?

2. Producing the magazine:

Obtaining submissions: Produce an entry form like the one in Figure 6-10 to have on hand at the library and distribute in classes. If you want submissions to have a theme, this is the place to convey that, along with any other criteria. Work with creative writing and other teachers to encourage students to submit materials. Do not, however, accept a packet of materials from a teacher unless the students have agreed to have it published.

Gathering submissions: Take everything and lock yourself and the editorial board away in a room somewhere. Make sure everything you have meets the criteria. If something is very good but misses the mark for some reason (too long, too short, etc.), then consider contacting the author.

Awarding prizes: If you got some financial help, you might want to award prizes to the best works by category and/or grade. Your editorial board should not choose the winners, but to save time they could choose the top ten or so works. Get other library staff, local college professors, local writers, or other experts to judge materials. Make sure these judges get a thank-you letter, a mention in the magazine, and a copy of the final product. Give the judges entry forms, criteria, and scoresheets.

3. Laying out the magazine

Preparing text: The text should be camera ready. Depending on your submission requirements and your aesthetic judgement, you can choose to have everything retyped or printed as is. It all depends on how professional you want the publication to look, how much time you and the editorial board have, whether other staff can assist you, and what kinds of technology you have available. Each piece should be "by-lined" with the YA's name, age, and school.

FIGURE 6-10   LITERARY MAGAZINE ENTRY FORM

REFLECTIONS
Literary/Graphic Arts Magazine

For and by
students
grades 7 - 12

Reflections
Reflections

CONTEST

Entries will be judged and prizes awarded

in two age categories: *(Grades 7 - 9 and Grades 10 - 12)*

SUBMISSION DEADLINE: MAY 31, 1991

CONTEST RULES

1. There is a maximum of *two* entries *per category* (poetry, prose, art).
2. There is a maximum of *four* entries *per person* (in all categories).
3. All literary entries must be *type-written, double spaced.*
4. There is a maximum of *three* pages per entry.
5. Poetry and prose: please send *copies only.* No manuscripts can be returned. Original artwork can be photocopied and returned.
6. Graphics must be *black and white*, no larger that 11" x 17". *Note:* Solid black areas do not reproduce well. Since the first-place art will be on the magazine cover, this must be taken into consideration by the judges.
7. Employees of Cuyahoga County Public Library are ineligible for the contest, but may submit items for publication.
8. Each entry must have a *completed* entry form with *original* signature attached.
9. After one-time publication in *Reflections* (c. 1991), all rights revert to the author/artist.

WE ARE LOOKING FOR:
Literary entries POEMS ● SHORT STORIES ● ANECDOTES
SHORT PLAYS ● HUMOR ● FANTASY ● SCIENCE FICTION ● "SLICE OF LIFE"

Graphic entries: PEN & INK ● BLOCK PRINT ● SCRATCH BOARD
SILK SCREEN ● PAINT ● COMPUTER GRAPHIC ● PHOTOGRAPH

To send in your works through any branch of Cuyahoga County Public Library, put them in an envelope marked "MYR/YA," so they will get to the Young Adult Department of Mayfield Regional, 473-0350.

REFLECTIONS Contest Entry Form
(A **completed** entry form must be attached to each entry. Photocopies of the form are acceptable, but each form should have an **original signature ***)

This work is for the following category:
☐ Poetry   ☐ Prose   ☐ Graphic art
                                                        ☐ Please return this original artwork.

Title of work (if there is one): _____

Name _____   Phone _____

Street Address _____   School _____

City   State   Zip   ☐ 7   ☐ 8   ☐ 9 ●   ☐ 10   ☐ 11   ☐ 12
                                            Grade as of 4/30/91

I certify this to be my own original work. Cuyahoga County Public Library has my permission to publish my work in *Reflections Magazine.*

CUYAHOGA COUNTY PUBLIC LIBRARY
Mayfield Regional
6080 Wilson Mills Road ● 473-0350

* Signed _____

Date: _____

Using illustrations: As part of this process, you could have a concurrent art contest and use the art submissions to illustrate the text. Just be careful with placement. (Don't put a smiling clown face next to a suicide poem.)

Arranging the text: Start with the "best of show" or another award winner on page one. Then distribute the other winning pieces throughout the text by dividing the number of pages by the number of winners (so that prize works appear every so many pages).

Pacing: Try to keep a balance of longer and shorter pieces. Play with balance by grouping contrasting pieces on one page and similar ones on the next. You will know when two things match up next to each other, and you will know when it is wrong. Once satisfied, let it sit for day, then read it over once more to see if it all holds together.

Final touches:
- Table of contents
- Acknowledgments or thank-you page, recognizing judges, businesses that donated prizes, and helpful teachers and library staff
- Title page with the library's address and names of contributing writers, editors, the library director, YA staff, and bibliographic information.

4. Distributing the magazine

Kickoff event: Organize a reception to honor everyone for all their hard work and show the staff and the community how YAs can have a positive library experience.
- Contact winners and ask them to read their work. Send a letter or postcard to everyone else who entered.
- Display the artwork used in the magazine. If possible, enlarge the art so it can placed on easels.
- Provide refreshments and entertainment.
- Invite everyone on the thank-you page.
- Award prizes, have readings, and acknowledge all who contributed their efforts.
- Introduce members of editorial staff and have a gift for each of them.

Visit schools: Make sure each school library and English teacher have copies. Send you thank-you notes to principals and to cooperative teachers.

Catalog: One copy should be cataloged for your YA collection. One copy should also be available for each agency.

General public: Write a press release about the magazine, including names of the winners and send it to local newspapers. Have additional copies available for those who are interested.

FIGURE 6-11 PROGRAM PLANNING WORKSHEET

1. Program approved?
   [ ] by supervisor
   [ ] by director
   [ ] off desk planning time approved

2. Title of program:

   _____

3. Description of program:

   _____
   _____
   _____

4. Date:
   [ ] check library calendar
   [ ] check school calendar
   [ ] check community calendar

5. Time: start:_____ end:_____

6. Place:
   [ ] meeting room
   [ ] YA area
   [ ] other:

7. Approx cost:
   [   ] speaker/fees
   [   ] supplies/materials
   [   ] staff time
   [   ] graphics/printing
   [   ] other
   [   ] TOTAL

8. Funding source:
   [   ] budget line
   [   ] Friends of the Library
   [   ] outside/donations
   [   ] other:
   [   ] TOTAL

9. Target audience:
   [ ]children [ ]YA [ ]adult [ ]all

10. Potential YA audience:
    [ ]boys   [ ]girls
    [ ]jr. high   [ ]senior high

11. Expected attendance:_____

FIGURE 6-11 PROGRAM PLANNING WORKSHEET, cont.

12. Timeline:

TASK:	ASSIGNED TO:	DATE:	DONE?

13. Confirmation
    [ ] contract sent
    [ ] contract returned
    [ ] follow up call

14. Publicity (how many?)
    [   ] flyers
    [   ] posters
    [   ] bookmarks
    [   ] booklists
    [   ] other:

    press releases sent to:
    [ ] local newspaper
    [ ] school newspaper
    [ ] Friends of the Library newsletter
    [ ] PTA/PTO newsletter
    [ ] radio
    [ ] TV
    [ ] other:

15. Promotion:
    [ ] all staff informed
    [ ] visits to schools planned
    [ ] book display
    [ ] YAs called/mailing list
    [ ] letter sent to:
        [ ] school groups
        [ ] community groups

FIGURE 6-11 PROGRAM PLANNING WORKSHEET, cont.

[ ] flyers/posters distributed to:
    [ ] schools
    [ ] community groups
    [ ] businesses
    [ ] other libraries
[ ] other:

16. Program details:
    [ ] room set-up
    [ ] equipment supplies
    [ ] refreshments
    [ ] speaker's introduction
    [ ] speaker's check
    [ ] evaluation form/pencils
    [ ] flyers for next program
    [ ] room clean-up
    [ ] other:

17. After program:
    [ ] thank-you letters
    [ ] tally evaluations
    [ ] self evaluation
    [ ] file all documents
    [ ] other:

18. What were the elements of success?

_____
_____
_____
_____

19. What were problems?

_____
_____
_____
_____

20. Notes for next time:

_____
_____
_____
_____

7 MARKETING AND MERCHANDISING

Marketing in libraries has received a great deal of attention recently. Managers are looking at their users and trying to find out about their non-users in an effort to plan and allocate resources better. For a long time libraries were primarily concerned with what products the library had: how many books, tapes, records, or magazines. Recently, the focus has shifted to the use of these products. The bridge between the library's input and its output is what marketing is all about.

7.1 MARKETING

Marketing is defined in many different ways, but a good definition is "getting your goods or services to your customers." It is not incorrect to call library patrons customers. Customers "buy" services, and libraries offer services. Putting up a display of horror titles, however, is not marketing. In this case, marketing is deciding why you are doing the display, when and where you are doing it, who the display is supposed to attract, and what you hope to accomplish.

It is next to impossible to merchandise YA collections if they are not all in one area. The goal of merchandising is to turn a passive YA collection into an active YA area. Unfortunately, because of space priorities or other factors in many libraries, it is not always possible to have a separate YA area. In this case, you must at least make sure that whatever materials you have for YAs are not near the children's room. A better location for a YA collection is near reference, magazines, or audiovisual materials. If these materials are not separated in any way, YAs will be discouraged from using the library because they will have to hunt and peck throughout the collection to find materials of interest.

When designing a YA area (Figure 7-1), two major concerns are YA privacy and staff access. You want an area that will allow YAs to talk in private, yet not so private that staff cannot easily monitor activity. You don't want it near areas where staff needs quiet to do their work, such as the reference desk or circulation desk. Finally, the YA area should be easy to identify, find, and enjoy.

MARKET SEGMENTS
The library market means the audience for library services. This market is subdivided in many ways. One division is by age, thus the

FIGURE 7-1 YA AREA DESIGN PLAN

A. Traffic and sightlines
1. Easy access
2. Magazines in direct sight
3. Most popular materials in front
4. Least popular items in back/kept low
5. Displays at eye level

B. Environment
1. Decorated: posters from magazines
2. Comfortable chairs
3. Table available for games/study
4. Bulletin board with local happenings
5. Place for student art/writings
6. Desk for YA staff near entrance
7. Listening station
8. Computer for games

C. Materials
1. Books: recreational
2. Books: informational
3. Books: educational
4. Magazines
5. Listening collection
6. Viewing collection
7. Flyers on upcoming program
8. Booklists
9. Suggestion box

D. Location
1. Not adjacent to children's room
2. Not adjacent to circulation desk
3. Not adjacent to "quiet" study area
4. Near front entrance
5. Clearly visible/identifiable
6. Allowing for both privacy and staff monitoring

E. Arrangement
1. Series shelved separately
2. New book display area
3. Multiple rotating display areas
4. Books shelved by genre not author
5. Shelves uncrowded: display on end
6. No rebound or without jacket books on display
7. Shelves reachable: not too high/low
8. Wheelchair accessible

F. If no separate YA is available, then:
1. Keep away from children's
2. Keep near magazines/reference

YA market segment. User groups or market segments can also be divided by:

1. Geographic factors
2. Economic factors
3. Social factors
4. Amount of library use
5. Reasons for library use
6. Types of library use
7. Reading interests
8. Library knowledge
9. Awareness of library services
10. Time spent in the library
11. Methods used to find materials
12. Non-users

Within the YA market, the segment can be divided further by:

1. Gender
2. Age and/or grade
3. School
4. Academic achievement
5. Clique
6. Reader or nonreader
7. How free time is spent
8. Special interests
9. Working vs. nonworking
10. College bound vs. non-college bound
11. Library card holders vs. non-holders
12. Attitudes about the library

You need to know as much about your market as possible. You don't want to plan GED programs in a community with virtually no dropout rate. Your planning of services will hinge on what you know.

USING SURVEYS

In Chapter 2, there was a sample user survey. This is really a potential user survey because you want it to reach those who are not already going to the library. After tabulating the results of the survey, you will have the following information about your market:

1. Amount of library use
2. Percentage of card holders
3. Why YAs use the library (and why they don't use it)
4. What they use (and don't use) the library for
5. Gender
6. Age, grade, and school

You can also use your survey results to answer the following questions:

1. Who is the "average" YA user?
2. Why do YAs use the library?
3. Why don't they?
4. What do YAs like most/least about the library?
5. What is the most surprising statistic?
6. What type of follow-up questions are needed?
7. What should the priorities of YA services be?
8. What programs or services could break down barriers between YAs and the library?

Once you have this information, you can begin to focus your efforts more directly. After determining which specific user groups within the YA market you want to focus on, you can begin looking for the meeting point between their interests and your services.

7.2 THE MARKETING PLAN

What can you do to serve the user better and reach the non-user? You can employ what is known as the "marketing mix," made up of four elements:

1. Products: what you offer
2. Price: what it costs you
3. Place: where you offer it
4. Promotion: how you tell people about what you offer

Let's begin with products. What products does your library have to offer YAs?

Products:

1. A building with chairs
2. Collections of print and nonprint materials
3. Information services
4. Staff
5. Programs and activities

Next, examine the other elements with regard to your YA services.

Price:

1. Cost to buy, prepare and house products
2. Staff cost
3. Cost of program and activities
4. At what other cost? (If you do YA, then what will you not be able to do?)

Place:

1. Where YA is offered in the library
2. How much space is available
3. Where YA is offered outside the library (outreach)

Promotion:

1. Inside the library
2. Outside the library
3. For programs and activities
4. Community and media relations

Once the objectives are stated, the mission defined, and the segment targeted, the various parts of the mix can come together to form a marketing plan (Figure 7-2). Obviously you can't do all of these things at the same time; the costs in terms of staff time would be too much. But this is an example of choosing one small segment of the potential library audience and designing products to meet their specific needs.

7.3 MERCHANDISING

Merchandising is an outgrowth of marketing. It is primarily concerned with the place element, or distribution. Merchandising

FIGURE 7-2 MARKETING PLAN

I. Identity YA market segments

II. Choose segment [reluctant readers]

    A. Characteristics of this user group

    B. Recreational interests [movies/videos?]

    C. Current awareness of group
        1. Of library services
        2. How can awareness be increased?
        3. What will move them to action?

III. Products

    A. Collections
        1. Video tapes
        2. Movie soundtracks on cd/tape
        3. Magazines about movies
        4. Books about movies
        5. Movie tie-ins
        6. Movie posters

    B. Services
        1. Circulation of above products
        2. Booktalking movie tie-ins
        3. Programming
            a. Film or video series
            b. Movie trivia contests
            c. read the movie discussion group
            d. make your own movie/video
            e. reading contest movie tie ins
            f. favorite movie star polls
            g. storyboard YA novels
            h. scripts for YA novels

IV. Price

    A. Cost of materials

    B. Staff cost

V. Place

    A. Within the library
        1. Decorate YA area with movie posters
        2. Create movie tie in display
        3. Move some videos in YA area
        4. Meeting room to show videos

FIGURE 7-2 MARKETING PLAN, cont.

    B. Outside the library
       1. Promote/booktalk in schools
       2. Work with local theater/video store

VI. Promotion

    A. Within the library
       1. Flyers/posters
       2. Book/movie list
       3. Movie posters

    B. Outside of library
       1. School visits
       2. Press releases

    C. Programs
       1. Kickoff film or other BIG event
       2. Ongoing contests/activities

    D. Priority
       1. This will the major YA fall project
       2. All materials have YA logo
       3. Try to get photo/article in school or
          local paper.

VII. Measures

    A. Formal
       1. Circulation
       2. Program attendance
       3. Restocking of displays
       4. Activity/contest participation

    B. Informal
       1. Comments from users
       2. Comments from parents/teachers/staff

VIII. Conclusion

By marketing to specific group [reluctant reader]
through use of high appeal items [movie/videos],
awareness of what the library offers to this user
group should increase, which should result in an
increase in library user/circulation by members

means presenting your products in an attractive, eye-catching fashion to encourage their use by your customers. In merchandising, the product is the collection; the cost is that of the materials and special shelving; the place is in the library (but a library designed for the customer rather than librarians); and the promotion strategy is allowing the products to promote themselves. The market segment this appeals to is the one that survey after survey tells us populates public libraries—the browsers. Merchandising is thus an example of a marketing strategy.

The merchandising idea was "born" in the mall bookstores and soon caught on in many libraries, but not without controversy. Few can doubt the effectiveness of merchandising techniques to increase circulation; there are just too many case studies documenting it. The argument is more philosophical: should libraries imitate bookstores not only in display but also in selection?

Supermarkets are expert merchandisers—lots of displays, materials arranged by broad subjects, and within those more narrowly, and lots of "point-of-purchase" sales. Waldenbooks and B. Dalton are also experts, using a lot of the same techniques as Piggly Wiggly: good lighting, covers facing out, displays in high-traffic areas, the use of bookdumps to push certain titles, signs to get customers to the right areas, and an entire storefront designed to show what is hot and new.

ARGUMENT FOR YA MERCHANDISING
In Gallo's survey (see section 3.1), YAs were asked, "How do you find the books you read?" Following are their responses:

1. Browsing (56%)
2. Friend's suggestion (28%)
3. Bookstore display (12%)
4. Library display (4%)
5. Teacher's suggestion (3%)
6. Librarian's suggestion (2%)

These findings have three key implications for merchandising: that YAs are browsers; that our advice and expertise don't matter much; and that library displays don't work.

The third finding might seem the most surprising, and even contradictory to the principles of merchandising. Aren't displays merchandising? Yes and no. Sticking a bunch of books about Thanksgiving and a cutout cardboard turkey on a table and leaving it up there for a month—and using the same display every year—is not merchandising. You are not making the items more attractive, you are not promoting them, you are not creating excitement, and you certainly are not appealing to a browser's interest.

By the same token, why are YA areas designed for us rather than them? If YAs are browsers, then shouldn't everything possible be done to design the YA area with this fact in mind? How often does a YA come into the library looking for one particular recreational book to read? Rarely. They are looking for choices, ideas, and authors that attract them.

YAs act on impulse. Impulse is the lifeblood of merchandising, as the *National Enquirer* and Milky Ways at the grocery checkout counter illustrate. Putting appealing materials near the circulation desk or at the front of the YA area encourages the impulse "buy." Some impulse items might be:

1. Nintendo how-to books
2. Matt Groening's *Life in Hell* series
3. *Garfield* or other comics
4. YA thrillers by Christopher Pike or R.L. Stine
5. Celebrity biographies
6. Movie tie-ins
7. Joke books
8. Multiple copies of new magazines
9. Oversize nonfiction
10. Horror books

These high-appeal materials will be noticed and checked out—and YA circulation will increase dramatically, not just of these items. Because you have created an inviting entrance, YAs will wonder what other "good stuff" might be in that YA area.

7.4 THE MERCHANDISING PLAN

Before developing a merchandising plan, lets review some key concepts:

Covers, not spines: YAs respond well to visual images, from music videos to posters. The covers of YA books are often their main selling point. Merchandising means creating space to arrange as many titles as possible to be shelved face out. Publishers put good money and a lot of thought into designing book jackets and covers, and librarians should use rather than lose that expertise.

Access, not advice: Since our advice is so rarely called upon, we should acknowledge that fact and use it to our advantage. If our role has changed from reader's advisor to presenter of materials, we should select the most popular items and plenty of them. Then we should shelve them in a way that increases access and makes the collection "user-friendly" for the browser.

Signals, not signs:
The YA area should be designed and decorated in such a way that it sends a clear signal to every YA: this area is for you. The area needs to be active: always changing displays, bookdumps, bulletin boards, posters. It should clearly highlight the uniqueness of the area, not just to YAs, but to other patrons and staff. The best YA area doesn't need a sign saying "YA Area"—everyone should be able to tell that.

Products, not preservation: It's not a rare book room, so you don't need to worry about preservation. You can buy a lot of materials that have a short shelflife, like magazines and paperbacks.

Desirable, not just available: By selecting materials, we make them available. By cataloging them, we make them accessible. By merchandising them, we make them desirable. It is not just giving YAs what they want; it is showing them what they want and making them want even more.

Patron, not librarian: Those schooled in the Dewey decimal system will hate your "merchandised" YA area. Staff or patrons looking for specific materials will be frustrated, but you can combat that frustration with training and documentation for staff and signage for patrons. Some will still complain, but remember your mission is to serve the YA constituency, not the adult reference staff.

Books, not a book: Your collection philosophy naturally changes; you buy fewer titles but more copies of each. You consider covers and the browsing appeal of materials. You begin to think not about each book, but about all the books.

Sell, not select: Merchandising is passive booktalking—it is creating excitement about titles. You will notice an increase in "sales" with merchandising. Circulation is just one measure of success, but it is a good one. Compare:

- Pre-merchandising circulation with post-merchandising circulation.
- YA circulation's percentage of total circulation then and now.
- "Sales" per square foot—how big is the YA area and what's the ratio of area to circulation? Find this out for other departments.
- Turnover rate then and now.
- Bang for the buck—compare circulation with budget. Compare this with other departments.

Plan, don't "plop": Merchandising tries to get the most out of the least, which makes good sense for YA services because they are usually poorly funded. Think out a strategy and put it in the form of a plan (Figure 7-?). Make sure everyone has a chance to see the plan and understand it. Make it clear that you are redesigning the YA area to increase circulation, not just "plopping" a handful of books on a table.

7.5 SUMMARY

Many libraries who think they are merchandising are not. Merchandising is not just putting books on display. It is the byproduct of a larger plan about what libraries should do in a community.

Merchandising works a lot like buying Oreo cookies. Most people who leave a supermarket with a bag of Oreos didn't have them on their shopping list when they came in. The cookies were just there, easy to find in all their temptation—easy to find at the end of an aisle or near the checkout, in a display just inviting you to take one.

FIGURE 7-3 MERCHANDISING PLAN

I. **Collection development**
  A. Weeding
    1. Make room for new purchases
    2. Have more space for display
    3. Does book "earn" its place on shelf?
    4. Sales per square feet: is space being used for maximum sales/circulation?
    5. Weed books which are tattered, without covers, etc. Replace with pbk versions.
  B. Selection
    1. Paperbacks paperbacks paperbacks
    2. Magazines
    3. Hot nonfiction
    4. Browsing items

II. **Shelving**
  A. Current
    1. Each shelf needs end space to display
    2. Rearrange to create more shelving
  B. New
    1. Zig-zag
    2. Bookstore style slanted shelves
    3. Bookdumps: cardboard and permanent
    4. Shelf end display racks

III. **Displays**
  A. Current
    1. Table or shelf top
    2. Put in high traffic area
    3. Use floor, book trucks, etc.
  B. New
    1. Cubes or display units
    2. Book easels
  C. Responsibilities
    1. Scheduling/planning/creating
    2. Shelving/maintaining
  D. Creating
    1. Use props
    2. Use signs
    3. Covers face out
    4. Multiple copies
    5. Eye level and in sightline
    6. Active, keep filled
    7. Change regularly
    8. Sign saying materials CAN be checked out
    9. Gimmicks
    10. Interactive

8 ISSUES IN YOUNG ADULT SERVICES

One of the things that makes YA service difficult is a constant feeling of being under attack—not just from within the library but also from outside. Many social and professional issues revolve around YAs, perhaps because adolescence is a time of transition and vulnerability. Society and libraries are torn between allowing YAs to behave independently and wanting to protect them. This chapter presents some of the larger questions about teenagers and their place in libraries and society.

8.1 CONFIDENTIALITY

SCENARIO #1:
A YA requests a copy of *The Satanic Bible*. Of course it is not on your shelf, but you manage to get ahold of a copy from another agency. You happen to call the house when the YA is not at home. A parent answers:

"This is the library calling. Is (name) there?"

"No, he's at school right now. Can I take a message?"

"Would you please tell him that a book has come in for him. We will hold it for one week."

"What is the book?"

"I'm sorry, but. . ."

"I'm his mother. I have a right to know what book it is."

Some libraries already have a policy in place to deal with this problem, which is not unique to YA services. Violating a patron's confidentiality by telling anyone who answers the phone what the patron has requested is bad business. (Would we show that person material the patron has checked out if they came into the library?) With YAs, however, the problem is more complex for two reasons. First, given the curious nature of YAs, many will be asking you for titles such as *The Satanic Bible, As Nasty As They Wanna Be, Go Ask Alice,* and *Forever.* Mom is the last person they want to have know about this in most cases. Some libraries will reveal this information to parents as long as the material is not controversial. But who decides what is controversial and what isn't? Maybe we think there is nothing controversial about telling someone's mother that he or she requested *Bambi* on videocassette, but maybe that YA doesn't have a VCR in the house. Mom may wonder where her child is watching movies (and what other kinds of movies he or she is watching).

SCENARIO #2:
An adult patron comes in with her YA son's overdue notice, a long list of unreturned items. She says she wants to pay the fines for him, but she wants to know not just what else he has overdue, but everything he has checked out. She insists that since she is the parent (and thus has financial responsibility) she has a right to know. Does this parent's "right" conflict with the YA's right to confidentiality? Does a parent's liability for library fines give him or her a right to know about a YA's borrowing habits? This puts the librarian in a terrible bind and a sticky legal position.

8.2 PRIVACY

Closely related to confidentiality rights are privacy rights. If we think of confidentiality primarily in relation to circulation records, then privacy is related to everything else. A person's library use is a private matter, and YAs are the most private of people. Because many YAs have, or at least feel they have, a secret life, their privacy is of paramount importance.

SCENARIO #1:
You've been working with a school principal to develop a cooperative library instruction program. The program is a success because this principal was so helpful. The same principal calls you up and asks for a favor. She asks if a certain student was in the library that day during school hours. You don't know what to say. Sometimes schools feel you have an obligation to report students who are skipping school and hanging out in the library. Some schools may also want you to enforce some of their conduct rules for them. Schools need to be made to understand that the right to privacy the library guarantees extends to everyone—including YAs.

SCENARIO #2:
An adult patron calls you up one day checking on her teenage son. She wants to know if he was in the library on a particular night last week. (As every kid knows, "Mom, I'm going to the library," is a great cover.) If YAs are in the library during obvious school hours, should staff approach them? If a parent calls and asks if his or her child is in the building, should we page the YA? If a YA is spending an extraordinary amount of time in the library, is that an issue?
Some of these issues relate to larger questions about privacy and

confidentiality for everyone in the library setting. Others are related to YAs' unique situation. They are old enough to have private lives, but their parents still have financial and legal responsibility for them. Certainly, if YAs' use of the library is to be a "positive experience," their knowing that use is a private matter is as important to them as it is to us.

8.3 SOCIAL RESPONSIBILITY

SCENARIO #1:
A young woman comes in and asks for information about marriage. As your reference interview continues, the subject gradually changes to wife abuse, then to dating violence. You begin to notice she seems upset and that she has a bruise on her face. You don't ask her "when the paper is due" because you've figured out that she doesn't need the information for school. Do you refer her to a battered woman's shelter? Do you give her 800 numbers or local hotlines to call? Would you do more or less for a teenager than for an adult patron? Should you contact a school counselor and ask that person to intervene? Should you do anything at all?

SCENARIO #2:
Did your library purchase tapes by Two Live Crew? If so, did anyone on staff listen to them or read the lyrics? If we consider sexism, racism, and outright "filth" to be social ills, are we promoting or sanctioning these ills by purchasing materials that exploit, advance, celebrate, or exemplify them? With YAs, the issue is more intense, since YA-hood is usually a time of character definition. Would you hand *American Psycho* to a YA who asked for the "grossest" book out there? If we want the library to be a positive experience for YAs, do we give them everything—even what we consider to be negative examples?

8.4 CENSORSHIP

No other issue involved in young adult services is discussed more often or is more important than censorship. YA materials seem to be challenged more than any others. The most recent debate over Two Live Crew involves those under 18. The issue of labeling records and cassettes is still alive, and in school and public libraries across the country YA books are still being challenged. There's not a lot to say about this issue that hasn't been said or written elsewhere. Each library needs a collection development policy, a statement regarding intellectual freedom, and a procedure for handling complaints about materials. Examples of all of these can be found in the ALA *Intellectual Freedom Manual.*[1]

The censorship battleground is now shifting to nonprint materials for a variety of reasons:

"Ratings": In the "outside" world books are not rated nor is access to them limited by age, with the exception of pornographic materials. A YA can go into any bookstore and purchase virtually any item. The same YA, however, is prohibited from attending certain films, from renting certain videotapes, and from purchasing certain tapes in many chain record stores. These examples are outside the library setting, but they raise an interesting question about standards. That libraries should reflect their community is a given, but what if the community doesn't reflect library standards?

Nonprint problems: As the entire culture becomes less interested in reading and the importance of nonprint materials increases, it seems only natural for the censors to follow suit. Not that opposition to some types of music is a new idea, but it certainly has picked up steam in the 1980s and will continue to do so as music pushes back old boundaries and stakes out new, bold territory. As certain forms (primarily rap music) gain in popularity, the move to stop them will also increase.

The new bandwagon: Book banning has a bad odor to it, but stopping YAs from listening to rap music doesn't seem to attract the same societal smell. Your community might be perfectly willing to "stand up" to book banners, but how many would join the crusade defending YAs' access to rap music or slasher movies?

Self-censorship: It would be interesting if the *Newsletter on Intellectual Freedom* began expanding its scope to cover censorship from the inside. Self-censorship is the only way to explain why many materials YAs need and want cannot be found in many collections. Under the guise of materials selection, many libraries decline to purchase items they fear will be challenged.

STORY #1:

One of the books I once nominated for YALSA's Quick Picks booklist (for reluctant readers) was the *New Pictorial History of Wrestling*. This is primarily a book of photos with short readable biographies on numerous professional wrestlers. It is by all definitions a book for the reluctant reader. It is easy reading, has lots of photos, and covers a subject of high interest to YAs. Not only did this book not make the list, but it received only two votes. The discussion around the book included statements such as, "I couldn't (or wouldn't) have this book in my library." People were concerned because the book, although mild by wrestling standards, contains two photos of wrestlers bleeding. The point is not that the book didn't make the list (because every book can't), but that these YA librarians would have not selected this book because of their own *personal* feelings about it.

STORY #2:

I worked in a large suburban library system during the fury over Two Live Crew. The group's answer to their censorship challenge was a tape called *Banned in the USA*, which quickly rose on the charts. It was also, if possible, even more graphic and potentially offensive than *As Nasty as They Wanna Be*. Only two branches in this system purchased the tape. Since the primary selection tool for music in this system was the *Billboard* charts, it certainly should have been selected, but it was not.

STORY #3:

Another system I worked in at one time decided to increase its magazine collection. One title in this collection was *Fangoria,* a fan magazine for people who like gory movies. The first issue the library purchased had a centerfold of a man with steel pipes driven through his skull with the ends sticking from his mouth, eyes, and ears. That was the first and last issue of *Fangoria* I selected for the library.

The line between selection and self-censorship gets very narrow in the non-book field. Why don't libraries choose *Hustler* for YAs? Certainly it would be popular. When we draw lines based on a variety of criteria, we select. When we do so based on our own personal agendas (or for fear of others), we self-censor. Librarians serving YAs face a real challenge because many in the community want to draw these lines for us, and we often find them hard to draw ourselves.

8.5 RESTRICTED ACCESS

Access is limited either directly (through a written policy) or indirectly (by simply not offering certain services to YAs). Although there may not be a written policy about Dialog searches for students, many libraries have an informal understanding not to do so, or at least not to offer the service as quickly to a student as they would to a business professional. There are outrageous examples of these double standards, such as labeling certain materials "for adults only." There are also more subtle ones. We often think nothing of "breaking up" a group of students gathered around a table talking, but many would be hesitant to "break up" a table full of adults doing exactly the same thing. Restricted access to videos was discussed earlier in Chapter 3. There sometimes is a touch of arrogance in our position, along with a plain old mistrust of teenagers. Every library staff should take a look at the big and little things they do to restrict access to young adults. (See Figure 8-1.)

8.6 LATCHKEY AND HOMELESS YAS

SCENARIO #1:
A pre-teen (age 12) comes to your library every day in the summer when you open and stays until you close. He doesn't bring a lunch with him nor does he seem to leave the building long enough to get something to eat. He doesn't cause any trouble—each day he reads, uses the computers, and sleeps.

YA services are targeted at getting YAs to want to use the library, and here is one that does—every day, five days a week, eight hours a day. But this is a problem. Is this a neglected child? Should you report this to child advocacy authorities? Should you try to contact the child's parents? Should you do anything? If you don't do anything, you might be committing a crime (depending on what state you work in), and you or the library will be responsible.

FIGURE 8-1   SELF EVALUATION: RESTRICTING ACCESS

<u>**yes**</u> <u>**no**</u> **Can YAs:**

[ ] [ ]   Have their own library cards?

[ ] [ ]   Check out non-YA books?

[ ] [ ]   Check out all formats (videos)?

[ ] [ ]   Use certain equipment?

[ ] [ ]   Have database searches performed?

[ ] [ ]   Have extended loan periods?

[ ] [ ]   Get items through Interlibrary loan?

[ ] [ ]   Book meeting rooms?

[ ] [ ]   Use special collections?

[ ] [ ]   Find "labeled" materials?

[ ] [ ]   Place reserves?

[ ] [ ]   Attend programs?

[ ] [ ]   Participate in Friends groups?

[ ] [ ]   Get in-depth reference assistance?

[ ] [ ]   Ask reference questions over phone?

[ ] [ ]   Find no YA limits on # of checkouts?

[ ] [ ]   Attend board meetings?

[ ] [ ]   Use OCLC?

[ ] [ ]   Meet/study in groups?

[ ] [ ]   Smoke on library property (if adults are allowed to)?

[ ] [ ]   Visit library during school hours?

[ ] [ ]   Find no limits on # allowed in building?

[ ] [ ]   Use telephones/fax machines?

[ ] [ ]   Other: _____

Where do you draw the line between the right to privacy and the need to protect children from harm?

SCENARIO #2:
An older teen, age 16, comes to your library every day in the winter when you open and stays until you close. This person primarily reads, sleeps, and smells real bad. He doesn't cause any trouble, but it is pretty obvious to the whole library staff that this person might be in some sort of trouble. Do you call anyone? Do you intervene?

With more working parents, libraries are having to face the issue of latchkey children. Some librarians believe, however, that there is no such thing as a latchkey young adult and that once a child reaches age 12, it is no longer our problem. While homeless persons are a fact of life that each library deals with in its own way, should libraries intervene in the case of homeless teenagers or children? This is another question of balancing our humanitarian instincts and sense of social responsibility with the right to privacy.

8.7 OUT-OF-SCHOOL/ NON-COLLEGE-BOUND YAS

If you develop a library instruction program, will it reach all classes, or will the school only send certain classes. It's a sure bet they will send the honors and college-track students. What about the YAs taking shop or home economics instead of advanced English? Can libraries find ways to build programs that make the library important to these students? They may need our help even more than the others. So why don't they get it more often?

Schools: Schools often want to push their stars and forget about their other students. Many school guidance counselors focus on getting YAs into college, but don't help those who don't want to go.

Fit: It is much easier to make a good fit for a library program with an honors English class than it is with a class in diesel engine repair.

Our backgrounds: Most of us working in this field didn't take shop and we didn't hang around with those who did. Our own kids probably don't take shop either. If anyone ever surveyed our profession, they might find that we tend to serve the students we recognize as being like ourselves. The fact that all professional librarians went to college alienates us from this group who don't have it in their future.

Stereotypes: Sometimes a school can give all non-college-bound YAs a bad reputation, which the library finds easy to buy into. We may tend to see only the apathetic kids and make no effort to meet the rest because we think they'll just be a headache too.

Another large group of YAs too often bypassed are those no longer in school. Because so much energy goes into making school contacts, we sometimes miss YAs who have left school. (We might do a GED program every now and them, but that is usually about it.) This is perhaps one of the toughest groups to reach. Anti-dropout programs could be one area of focus for the public library. Many of the services and resources libraries have to offer could certainly be of use to at-risk students. We also can identify the agencies within the community that have this as their target group and work cooperatively with them.

8.8 LACK OF DIVERSITY

When I was working in a community with a large Puerto Rican community I was amazed at the lack of YA literature for this group. Even though there have been several articles written about library services to Hispanics, there are no current YA novels written in English for this audience. Similar situations exist for almost every other special population. There seems to be no real growth in books for African-American youth. Although there have been a few more titles of interest to Asian American YAs recently, that field is still quite small. The only growth seems to be in books dealing with gay characters. But overall, YA literature remains predominantly white, suburban, straight, and middle class. Because there is so little literature available for special populations, it is difficult to encourage them to read more. And if they do want to read more, unfortunately there is little available to them. Some major authors are listed in Appendix C.

8.9 DEFINING YA SERVICES

It seems only appropriate that, since the teen years are a time of confusion about identity, libraries should suffer the same confusion in defining services to YAs. Libraries don't seem to know whether to call collections YA areas or teen areas, or anything at all. While many libraries focus YA services on older YAs by providing formal educational support through library instruction and reference materials, others focus on middle school students with booktalking and "fun" programs. At the beginning of this book, YA-hood was defined as a time when youth don't want to consider themselves children but are not yet recognized as adults. Former YALSA president Christy Tyson once said:

> Libraries and their librarians use the term young adult in order to be able to plan, budget, and evaluate services for a specific age group, usually based on the configuration of their local schools. This has left our specialty with a bewildering service range that spans ages from 10 through 21.[2]

Why the problem in getting a clear cut definition of both YA and YA service?

Institutional reality: If a library has a YA department and a children's department it is a sure bet that grades five through eight are a battleground. For whatever reasons, many children's librarians don't serve these grades, yet because of tradition, turf protection, and simple budget realities (the bigger your age range, the bigger your materials budget and staff), they are not willing to "give up" these grades. Many students in this grade range are served not by children's but YA librarians for both informational and recreational materials, but YA doesn't get the allocation or the credit for this.

Physical reality: If we match up YA with the onset of puberty, we have to be aware that research has shown puberty to occur earlier in every decade since 1940. The same research has also indicated that "biologically, today young adolescents are approximately two years in advance of the young people for whom the first junior high schools in America were established."[3]

Social reality: Our YA years don't match up with today's YA years. Noted YA commentator Audrey Eaglen noted that libraries need to "recognize and accept that the world in which today's young people are living is a different one from that in which we grew up."[4] Maybe we weren't ready for *Forever* when we were 12, but today's YAs, if not ready, are at least interested.

School reality: A Carnegie Council for Adolescent Development committee found that the middle grade and junior high schools "are potentially society's most powerful force to recapture millions of youth adrift."[5] There is recognition that the time to influence a child's identity is occurring much sooner.

Psychological reality: Psychologist David Elkin discusses the variety of pressures on young adults today that are making them grow up too fast.[6] YAs are finding the pressures around them greater, occurring sooner in their lives, and more difficult to deal with.

Age reality: Because of all the physical, social, and psychological realities mentioned above, students in grades five and six often think of themselves of young adults or teenagers. Cathy Hakala-Ausperk surveyed fifth and sixth graders about their reading preferences and which part of the library (children's or young adult) they would rather use. Her findings (Figure 8-2) show that there is a clear and strong preference by persons in this age group to want to feel "grown up," demonstrated by their desire to use the young adult area and read young adult materials. She concluded that:

> While many different arguments can be made as to why these youths feel so strongly about not wanting to use a children's room, only one thing really matters in the end—it *is* their choice. If librarians, in striving to protect the established service parameters of their areas, seek only to discount results such as these rather than face change, and perhaps, the surroundings of a piece of their audience, these patrons they are fighting over may simply leave and never come back. If the preferences of these youth are ignored, they might end up as patrons lost—from both rooms—for quite a while.[7]

If we redefine YA, then how do we define YA services? If we reprioritize library roles to include YA, what all does that mean? If we want YA services, yet cannot or will not hire qualified, energetic YA librarians and give them support to implement a program of YA service, then what levels of service can be provided? Thus, by

FIGURE 8-2 READING ROOM PREFERENCES

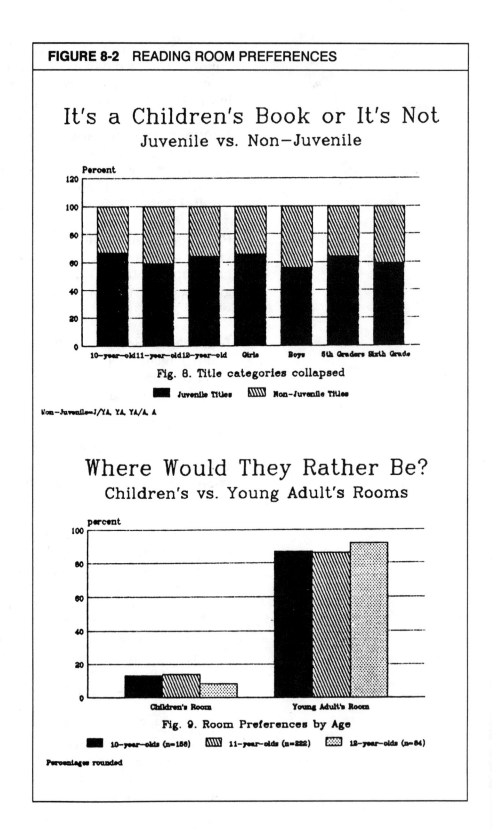

It's a Children's Book or It's Not
Juvenile vs. Non—Juvenile

Fig. 8. Title categories collapsed

■ Juvenile Titles   ▨ Non-Juvenile Titles

Non—Juvenile=J/YA, YA, YA/A, A

Where Would They Rather Be?
Children's vs. Young Adult's Rooms

Fig. 9. Room Preferences by Age

■ 10-year-olds (n=156)   ▨ 11-year-olds (n=222)   ▨ 12-year-olds (n=64)

Percentages rounded

FIGURE 8-3   YA SERVICE LEVELS CHECKLIST

1. Materials to meet basic formal educational support needs [reference; nonfiction; fiction classics]

2. Services to meet basic formal educational support needs [reference service]

3. Materials to meet basic informational needs [books about YA life and choices]

4. Materials to meet basic recreational reading needs [fiction and magazines]

5. Space for YA materials [separate YA collection]

6. Space for YAs to gather [separate YA area]

7. Services to meet basic formal educational support needs [library tours]

8. Services to meet basic recreational reading needs [readers advisory service]

9. Services to meet basic library literacy needs [library instruction]

10. Services to encourage YA recreational reading [booktalking]

11. Services to meet YA developmental needs and encourage library use [programming]

12. Materials to meet YA nonreading recreational needs [non-print collections]

13. Materials to meet special needs [reluctant reader, rampant reader, homework collections, etc.]

14. Services to meet special recreational, educational or informational needs [cooperative programming]

15. Space to promote YA reading [merchandised YA collection]

16. Services to increase use of library by YAs [marketing YA services]

way of conclusion and also as a beginning, what are the levels of YA service available? What should be the base level that all libraries should provide and how would services be prioritized after that? (Figure 8-3)

These steps demonstrate what range of services are available within YA. From the most basic (having materials) to the most complex (marketing services), each step represents more of a commitment on the part of the organization to the YA patron. Each step is one step closer to providing 100% quality library service to help ensure that 25% of all patrons have a positive library experience.

ENDNOTES

1. *Intellectual Freedom Manual,* Chicago: American Library Association, 1988.
2. Christy Tyson, "What's In a Name?" *School Library Journal* (December 1990): 47.
3. Joan Lipstiz, *Successful Schools for Young Adolescents,* New Brunswick, NJ: Transaction Books, 1984, p. 6.
4. Audrey Eaglen, "An Immodest Proposal," *School Library Journal* (August 1989): 92.
5. Carnegie Council of Adolescent Development, *Turning Points: Preparing Youth for the 21st Century,* Washington, DC: Carnegie Council, 1989, p. 10.
6. David Elkind, *All Grown Up and No Place to Go,* Reading, MA: Addison-Wesley, 1984.
7. Cathy Hakala-Ausperk, "Are Young Adults Getting Younger?" Master's Research Paper, Kent State University School of Library Science, 1991, p. 26.

APPENDIX A

NCES SURVEY HIGHLIGHTS

The following tables are excerpted from the National Center for Education Statistics (NCES) Survey Report, *Services and Resources for Young Adults in Public Libraries,* published in July 1988. The survey took place in the fall of 1987. Questionnaires were sent to 846 libraries (540 main libraries and 306 branch libraries), with a response rate of 98 percent. Data were collected for individual library buildings rather than for library systems.

Table 1.--Percentage of public libraries that have a young adult section or collection, composition of the young adult collection, and mean percent of budget used for the young adult collection, by library characteristic: United States, fall 1987

Library characteristic	Percentage of public libraries with a young adult section or collection	Mean percentage[1] of young adult collections that are:			Mean percentage[2] of library budget used for the young adult collection
		Books	Other printed materials	Audio-visual materials	
Total.........................	84	91	6	3	15
Patrons per week					
Less than 200	78	91	7	2	19
200-999........................	86	92	5	3	14
1,000 or more	88	91	5	4	10
Type of library					
Main without branches...	83	92	5	3	16
Main with branches........	84	92	5	4	11
Branch...........................	86	90	7	4	14
Young adult librarian					
Have..............................	98	88	7	5	14
Do not have....................	82	92	6	3	15

[1]Based on libraries with a young adult section/collection. Percentages may not add to 100 because of rounding.

[2]Based on libraries with a young adult section/collection.

Table 3.-- Percentage of public libraries that have a young adult librarian, percentage serving young adults with other types of librarians, and percentage requiring continuing training in young adult services and materials, by library characteristic: United States, fall 1987

Library characteristic	Public libraries with a young adult librarian	Public libraries serving young adults with other types of librarians[1]						Public libraries requiring continuing training in young adult services and materials[3]
		Generalist	Adult	Adult/Young adult	Children's	Reference	Other[2]	
Total.................	11	45	22	3	12	5	14	19
Patrons per week								
Less than 200.............	2	59	22	2	3	*	14	16
200-999.................	9	43	21	3	16	4	13	17
1,000 or more.............	26	28	20	3	22	15	13	25
Type of library								
Main without branches.............	8	44	24	2	13	4	12	19
Main with branches.............	19	26	21	1	26	13	12	10
Branch.............	13	50	18	4	8	3	16	20
Young adult section								
Have.............	12	45	21	3	12	5	14	21
Do not have.............	1	46	24	1	12	4	13	6
Young adult librarian								
Have.............	11	-	-	-	-	-	-	42
Do not have.............	-	45	22	3	12	5	14	16

* Less than 1 percent.

[1] Based on libraries with a young adult librarian. Percentage may not add to 100 because of rounding.

[2] These libraries indicated that someone other than a generalist, adult librarian, adult/young librarian, children's librarian, adult/young librarian or reference librarian was the primary provider of services to you adults. Included in this category are library administrators, fiction specialists, reader's advisor, and library technician or other nonprofessionals.

[3] Based on all libraries.

Table 6.--Percentage of public libraries indicating moderate or heavy use of various sections of their libraries during the last 12 months by 12- to 18-year-olds, by library characteristic: United States, fall 1987

Library characteristic	Moderate or heavy use by 12- to 18-year-olds			
	Children's section	Young adult* section	Adult circulation	Adult reference
Total..............................	38	74	67	75
Patrons per week				
Less than 200	34	65	57	58
200-999..	37	77	65	81
1,000 or more...................................	45	81	85	88
Type of library				
Main without branches......................	34	71	65	73
Main with branches	47	75	73	87
Branch	41	79	69	75
Young adult section				
Have..	38	74	67	75
Do not have	37		68	73
Young adult librarian				
Have..	54	86	78	89
Do not have	36	73	66	73

*Based on libraries with a young adult section or collection--84 percent of all libraries.

Table 7.--Percentage of public libraries reporting moderate or heavy use during the last 12 months by 12- to 18-year-olds during the following times, by library characteristic: United States, fall 1987

| Library characteristic | Moderate or heavy use by 12- to 18-year-olds during | | | | |
| | The school year | | | | Vacations |
	School hours	After school hours (3-6 p.m.)	Evening hours[1]	Weekends[2]	
Total.............................	12	76	53	48	54
Patrons per week					
Less than 200	14	59	26	25	62
200-999............................	13	82	59	51	56
1,000 or more......................	7	90	81	74	42
Type of library					
Main without branches......................	11	71	54	47	50
Main with branches...........................	17	82	68	66	54
Branch....................................	11	82	50	46	61
Young adult section					
Have..........................	12	77	56	49	56
Do not have..........................	11	70	41	42	46
Young adult librarian					
Have..........................	16	92	79	78	55
Do not have..........................	11	74	50	45	54

[1]Thirteen percent of libraries were closed during evening hours.

[2]Thirteen percent of libraries were closed on weekends.

APPENDIX B

CORE COLLECTION
The following is a core paperback fiction collection for YAs. Materials here are those YAs would find on their own, rather than "classics" they are assigned to read. Those 150 titles marked with a "*" should be in any YA collection because of their popularity and/or quality.

For full publisher names and addresses, see Appendix D. Sources used to compile this list:

American Library Association/Young Adult Library Services Association lists:

> Contemporary Classics for Junior High
> Contemporary Classics for Young Adults
> Nothin' But the Best: Best of the Best Books
> Outstanding Books for the College Bound: Fiction
> *Books in Print* 1991-92
> *Forthcoming Books In Print*, August 1991.
> Ingram paperback advances January 1990 - August 1991
> *Junior High Library Catalog* 1990.
> *Paperbacks for Young People* 1990-91 (Bookman, Inc.)
> *Senior High Library Catalog* 1988 (and supplements)

Adams, Douglas. *Hitchhiker's Guide to the Galaxy*. $4.95. 0-671-70159-2. Pocket.

*Adams, Nicholas. *Horror High* series. $3.50 each. Harper.

Adams, Richard. *Watership Down*. $5.95. 0-38000293-0. Avon.

Alexander, Lloyd. *Beggar Queen*. $2.95. 0-440-90548-6. Dell.

———. *Kestrel*. $2.95. 0-440-94393-0. Dell.

———. *Westmark*. $2.95. 0-440-99771-3. Dell

*Andrews, V.C. *Dawn*. $5.95. 0-671-67068-9. Pocket.

———. *Flowers in the Attic*. $5.95. 0-671-72941-1. Pocket.

———. *Garden of Shadows*. $5.95. 0-671-72942-X. Pocket.

———. *Gates of Paradise*. $5.95. 0-671-72943-8. Pocket.

———. *Heaven*. $5.95. 0-671-72944-6. Pocket.

———. *If There Be Thorns*. $5.95. 0-671-72945-4. Pocket.

———. *My Sweet Audrina*. $5.95. 0-671-72946-2. Pocket.

———. *Petals on the Wind*. $5.95. 0-671-72947-0. Pocket.

———. *Secrets of the Morning*. $5.95. 0-671-69512-6. Pocket.

———. *Seeds of Yesterday*. $4.95. 0-317-63632-4. New American Library.

———. *Web of Dreams*. $5.95. 0-671-72949-7. Pocket.

Anthony, Piers. *Total Recall*. $4.50. 0-380-70874-4. Avon.

Arrick, Fran. *Tunnel Vision*. $2.95. 0-440-98579-X. Dell.

Asimov, Isaac. *Foundation*. $5.95. 0-345-33627-5. Del Rey.

———. *Foundation & Earth*. $4.95. 0-345-33996-7. Del Rey.

———. *Foundation & Empire*. $4.95. 0-345-33628-3. Del Rey.

———. *Foundation's Edge*. $4.95. 0-345-30898-0. Del Rey.

———. *Robot City* series. $3.95 each. Ace.

Atwood, Margaret. *Handmaid's Tale*. $5.95. 0-449-21260-2. Fawcett.

Auel, Jane. *Clan of the Cave Bear*. $5.95. 0-553-25042-6. Bantam.

Avi. *Fighting Ground*. $3.50. 0-06-440185-5. Harper.

*Baldwin, James. *If Beale Street Could Talk*. $4.95. 0-440-34060-8. Dell.

Bates, A. *Final Exam*. $2.95. 0-590-43291-5. Scholastic.

———. *Mother's Helper*. $2.95. 0-590-44582-0. Scholastic.

———. *Party Line*. $2.75. 0-590-42439-4. Scholastic.

Beagle, Peter. *Last Unicorn*. $4.95. 0-345-35367-6. Del Rey.

Behrens, Michael. *At the Edge*. $2.95. 0-590-75610-2. Avon.

Bennett, Jay. *Death Ticket*. $2.75. 0-380-89597-8. Avon.

————. *Executioner*. $2.95. 0-380-79160-9. Avon.

Blair, Cynthia. *Pratt Twins* series. $2.95 each. Fawcett.

Blatty, William Peter. *Exorcist*. $4.50. 0-553-27010-9. Bantam.

*Blume, Judy. *Are You There God? It's Me, Margaret*. $3.25. 0-440-40419-3. Dell.

————. *Deenie*. $2.95. 0-440-93259-9. Dell

————. *Forever*. $3.95. 0-671-69530-4. Pocket.

————. *It's Not the End of the World*. $3.50. 0-440-94140-7. Dell.

————. *Just As Long as We're Together*. $3.50. 0-440-40075-9. Dell.

————. *Then Again, Maybe I Won't*. $3.25. 0-440-98659-9. Dell.

————. *Tiger Eyes*. $3.50. 0-440-98469-6. Dell.

Borland, Hal. *When the Legends Die*. $3.50. 0-553-25738-2. Bantam.

*Bradbury, Ray. *Fahrenheit 451*. $3.95. 0-345-34296-8. Del Rey.

————. *Martian Chronicles*. $3.50. 0-553-26353-3. Bantam.

————. *Something Wicked This Way Comes*. $3.50. 0-553-25774-9. Bantam.

Bradley, Marion Zimmer. *Mists of Avalon*. $9.95. 0-345- 33385-3. Ballantine.

*Brancato, Robin. *Winning*. $3.95. 0-394-80751-0. Bantam.

Bridgers, Sue Ellen. *All Together Now*. $2.75. 0-553-268457. Bantam.

————. *Home Before Dark*. $2.50. 0-553-26432-X. Bantam.

————. *Notes for Another Life*. $2.95. 0-553-27185-7. Bantam.

————. *Permanent Connections*. $3.50. 0-06-447020-2. Harper.

Brin, David. *The Postman*. $4.95. 0-553-27874-6. Bantam.

*Brooks, Bruce. *Midnight Hours Encores*. $3.50. 0-06- 4470210. Harper.

————. *Moves Make the Man*. $2.95. 0-06-4470229. Harper.

————. *No Kidding*. $3.50. 0-06-4470512. Harper.

Brooks, Terry. *Magic Kingdom For Sale - Sold*. $5.95. 0- 345-31758-0. Del Rey.

*Bunting, Eve. *Someone is Hiding On Alcatraz Island*. $2.75. 0-425-10294-7. Berkley.

————. *Sudden Silence*. $3.50. 0-449-70362-2. Fawcett.

Burgess, Anthony. *Clockwork Orange*. $5.95. 0-345-35443-5. Ballantine.

Card, Orson Scott. *Ender's Game & Speaker for the Dead*. $3.95. 0-317-57062-5. Tor.

Carter, Alden. *Sheila's Dying*. $2.75. 0-590-42045-3. Scholastic.

*Childress, Alice. *Hero Ain't Nothin' But A Sandwich*. $2.95. 0-380-00132-2. Avon.

————. *Rainbow Jordan*. $2.95. 0-380-589745. Avon.

Christie, Agatha. *And Then There Were None*. $3.95. 0-671- 70606-X. Pocket.

————. *Murder of Roger Ackroyd*. $3.95. 0-671-70118-5. Pocket.

Clancy, Tom. *Hunt for Red October*. $5.95. 0-425-12027-9. Berkley.

Clark. Mary Higgins. *Cradle Will Fall*. $4.95. 0-440-11545- 0. Dell.

————. *Cry in the Night*. $4.95. 0-440-11065-3. Dell.

————. *Stillwatch*. $4.95. 0-440-18305-7. Dell.

————. *Stranger is Watching*. $4.95. 0-440-181275-5. Dell.

————. *Where Are the Children?* $4.95. 0-440-19593-4. Dell.

Clarke, Arthur C. *2001: A Space Odyssey*. $3.95. 0-451- 15580-7. New American Library.

————. *Childhood's End*. $4.95. 0-345-34795-1. Del Rey.

Collier, James. *My Brother Sam is Dead*. $2.50. 0-590- 407376. Scholastic.

Conford, Ellen. *Alfred G. Graebner Memorial High School Handbook of Rules and Regulations.* $2.75. 0-671-67247- 9. Pocket.

———. *Things I Did For Love.* $2.95. 0-553-27374-4. Bantam.

Cook, Robin. *Coma.* $4.95. 0-451-15953-5. New American Library.

———. *Godplayer.* $4.95. 0-451-15728-1. New American Library.

Cooney, Caroline. *Cheerleader.* $2.95. 0-590-44316-X. Scholastic.

———. **Face on the Milk Carton.* $3.50. 0-553-28958-6. Bantam.

Cooney, Linda. *Freshman Dorm* series. $3.50 each. Harper.

Cooper, Susan. *Dark is Rising.* $2.95. 0-689-71087-9. Collier.

———. *Greenwitch.* $2.95. 0-689-71088-7. Macmillan.

———. *Grey King.* $2.95. 0-689-71089-5. Macmillan.

*Cormier, Robert. *After the First Death.* $3.95. 0-440- 20835-1. Dell.

———. **Beyond the Chocolate War.* $3.25. 0-440-90580-X. Dell.

———. **Bumblebee Flies Anyway.* $3.25. 0-440-90871-X. Dell.

———. **Chocolate War.* $3.50. 0-440-94459-7. Dell.

———. *Fade.* $4.50. 0-440-20487-9. Dell.

———. **I Am the Cheese.* $3.25. 0-440-94060-5. Dell.

*Crutcher, Chris. *Chinese Handcuffs.* $3.25. 0-440-20837-8. Dell.

———. **Crazy Horse Electric Game.* $3.25. 0-440-20094-6. Dell.

———. **Running Loose.* $3.25. 0-440-97570-0. Dell.

———. **Stotan!* $3.25. 0-440-20080-6. Dell.

*Cusick, Richie. *April Fools.* $2.95. 0-590-43115-3. Scholastic.

———. **Lifeguard.* $2.50. 0-590-41549-2. Scholastic.

———. *Teacher's Pet.* $2.95. 0-590-43114-5. Scholastic.

———. *Trick or Treat*. $2.75. 0-590-42456-4. Scholastic.

———. *Vampire*. $3.50. 0-671-70956-9. Pocket.

Daly, Maureen. *Seventeenth Summer*. $2.95. 0-671-61931-4. Pocket.

Danziger, Paula. *Can You Sue Your Parents for Malpractice?* $3.25. 0-440-91066-8. Dell.

———. *Cat Ate My Gymsuit*. $3.25. 0-440-41612-4. Dell.

———. *There's A Bat in Bunk Five*. $2.95. 0-440-40098-8. Dell

Davidson, Nicole. *Crash Course*. $2.95. 0-380-75964-0. Avon.

———. *Winterkill*. $2.95. 0-380-75965-9. Avon.

Davis, Jenny. *Good-bye and Keep Cold*. $2.95 0-440-20481-X. Dell.

———. *Sex Education*. $2.95. 0-440-20483-6. Dell.

*Davis, Jim. *Garfield* series. $6.95 each. Ballantine.

Dickinson, Peter. *Eva*. $3.50. 0-440-20766-5. Dell.

*Dixon, Franklin. *Hardy Boys Case File* series. $2.95. Pocket.

Donaldson, Stephen. *Lord Foul's Bane*. $4.95. 0-345-348656. Del Rey.

———. *One Tree*. $4.95. 0-345-34869-9. Del Rey.

Duncan, Lois. *Don't Look Behind You*. $3.50. 0-440-20729-0. Dell.

———. *I Know What You Did Last Summer*. $2.95. 0-671-63970-6. Pocket.

———. *Killing Mr. Griffin*. $3.50. 0-440-94515-1. Dell.

———. *Locked in Time*. $3.50. 0-440-94942-4. Dell.

———. *Stranger with My Face*. $3.25. 0-440-98356-8. Dell.

———. *Summer of Fear*. $3.50. 0-440-98324-X. Dell

———. *Twisted Window*. $3.50. 0-440-20184-5. Dell.

Ellis, Bret Easton. *Less Than Zero*. $3.95. 0-14-010927-7. Penguin.

Ellis, Carol. *My Secret Admirer*. $2.75. 0-590-42515-3. Scholastic.

Erdrich, Louise. *Tracks*. $8.95. 0-06-097245-9. Harper.

*Ferguson, Alane. *Show Me the Evidence*. $2.95. 0-380- 70962-7. Avon.

Finney, Jack. *Time and Again*. $10.95. 0-671-24295-4. Simon and Schuster.

*Forshay-Lunsford, Lin. *Walk Through Cold Fire*. $2.75. 0-440-99322-9. Dell.

Fox, Paula. Moonlight Man. $3.25. 0-440-20079-2. Dell.

———. *Slave Dancer*. $2.95. 0-440-96132-7. Dell.

Frank, Pat. *Alas Babylon*. $3.95. 0-553-26314-5. Bantam.

Gaines, Ernest. *Autobiography of Miss Jane Pittman*. $3.95.0-553-26357-9. Bantam.

*Gallo, Donald. *Connections: Short Stories by Outstanding Writers for Young Adults*. $3.50. 0-440-20768-1. Dell.

———. *Sixteen: Short Stories by Outstanding Young Adult Writers*. $3.50. 0-440-97757-6. Dell.

———. *Visions: Nineteen Short Stories by Outstanding Writers for Young Adults*. $3.25. 0-440-20208-6. Dell

*Garden, Nancy. *Annie on My Mind*. $3.50. 0-374-40413-5. Farrar, Straus & Giroux.

Gardner, John. *Grendel*. $4.95. 0-394-74056-4. Random House.

———. *License Renewed*. $4.50. 0-425-12463-0. Berkley.

Golding, William. *Lord of the Flies*. $4.95. 0-399-50148-7. Putnam.

Greenberg, Jan. *No Dragons to Slay*. $3.95. 0-374-45509-0. Farrar, Straus & Giroux.

Greenberg, Joanna. *I Never Promised You a Rose Garden*. $3.95. 0-451-16031-2. New American Library.

*Greene, Bette. *Summer of My German Soldier*. $3.50. 0-553-27247-0. Bantam.

*Groening, Matt. *Childhood is Hell.* $6.95. 0-679-72055-3. Pantheon.

————. *Love is Hell.* $6.95. 0-394-74454-3. Pantheon.

————. *Work is Hell.* $6.95. 0-394-74864-6. Pantheon.

Guest, Judith. *Ordinary People.* $5.95. 0-345-33505-8. Ballantine.

Guy, Rosa. *The Disappearance.* $3.25. 0-440-92064-7. Dell.

————. *The Friends.* $2.95. 0-553-26519-9. Bantam.

Hamilton, Virginia. *A Little Love.* $2.50. 0-425-08424-8. Berkley.

————. *M.C. Higgins the Great.* $3.95. 0-02-043490-1. Collier.

————. *Sweet Whispers, Brother Rush.* $2.95. 0-380-65193-9. Avon.

————. *A White Romance.* $3.95. 0-15-295888-6. Harcourt Brace Jovanovich.

Hart, Bruce and Carol. *Breaking Up is Hard to Do.* $3.50. 0-380-89970-1. Avon.

————. *Cross Your Heart.* $3.50. 0-380-89971-X. Avon

————. *Now or Never.* $3.50 0-380-75963-2. Avon.

————. *Sooner or Later.* $3.50. 0-380-42978-0. Avon.

————. *Waiting Games.* $3.50. 0-380-79012-2. Avon.

Head, Ann. *Mr. and Mrs. Bo Jo Jones.* $3.95. 0-451-16319-2. New American Library.

Heinlein, Robert. *Stranger in a Strange Land.* $5.50. 0-441-79034-8. Ace.

Herbert, Frank. *Dune.* $4.95. 0-441-17271-7. Ace.

Hesse, Hermann. *Siddhartha.* $3.50. 0-553-20884-5. Bantam.

————. *Steppenwolf.* $4.50. 0-553-27990-4. Bantam.

*Hinton, S.E. *The Outsiders.* $3.25. 0-440-96769-4. Dell

————. *Rumble Fish.* $3.25. 0-440-974534-4. Dell.

————. *Taming the Star Runner*. $3.25. 0-440-20479-8. Dell

————. *Tex*. $3.25. 0-440-97850-5. Dell.

————. *That Was Then, This is Now*. $3.25. 0-440-98652-4. Dell.

Hoh, Diane. *The Accident*. $2.95. 0-590-44330-5. Scholastic.

————. *Funhouse*. $2.95. 0-590-43050-5. Scholastic.

*Holman, Felice. *Slake's Limbo*. $3.95. 0-689-71066-6. Macmillan.

Hunt, Irene. *Across Five Aprils*. $2.75. 0-425-10241-6. Berkley.

Irving, John. *Prayer for Owen Meany*. $5.95. 0-345-36199-2. Ballantine.

————. *World According to Garp*. $5.95. 0-345-36676-X. Ballantine

Irwin, Hadley. *Abby, My Love*. $2.50. 0-451-14501-1. New American Library.

————. *Kim/Kimi*. $3.95. 0-14-32593-X. Penguin.

Jackson, Shirley. *The Lottery*. $8.95. 0-374-51681-2. Farrar, Straus & Giroux.

Jones, Diane. *Howl's Moving Castle*. $3.50. 0-441-34664-2. Ace.

*Keene, Carolyn. *Nancy Drew Files* series. $2.95 each. Pocket.

————. *River Heights* series. $2.95 each. Pocket.

Kerr, M.E. *Dinky Hocker Shoots Smack!* $3.95. 0-06-447006-7. Harper.

————. *Fell*. $3.25. 0-06-447031-8. Harper.

————. *Gentlehands*. $2.75. 0-553-26677-2. Bantam.

————. *Night Kites*. $3.25. 0-06-447035-0. Harper.

*Kesey, Ken. *One Flew Over the Cuckoo's Nest*. $4.95. 0-451-15826-1. New American Library.

Keyes, Daniel. *Flowers for Algernon*. $3.50. 0-553-25665-3. Bantam.

King, Stephen. *The Bachman Books*. $5.95. 0-451-14736-7. New American Library.

———. *Carrie*. $3.95. 0-451-14744-3. New American Library.

———. *Christine*. $4.95. 0-451-16944-4. New American Library.

———. *Creepshow*. $7.95. 0-452-25380-2. New American Library.

———. *Cujo*. $4.95. 0-451-16135-1. New American Library.

———. *Cycle of the Werewolf*. $9.95. 0-451-82219-6. New American Library.

———. *Dark Half*. $5.95. 0-451-16731-7. New American Library.

———. *Dead Zone*. $4.95. 0-451-15575-0. New American Library.

———. *Different Seasons*. $5.95. 0-451-16753-8. New American Library.

———. *Drawing of the Three*. $5.95. 0-451-16352-4. New American Library.

———. *Eyes of the Dragon*. $4.95. 0-451-16658-2. New American Library.

———. *Firestarter*. $4.50. 0-451-15031-7. New American Library

———. *Gunslinger*. $5.95. 0-451-16052-5. New American Library.

———. *It*. $5.95 0-451-15927-6. New American Library.

———. *Misery*. $5.95. 0-451-15355-3. New American Library.

———. *Nightshift*. $4.95. 0-451-16045-2. New American Library.

———. *Pet Sematary*. $4.95. 0-451-15775-3. New American Library.

———. *Salem's Lot*. $4.95. 0-451-16588-8. New American Library.

———. *The Shining*. $4.95. 0-451-16091-6. New American Library.

———. *Silver Bullet*. $9.95. 0-451-82128-9. New American Library

———. *Skeleton Crew*. $4.95. 0-451-14293-4. New American Library.

———. *The Stand: Complete and Uncut*. $6.99. 0-451-16953-0. New American Library.

———. *Tommyknockers*. $5.95. 0-451-15931-0. New American Library.

Klein, Norma. *Breaking Up*. $2.50. 0-380-55830-0. Avon.

———. *Family Secrets.* $3.50. 0-449-70195-6. Fawcett.

———. *Going Backwards.* $2.50. 0-590-40329-X. Scholastic.

———. **It's Okay If You Don't Love Me.* $3.50. 0-449-70236-7. Fawcett.

———. *Just Friends.* $3.95. 0-449-70352-5. Fawcett.

———. **Love is One of the Choices.* $3.50. 0-449-70273-1. Fawcett.

———. **My Life as a Body.* $3.50. 0-449-70265-0. Fawcett.

———. *No More Saturday Nights.* $3.50. 0-449-70304-5. Fawcett.

———. *Now That I Know.* $2.95. 0-553-28115-1. Bantam.

———. *Older Men.* $2.95. 0-449-70261-8. Fawcett.

———. *That's My Baby.* $3.50 0-449-70356-8. Fawcett.

*Knowles, John. *A Separate Peace.* $3.95. 0-553-27574-7. Bantam.

*Koetge, Ron. *Arizona Kid.* $3.50. 0-380-70776-4. Avon.

———. *Where the Kissing Never Stops.* $2.95. 0-440-20167-5. Dell.

Koontz, Dean. *Midnight.* $4.95. 0-425-11870-3. Berkley.

———. *Strangers.* $4.95. 0-425-11992-0. Berkley.

———. *Watchers.* $4.95. 0-425-10746-9. Berkley.

———. *Whispers.* $4.95. 0-425-09760-9. Berkley.

Korman, Gordon. *Don't Care High.* $2.95. 0-590-43129-3. Scholastic.

Kosinski, Jerzy. *Painted Bird.* $4.95. 0-553-26520-2. Bantam

Larimer, Tamela. *Buck.* $2.50. 0-380-75172-0. Avon.

*Larson, Gary. *Far Side* series. $5.95 each. Andrews & McMeel.

*Lee, Harper. *To Kill a Mockingbird.* $3.50. 0-446-31049-2. Warner.

Lee, Stan. *Invincible Iron Man.* $6.95. 0-939766-97-3. Marvel Comics.

———. *Uncanny X-Men.* $6.95. 0-939766-96-5. Marvel Comics.

LeGuin, Ursula. *Farthest Shore*. $4.95. 0-553-26847-3. Bantam.

———. *Wizard of Earthsea*. $4.95. 0-553-26250-5. Bantam.

L'Engle, Madeleine. *Many Waters*. $3.50. 0-440-95252-2. Dell.

———. *Swiftly Tilting Planet*. $3.50. 0-440-90158-8. Dell.

———. *Wind in the Door*. $3.50. 0-440-98761-X. Dell.

———. *Wrinkle in Time*. $3.50. 0-440-99805-0. Dell.

Lester, Julius. *To Be a Slave*. $2.50. 0-590-40682-5. Scholastic.

Levitin, Sonia. *Incident at Loring Grove*. $2.95. 0-449-703479-X. Fawcett.

Levy, Marilyn. *Putting Heather Together Again*. $3.50. 0-449-70312-6. Fawcett.

*Lipsyte, Robert. *The Contender*. $2.95. 0-06-447039-3. Harper.

Littke, Lael. *Prom Dress*. $2.75. 0-590-41929-3. Scholastic.

Lowry, Lois. *Summer to Die*. $2.95. 0-553-26297-1. Bantam.

McCaffrey, Anne. *Dragonsinger*. $3.95. 0-553-25854-0. Bantam

———. *Dragonsong*. $3.95. 0-553-25852-4. Bantam.

*McDaniel, Lurlene. *Goodbye Doesn't Mean Forever*. $2.95. 0-553-28007-4. Bantam

———. *Somewhere Between Life and Death*. 0-553-28349-9. Bantam.

———. *Time to Let Go*. $2.95. 0-553-28350-2. Bantam.

———. *Too Young To Die*. $2.95. 0-553-28008-2. Bantam.

McKinley, Robin. *Blue Sword*. $3.95. 0-441-06880-4. Ace.

———. *Hero and the Crown*. $3.50. 0-441-32809-1. Berkley.

———. *Outlaws of Sherwood*. $3.95. 0-441-64451-1. Berkley.

Mad series. $3.50 each. Warner Books.

Malamud, Bernard. *The Fixer*. $3.95. 0-671-69851-6. Pocket.

———. *The Natural.* $4.50 0-380-50609-2. Avon.

Martin, Ann. *Slam Book.* $2.75. 0-590-41838-6. Scholastic.

Mason, Bobbie Ann. *In Country.* $5.95. 0-06-080959-0. Harper.

Mazer, Harry. *I Love You Stupid!* $2.95. 0-380-61432-4. Avon.

———. *Last Mission.* $3.25. 0-440-94797-9. Dell.

———. *Snowbound.* $3.25 0-440-96134-3. Dell.

———. *When the Phone Rang.* $2.50. 0-590-40383-4. Scholastic.

*Mazer, Norma Fox. *After the Rain.* $3.50. 0-380-75025-2. Avon.

———. *Silver.* $2.95. 0-380-75026-0. Avon.

———. *Taking Terri Mueller.* $3.50. 0-380-79004-1. Avon.

Michaels, Barbara. *Black Rainbow.* $4.95. 0-425-12481-9. Berkley.

Miklowitz, Gloria. *Goodbye Tomorrow.* $3.25. 0-440-20081-4. Dell.

———. *Secrets Not Meant to Be Kept.* $3.25. 0-440-20314-7. Dell.

Miller, Frances. *Aren't You the One Who?* $3.50. 0-449-70286-3. Fawcett.

———. *Cutting Loose.* $3.95. 0-449-70384-3. Fawcett.

———. *Losers and Winners.* $3.50. 0-449-70151-4. Fawcett.

———. *Truth Trap.* $2.95. 0-449-70247-2. Fawcett.

*Miller, Frank. *Batman: The Dark Knight Returns.* $12.95. 0-446-385050-0. Warner.

———. *Batman: Year One.* $9.95. 0-446-38923-4. Warner.

Montgomery, L.M. *Anne of Green Gables.* $2.95. 0-553-21313-X. Bantam.

———. *Anne of Avonlea.* $2.95. 0-553-21314-8. Bantam

———. *Anne of the Island.* $2.95. 0-553-21371-2. Bantam.

———. *Anne of Windy Poplars.* $2.95 0-553-21316-4. Bantam.

————. *Anne's House of Dreams.* $2.95. 0-553-21318-0. Bantam.

————. *Anne of Ingleside.* $2.95 0-553-26921-6. Bantam.

————. *Rainbow Valley.* $3.50. 0-553-26921-6. Bantam.

————. *Rilla of Ingelside.* $3.50 0-553-26922-4. Bantam.

Moore, Alan. *Saga of Swamp Thing.* $10.95. 0-446-38690-1. Warner.

Morrison, Toni. *Bluest Eye.* $3.95. 0-671-53146-8. Pocket.

*Myers, Walter Dean. *Fallen Angels.* $3.50. 0-590-40943-3. Scholastic.

————. *Hoops.* $3.25. 0-440-93884-8. Dell.

————. *Scorpions.* $2.95. 0-06-447066-0. Harper.

Naylor, Phyllis. *Year of the Gopher.* $3.50. 0-553-27131-8. Bantam.

Nelson, Peter. *Night of Fire.* $2.95. 0-671-70583-0. Pocket.

Neufeld, John. *Lisa, Bright and Dark.* $2.95. 0-451-16093-2. New American
    Library.

O'Brien, Robert. *Z for Zachariah.* $3.95. 0-02-044650-0. Macmillan.

O'Brien, Tim. *Going After Cacciato.* $4.95. 0-440-32965-5. Dell.

O'Neal, Zibby. *In Summer Light.* $3.50. 0-553-25940-7. Bantam

————. *Language of Goldfish.* $3.95. 0-14-034540-X. Penguin.

Parks, Gordon. *Learning Tree.* $4.94. 0-449215040-0. Fawcett.

*Pascal, Francine. *Sweet Valley High* series. $2.95. Bantam.

Paterson, Katherine. *Jacob Have I Loved.* $2.95. 0-380-56499-8. Avon.

*Paulsen, Gary. *Hatchet.* $3.95. 0-14-032724-X. Penguin.

*Peck, Richard. *Are You in the House Alone?* $3.25. 0440-90227-4. Dell.

————. *Father Figure.* $2.95. 0-440-200695. Dell.

————. *Princess Ashley.* $3.25. 0-440-97339-2. $2.95. Dell.

————. *Remembering the Good Times*. $3.25. 0-440-97339-2. Dell.

Petersen, P.J. *Would You Settle for Improbable?* $3.25. 0-440-99733-X. Dell.

Pfeffer, Susan. *About David*. $3.25. 0-440-90022-0. Dell.

————. *Year Without Michael*. $3.50. 0-553-27373-6. Bantam.

Pierce, Meredith. *The Darkangel*. $2.95. 0-8125-4900-7. Tor.

————. *Gathering of Gargoyles*. $2.95. 0-8125-4902-3. Tor.

*Pike, Christopher. *Bury Me Deep*. $3.50. 0-671-69057-4. Pocket.

————. *Chain Letter*. $2.75. 0-380-89968-X. Avon.

————. *The Dance*. $2.95. 0-671-70011-1. Pocket.

————. *Die Softly*. $3.50. 0-671-69056-5. Pocket.

————. *Fall into Darkness*. $2.95. 0-671-67655-5. Pocket.

————. *Gimme a Kiss*. $2.95. 0-671-68807-3. Pocket.

————. *The Graduation*. $2.95. 0-671-70012-X. Pocket.

————. *Last Act*. $2.95. 0-671-68781-6. Pocket

————. *The Party*. $2.95. 0-671-68808-1. Pocket.

————. *Remember Me*. $2.95. 0-671-67654-7. Pocket.

————. *Scavenger Hunt*. $2.95. 0-671-67654-7. Pocket.

————. *See You Later*. $2.95. 0-671-67657-1. Pocket.

————. *Slumber Party*. $2.75. 0-590-43014-9. Scholastic.

————. *Spellbound*. $2.95. 0-671-68793-X. Pocket.

————. *Weekend*. $2.75. 0-590-42968-X. Scholastic.

————. *Witch*. $3.50. 0-671-69055-8. Pocket.

*Plath, Sylvia. *The Bell Jar*. $4.50. 0-553-27835-5. Bantam.

Platt, Kin. *The Boy Who Could Make Himself Disappear.* $3.25. 0-440-90837-X. Dell.

Potok, Chaim. *The Promise.* $4.95. 0-449-20910-5. Fawcett.

Pullman, Philip. *Ruby in the Smoke.* $3.25. 0-394-89598-4. Knopf.

————. *Shadow in the North.* $3.25. 0-394-82599-3. Knopf.

Pynchon, Thomas. *V.* $4.95. 0-553-24686-0. Bantam.

Rand, Ayn. *Anthem.* $4.50. 0-451-16683-3. New American Library.

*Raskin, Ellen. *Westing Game.* $2.95. 0-380-67991-4. Avon.

Rawls, Wilson. *Summer of the Monkeys.* $3.50. 0-440-98175-1. Dell.

————. *Where the Red Fern Grows.* $3.25. 0-553-25585-1. Bantam.

Rice, Anne. *Interview with the Vampire.* $5.95. 0-345-33766-2. Ballantine.

Robbins, Tom. *Jitterbug Perfume.* $5.99. 0-553-26844-9. Bantam.

*Salinger, J.D. *Catcher in the Rye.* $3.95. 0-53-25025-6. Bantam.

Santiago, Danny. *Famous All Over Town.* $8.95. 0-452-25974-6. New American Library.

*Saul, John. *Creature.* $5.95. 0-553-28411-8. Bantam.

————. *Punish the Sinners.* $5.95. 0-440-17084-2. Dell.

————. *Sleepwalk.* $5.95. 0-553-28834-2. Bantam.

————. *Suffer the Children.* $5.95. 0-440-18293-X. Dell.

Schulz, Charles. *Peanuts* series. $2.95 each. Fawcett.

Sebestyn, Ouida. *Girl in the Box.* $3.50. 0-553-28261-1. Bantam.

Sleator, William. *Interstellar Pig.* $3.50. 0-553-25564-9. Bantam.

Sparks, Beatrice. *Jay's Journal.* $2.95. 0-671-66747-5. Dell.

Spencer, Scott. *Endless Love.* $4.95. 0-345-35624-1. Ballantine.

Spiegelman, Art. *Maus.* $9.95. 0-394-74723-2. Pantheon.

Star Trek series. $4.95 each. Pocket.

Star Trek: The Next Generation series. $4.95 each. Pocket.

Steinbeck, John. *Grapes of Wrath*. $3.95. 0-14-004239-3. Penguin.

———. *Of Mice and Men*. $2.75. 0-553-26675-6. Bantam.

Steiner, Barbara. *Photographer*. $2.95. 0-380-75758-3. Avon.

Stewart, Mary. *Crystal Cave*. 0-449-20644-0. Fawcett.

———. *Hollow Hills*. 0-449-20645-9. Fawcett.

———. *Last Enchantment*. 0-449-20646-7. Fawcett.

*Stine, R.L. *The Babysitter*. $2.75. 0-590-41858-0. Scholastic.

———. *Babysitter II*. $2.95. 0-590-44332-1. Scholastic.

———. *Beach Party*. $2.95. 0-590-43278-8. Scholastic.

———. *Blind Date*. $2.75. 0-590-43125-0. Scholastic.

———. *The Boyfriend*. $2.95. 0-590-43279-6. Scholastic.

———. *Curtains*. $2.95. 0-671-69498-7. Pocket.

———. *Fear Street* series. $2.95 each. Pocket.

———. *The Snowman*. $2.95. 0-590-43280-X. Scholastic.

———. *Twisted*. $2.75. 0-590-43139-0. Scholastic.

*Strasser, Todd. *Angel Dust Blues*. $2.95. 0-440-90956-2. Dell.

———. *Beyond the Reef*. $3.50. 0-440-20881-5. Dell.

———. *Friends till the End*. $3.25. 0-440-92625-4. Dell.

———. *Very Touchy Subject*. $2.95. 0-440-98851-9. Dell.

Strieber, Whitley. *Wolf of Shadows*. $3.95. 0-449-21089-8. Fawcett.

Sweet Dreams series. $2.95 each. Bantam.

Taylor, Mildred. *Let the Circle Be Unbroken*. $3.50. 0-553-23426-6. Bantam.

————. *Roll of Thunder, Hear My Cry.* $3.50. 0-553-25450-2. Bantam.

Taylor, Theodore. *The Cay.* $3.50. 0-380-01003-8. Avon.

Thompson, Julian. *Discontinued.* $3.50. 0-590-40116-5. Scholastic.

————. *Grounding of Group Six.* $3.50. 0-380-83386-7. Avon.

————. *Question of Survival.* $2.50. 0-380-87775-9. Avon.

————. *Simon Pure.* $3.50. 0-590-41823-8. Scholastic.

*Tolkien, J.R.R. *Fellowship of the Ring.* $4.95. 0-345-33970-3. Ballantine.

————. *The Hobbit.* $5.95. 0-345-33968-1. Ballantine.

————. *Return of the King.* $5.95. 0-345-33973-8. Ballantine.

————. *Two Towers.* $5.95. 0-345-33971-1. Ballantine.

Voigt, Cynthia. *Dicey's Song.* $3.50. 0-449-70276-6. Fawcett.

————. *Homecoming.* $3.50. 0-449-70254-5. Fawcett.

————. *Izzy, Willy-Nilly.* $3.50. 0-449-70241-6. Fawcett.

————. *Solitary Blue.* $3.50. 0-449-70268-5. Fawcett.

————. *Sons from Afar.* $3.50. 0-449-70293-6. Fawcett.

Vonnegut, Kurt. *Cat's Cradle.* $4.95. 0-440-11149-8. Dell.

————. *Slaughterhouse Five.* $5.95. 0-440-18029-4. Dell.

*Walker, Alice. *Color Purple.* $4.50. 0-671-64745-8. Pocket.

Watterson, Bill. *Authoritative Calvin & Hobbes.* $12.95. 0-8362-1822-1. Andrews & McMeel.

————. *Calvin & Hobbes.* $7.95. 0-8362-2088-9. Andrews & McMeel.

————. *Calvin & Hobbes Lazy Sunday Book.* $9.95. 0-8362-1852-3. Andrews & McMeel.

————. *Essential Calvin & Hobbes.* $12.95. 0-8362-1805-1. Andrews & McMeel.

———. *Something Under the Bed is Drooling.* $7.95. 0-8362-1825-6. Andrews & McMeel.

———. *Weirdos from Another Planet.* $7.95. Andrews & McMeel.

———. *Yukon Ho!* $7.95. 0-8362-1853-3. Andrews & McMeel.

Weis, Margaret. *Dragonlance* series. 4.95 each. TSR.

———. *Rose of the Prophet* series. 4.95 each. Bantam

———. *Star of the Guardians* series. $4.95 each. Bantam.

*White, Robb. *Deathwatch.* $3.50. 0-440-91740-9. Dell.

White, T.H. *Once and Future King.* $5.50. 0-441-63740-4. Ace.

Wiesel, Elie. *Night.* $2.95. 0-553-20807-1. Bantam.

Willard, Nancy. *Things Invisible to See.* $3.95. 0-553-27652-2. Bantam.

Willey, Margaret. *Saving Lenny.* $2.99. 0-553-29204-8. Bantam.

Wright, Richard. *Native Son.* $4.95. 0-06-080977-9. Harper.

Yolen, Jane. *Dragon's Blood.* $3.50. 0-440-91802-2. Dell.

———. *Heart's Blood.* $3.25. 0-440-93385-4. Dell.

———. *Sending of Dragons.* $3.50. 0-440-20309-0. Dell.

*Zindel, Paul. *My Darling, My Hamburger.* $3.50. 0-553-27324-8. Bantam.

———. *Pigman.* $3.50. 0-553-26321-8. Bantam.

———. *Pigman's Legacy.* $3.50. 0-553-26599-7. Bantam.

APPENDIX C

CORE LIST BY AUTHOR AND GENRE

Realistic:

Arrick, Fran
Baldwin, James
Behrens, Michael
Blume. Judy
Brancato, Robin
Bridgers, Sue Ellen
Brooks, Bruce
Bunting, Eve
Carter, Alden
Childress, Alice
Cooney, Caroline
Cormier, Robert
Crutcher, Chris
Davis, Jenny
Forshay-Lunsford, Cin
Fox, Paula
Greenberg, Jan
Greenberg, Joanna
Guy, Rosa
Hamilton, Virginia
Hinton, S.E.
Holman, Felice
Irwin, Hadley
Kerr, M.E.
Klein, Norma
Koetge, Ron
Larimer, Tamela
Levy, Marilyn
Lipsyte, Robert
Lowry, Lois
McDaniel, Lurlene
Mazer, Harry
Mazer, Norma Fox
Milkowitz, Gloria
Myers, Walter Dean

Naylor, Phyllis
Neufeld, John
O'Neal, Zibby
Paterson, Katherine
Peck, Richard
Petersen, P.J.
Pfeffer, Susan Beth
Platt, Kin
Sebestyn, Ouida
Strasser, Todd
Voigt, Cynthia
Willey, Margaret
Zindel, Paul

Science Fiction/Fantasy:

Adams, Douglas
Adams, Richard
Alexander, Lloyd
Anthony, Piers
Asimov, Isaac
Beagle, Peter
Bradbury, Ray
Bradley, Marion Zimmer
Brin, David
Brooks, Terry
Card, Orson Scott
Clarke, Arthur C.
Cooper, Susan
Dickinson, Peter
Donaldson, Stephen
Frank, Pat
Heinlein, Robert
Herbert, Frank
Jones, Diane Wynne
LeGuin, Ursula
L'Engle, Madeleine

McCaffrey, Anne
McKinley, Robin
O'Brien, Robert
Pierce, Meredith Anne
Star Trek series
*Star Trek Next
    Generation* series
Stewart, Mary
Tolkien, J.R.R.
Weis, Margaret
White, T.H.
Yolen, Jane

Romance Authors:

Blair, Cynthia
Cooney, Linda
Daly, Maureen
Garden, Nancy
Greene, Bette
Hart, Bruce and Carol
Klein, Norma
Koetge, Ron
Mazer, Harry
Mazer, Norma Fox
Pascal, Francine
Sweet Dreams series
Willard, Nancy

Horror:

Andrews, V.C.
Blatty, William Peter
Cook, Robin
Jackson, Shirley
King, Stephen
Koontz, Dean
Michaels, Barbara
Rice, Anne
Saul, John
Strieber, Whitley

Mystery/Suspense:

Adams, Nicholas
Bates, A.
Bennett, Jay
Bunting, Eve
Christie, Agatha
Clark, Mary Higgins
Cusick, Richie
Davidson, Nicole
Dixon, Franklin
Duncan, Lois
Ellis, Carol
Ferguson, Alane
Gardner, John
Hoh, Diane
Keene, Carolyn
Levitin, Sonia
Littke, Lael
Miller, Frances
Pike, Christopher
Pullman, Philip
Raskin, Ellen
Steiner, Barbara
Stine, R.L.

Adventure:

Clancy, Tom
Mazer, Harry
Paulsen, Gary
Petersen, P.J.
Rawls, Wilson
Thompson, Julian
White, Robb

Humor:

Conford, Ellen
Danziger, Paula
Irving, John
Korman, Gordan
Robbins, Tom
Thompson, Julian

Vonnegut, Kurt
Zindel, Paul

Comics/Graphic Novels:

Davis, Jim
Groening, Matt
Larson, Gary
Lee, Stan
Mad series
Miller, Frankie
Moore, Alan
Schulz, Charles
Spiegelman, Art
Watterson, Bill

Historical:

Auel, Jean
Avi
Collier, James

Gaines, Ernest
Hunt, Irene
Lester, Jules
Montgomery, L.M.
Taylor, Mildred
Wiesel, Elie

African American:

Baldwin, James
Childress, Alice
Gaines, Ernest
Guy, Rosa
Hamilton, Virginia
Lester, Julius
Morrison, Toni
Myers, Walter Dean
Parks, Gordon
Taylor, Mildred
Walker, Alice
Wright, Richard

APPENDIX D

ADDRESSES OF MAJOR YOUNG ADULT PUBLISHERS

(Source: *Books in Print* 1990-91, 1991-92)

Mass Market Paperback:

Pocket Books, Inc. (Archway, Minstrel)
1230 Avenue of the Americas
New York, NY 10020

Avon Books
105 Madison Avenue
New York, NY 10016

Ballantine Books, Inc. (Del Rey, Fawcett, Ivy)
201 East 50th Street
New York, NY 10022

Bantam Doubleday Dell
666 Fifth Avenue
New York, NY 10103

Harper & Row Publishers, Inc.
10 East 53rd Street
New York, NY 10022

Literacy Volunteers of New York City
121 Sixth Avenue
New York, NY 10013

New American Library (DAW, Signet)
1633 Broadway
New York, NY 10019

Penguin Books
375 Hudson Street
New York, NY 10014

Scholastic, Inc. (Apple, Point)
730 Broadway
New York, NY 10003

Turman Publishing Company
1319 Dexter Avenue, North
Suite 30
Seattle, WA 98109

Willowisp Press, Inc.
401 East Wilson Bridge Road
Worthington, OH 43085

Science Fiction/Fantasy Publishers:

Berkley Publishing Group (Ace)
200 Madison Avenue
New York, NY 10016

Baen Books
260 Fifth Avenue
New York, NY 10001

Tor Books
49 West 24th Street
New York, NY 10010

Warner Books, Inc.
666 Fifth Avenue
New York, NY 10103

Zebra Books
475 Park Avenue South
New York, NY 10016

Hardback Fiction Publishers:

Delacorte Press
666 Fifth Avenue
New York, NY 10103

Farrar, Straus & Giroux, Inc.
19 Union Square West
New York, NY 10003

Harcourt Brace Jovanovich, Inc. (Gulliver)
1250 Sixth Avenue
San Diego, CA 92101

HarperCollins
10 East 53rd Street
New York, NY 10022

Henry Holt & Co.
115 West 18th Street
New York, NY 10011

Holiday House, Inc.
40 East 49th Street
New York, NY 10017

Houghton Mifflin Co. (Clarion)
1 Beacon Street
Boston, MA 02108

Little, Brown & Co.
34 Beacon Street
Boston, MA 02108

Macmillan Publishing Co., Inc.
(Atheneum, Bradbury, Collier, Crowell-Collier,
Four Winds, McElderry, Scribner)
866 Third Avenue
New York, NY 10022

William Morrow and Company (Greenwillow)
105 Madison Avenue
New York, NY 10016

Penguin USA (Dial, E.P. Dutton,
Cobblehill, Lodestar, Viking)
375 Hudson Street
New York, NY 10014

Random House, Inc. (Knopf)
201 East 50th Street
New York, NY 10022

Putnam Publishing Group (Philomel)
200 Madison Avenue
New York, NY 10016

Scholastic, Inc.
730 Broadway
New York, NY 10003

Walker Educational Book Corp.
720 Fifth Avenue
New York, NY 10019

Franklin Watts, Inc. (Orchard)
387 Park Avenue South
New York, NY 10016

YA Nonfiction publishers (many of the above also publish nonfiction):

Crestwood House, Inc.
866 Third Avenue
New York, NY 10022

Enslow Publishers, Inc.
P.O. Box 777
Hillside, NJ 07205

Greenhaven Press
P.O. Box 289009
San Diego, CA 92128

Millbrook Press
18 West 55th Street
New York, NY 10019

Peterson's Guides, Inc.
P.O. Box 2123
Princeton, NJ 08543

Rosen Publishing Group, Inc. (Blackbirch)
29 East 21st Street
New York, NY 10010

Simon & Schuster, Inc.
(Julian Messner, Silver Burdett)
1230 Avenue of the Americas
New York, NY 10020

Workman Publishing Co., Inc.
708 Broadway
New York, NY 10003

Comics/Comic Book Publishers:

Andrews & McMeel
4900 Main Street
Kansas City, MO 64112

Marvel Comics
387 Park Avenue South
New York, NY 10016

Pantheon Books
201 East 50th Street
New York, NY 10022

Warner Books, Inc.
666 Fifth Avenue
New York, NY 10103

APPENDIX E

ADDRESSES OF MAGAZINES FOR YOUNG ADULTS
Source: *Standard Periodical Directory*, 14th ed., 1991. A "*"
indicates an essential magazine for a YA collection. (Subscription
prices are for one year.)

General Interest

Boys' Life
P.O. Box 152079
Irving, TX 75015 ($13.20)

Sassy*
1 Times Square
New York, NY 10036 ($14.97)

Seventeen*
850 Third Avenue
New York, NY 10022 ($12.95)

Teen*
6725 Sunset Blvd.
Los Angeles, CA 90028 ($15.95)

Young Miss (aka YM)
685 Third Avenue
New York, NY 10017 ($12.95)

Music

Fanzines:

Bop*
3500 West Olive Avenue, #850
Burbank, CA 91505 ($15.00)

Dream Guys
253 East 62nd Street
New York, NY 10021 ($18.00)

Hip Hop
127 East 59th Street
New York, NY 10022 ($12.00)

Sixteen*
157 West 57th Street
New York, NY 10019 ($18.95)

Splice
10 Columbus Circle, #1300
New York, NY 10019 ($12.95)

Super Teen
355 Lexington Avenue
New York, NY 10017 ($27.00)

Teen Beat*
233 Park Avenue South
New York, NY 10016 ($21.00)

Teen Machine
355 Lexington Avenue
New York, NY 10017 ($27.00)

Tiger Beat
1086 Teaneck Road
Teaneck, NJ 07666 ($18.00)

General:

Creem
Box 931869
Sunset Station
Los Angeles, CA 90093 ($16.00)

Rolling Stone*
745 Fifth Avenue
New York, NY 10151 ($19.95)

Spin*
965 Broadway
New York, NY 10023 ($24.00)

Metal:

Circus*
3 West 18th Street
New York, NY 10011 ($19.00)

Hit Parader
Charlton Building
Derby, CT 06418 ($24.00)

Metal Edge
355 Lexington Avenue
New York, NY 10017 ($20.00)

Metal Mania
475 Park Avenue South
New York, NY 10016 ($15.00)

Rip*
9171 Wilshire Blvd
Beverly Hills, CA 90210 ($18.00)

Song Hits
Charlton Building
Derby, CT 06418 ($20.00)

Rap:

Black Beat
355 Lexington Avenue
New York, NY 10017 (price n.a.)

Fresh
19431 Business Center Drive, #27
Northridge, CA 91324 ($45.00)

Full Effect
25 West 39th Street
New York, NY 10018 ($18.00)

Rappin'
Charlton Building
Derby, CT 06418 ($18.00)

Right On
355 Lexington Avenue
New York, NY 10017 ($9.95)

Spice
475 Park Avenue South
New York, NY 10016 ($18.00)

Word Up*
63 Grand Avenue, #230
River Edge, NJ 07661 (price n.a.)

Alternative:

Option
2345 Wilshire Blvd., #2
Los Angeles, CA 90064 ($15.00)

Sports

General:

Inside Sport
990 Grove Street
Evanston, IL 60201 ($18.00)

Sport*
119 West 40th Street
New York, NY 10018 ($12.00)

Sporting News
1212 North Lindbergh Blvd.
St. Louis, MO 63132 ($38.64)

Sports Illustrated
Time-Life Building
Rockefeller Center
New York, NY 10020 ($69.66)

Big sports:

Baseball Digest
Basketball Digest
Football Digest
Hockey Digest
Century Publishing
990 Grove Street
Evanston, IL 60201 ($22.00 each)

Skating:

Thrasher*
1303 Underwood Avenue
San Francisco, CA 94124 ($16.50)

Transworld Skateboarding
3712 Escondido
Los Angeles, CA 92033 ($19.95)

Wrestling:

Inside Wrestling
Pro Wrestling Illustrated
Sports Review Wrestling
The Wrestler
G.C. London Publishing
Box 48
Rockville Center, NY 11571 ($19.00 each)

WWF Magazine*
Box 3857
Stamford, CT 06905 ($20.00)

Martial arts:

Black Belt
1813 Victory Place
Burbank, CA 91510 ($21.00)

TaeKwon Do Times
1423 18th Street
Bettendorf, IA 52722 ($9.99)

Boxing:

The Ring
130 West 37th Street
New York, NY 10018 ($18.00)

KO
Box 48
Rockville Center, NY 11570 ($18.00)

Sports cards:

Becket Baseball Card Monthly
4887 Alpha Road, #200
Dallas, TX 75244 (price n.a.)

Sports Card Trader
990 Grove Street
Evanston, IL 60201 ($29.95)

Bodybuilding:

Bodybuilding Lifestyles
1055 Summer Street
Stamford, CT 06905 ($12.95)

Joe Weider's Muscle and Fitness
21100 Erwin Street
Woodland Hills, CA 91367 (price n.a.)

Outdoor sports:

Field and Stream
Outdoor Life
Skiing
2 Park Avenue South
New York, NY 10016 ($15.94 each)

Technology

Cars:

Car and Driver
Road and Track
1633 Broadway
New York, NY 10019 ($19.94)

Hot Rod*
Motor Trend
6725 Sunset Blvd.
Los Angeles, CA 90028 ($19.94)

Cycles:

Bicycling
33 East Minor
Emmaus, PA 18049 ($30.00)

BMX Action
Freestylin' BMX
3162 Kashiwa Street
Torrance, CA 90505 ($16.50)

Computers:

Compute!
324 West Wendover Avenue
Greensboro, NC 27408 ($24.00)

Game Players
300-A Westgate Drive
Greensboro, NC 27407 ($17.00)

Game Pro
P.O. Box 2096
Knoxville, IN 50198 ($19.97)

Nintendo Power*
P.O. Box 97043
Redmond, WA 98073 ($15.00)

Movies:

Cinefantisque
P.O. Box 270
Oak Park, IL 60303 ($27.00)

Fangoria
Gorezone
Starlog
475 Park Avenue South
New York, NY 10016 ($19.98 each)

Humor

Cracked
535 Fifth Avenue
New York, NY 10017 ($10.00)

Mad*
485 Madison Avneue
New York, NY 10022 ($7.00)

National Lampoon
155 Avenue of the Americas
New York, NY 10013 ($10.95)

Spy
295 Lafayette Street
New York, NY 10012 ($21.77)

Games

Dragon (Dungeons & Dragons)
Box 756
Lake Geneva, WI 53147 ($30.00)

Games
810 Seventh Avenue
New York, NY 10019 ($11.97)

Current Affairs

News For You
Box 131
Syracuse, NY 13210 (price n.a.)

Scholastic Update
730 Broadway
New York, NY 10003 ($19.00)

Adult Magazines with High Teen Appeal

Ebony
Elle
Entertainment Weekly
Essence
Glamour
Globe (tabloid)
In Fashion
Jet
Life
Mademoiselle
National Enquirer*
Newsweek
People
Premiere
Time
Us
USA Today (newspaper)
Vogue
Weekly World News*

APPENDIX F

ADDRESSES OF PROFESSIONAL PERIODICALS
(Subscription prices are for one year.)

YA only:

ALAN Review
National Council of Teachers of English
1 University Heights
Asheville, NC 28804 ($15.00)

Kliatt Young Adult Paperback Book Guide
425 Watertown Street
Newton, MA 02158 ($33.00)

Voice of Youth Advocates
Scarecrow Press
P.O. Box 4167
Metuchen, NJ 08840 ($27.00)

YA and children (school focus):

Appraisal: Science Books for Young People
605 Commonwealth Avenue
Boston, MA 02215 ($26.00)

The Book Report
5701 North High Street, #1
Worthington, OH 43085

Bulletin of the Center for Children's Books
5270 South Woodlawn
Chicago, IL 60637 ($29.00)

Emergency Librarian
Dept 284, Box C34069
Seattle, WA 98124 ($40.00)

Horn Book
14 Beacon Street
Boston, MA 02108 ($36.00)

Interracial Books for Children Bulletin
1841 Broadway, #500
New York, NY 10023 ($24.00)

School Library Journal
249 West 17th Street
New York, NY 10011 ($63.00)

General media:

Booklist
50 East Huron Street
Chicago, IL 60611 ($56.00)

Kirkus Reviews
200 Park Avenue South
New York, NY 10003 ($225.00)

Keeping up with trends:

English Journal
National Council of Teachers of English
1111 Kenyon Road
Urbana, IL 61801 ($20.00)

Journal of Reading
International Reading Association
Box 8139
Newark, DE 19711 ($33.00)

Journal of Youth Services
School Library Media Quarterly
50 East Huron Street
Chicago, IL 60611 ($35.00)

Media and Methods
American Society of Educators
1429 Walnut Street
Philadelphia, PA 19102 ($29.00)

Wilson Library Bulletin (YA Perplex column)
950 University Avenue
Bronx, NY 10452

YA Hotline
School of Library Service
Dalhousie University
Halifax, Nova Scotia, Canada B3h 4H8 ($9.50)

BIBLIOGRAPHY

This is a bibliography of additional materials about YA services. Unlike the tools previously listed in both the text and in accompanying documents, these materials are for background information and further reading.

PART ONE: YOUNG ADULTS AND LIBRARIES

Overviews/Histories:

Adolescents, Literature and Work with Youth, edited by J. Pamela Weiner and Ruth Stein. New York: Haworth Press, 1985.

Atkinson, Joan. "Pioneers in Public Library Service to Young Adults." *Top of the News* (Fall 1986): 27-44.

Braverman, Miriam. *Youth, Society and the Public Library*. Chicago: American Library Association, 1979.

Broderick, Dorothy. "On Saying YeSS to Youth." *Illinois Libraries* (June 1986): 387-92.

———— "Serving Young Adults: Why We Do What We Do." *Voice of Youth Advocates* (October 1989): 2-6.

Chelton, Mary Kay. "Educational and Recreational Services of the Public Library for Young Adults." *Library Quarterly* (October 1978): 488-498.

Directions for Library Services to Young Adults. American Library Association/ Young Adult Services Division, Services Statement Development Committee. Chicago: American Library Association, 1977.

Edwards, Margaret. *The Fair Garden and the Swarm of Beasts*, 2nd ed. New York: Hawthorne Books, 1974.

Libraries and Young Adults: Media, Services and Librarianship, edited by JoAnn V. Rogers. Littleton, CO: Libraries Unlimited, 1979.

"Library Services to Youth: Preparing for the Future," edited by Linda Waddle. *Library Trends* (Summer 1988).

Managers and Missionaries: Library Services to Children and Young Adults in the Information Age, edited by Leslie Edmonds. Urbana: University of Illinois, 1988.

Meeting the Challenge: Library Services to Young Adults, edited by Andre and Ann Gagnon. Ottawa: Canadian Library Association, 1984.

Miller, Marilyn. "Changing Priorities for Service to Children and Adolescents in School and Public Libraries," in *Managers and Missionaries*: 5-16.

New Directions for Young Adult Services, edited by Ellen LiBretto. New York: Bowker, 1983.

Pape, Marion. "Breaking Down the Barriers to Services for Young Adults in Public Libraries," in *Meeting the Challenge*: 23-30.

Reaching Young People Through Media, edited by Nancy Bach Pillon. Littleton, CO: Libraries Unlimted, 1983.

Rogers, JoAnn. "Trends and Issues in Young Adult Services," in *Libraries and Young Adults*: 67-74.

VOYA Reader, edited by Dorothy Broderick. Metuchen, NJ: Scarecrow Press, 1990.

Wilson, Evie. "Librarian as an Advocate for Youth," in *Reaching Young People Through Media*: 103-115.

"Young Adult Service in the Public Library," edited by Audrey Biel. *Library Trends* (October 1968).

Young Adult Services in the Public Library. American Library Association, Committee on Standards for Work with Young Adults in Public Libraries. Chicago: American Library Association, 1960.

"Youth Services," edited by Linda Ward Callaghan. *Illinois Libraries* (January 1988).

Predictions:

Downen, Thomas Wm. "YA Services: 1993," unpublished paper (1979?).

Heller, Dawn. "Developing a Youth Agenda for the Information Age," in *Managers and Missionaries*: 157-162.

Hodges, Gerald. "The Future of Youth Services: Developmental, Demographic, and Educational Concerns." *Top of the News* (Winter 1987): 167-175.

Libraries Serving Youth: Directions for Service in the 1990's. New York: New York Library Association, 1987.

Mathews, Virginia, et al. "Kids Need Libraries: School and Public Libraries Preparing the Youth of Today for the World of Tomorrow." *Journal of Youth Services* (Spring 1990): 197-207.

Statistics/Measurement:

Chelton, Mary Kay. "Developmentally Based Performance Measures for Young Adult Services." *Top of the News* (Fall 1984): 39-52.

———— "The First National Survey of Services and Resources for Young Adults in Public Libraries." *Journal of Youth Services* (Spring 1989): 224-31.

Hodges, Gerald. "Evaluation and Measurement of Youth Services," in *Managers and Missionaries*: 147-156.

McClure, Charles, et al. *Planning and Role Setting for Public Libraries: A Manual of Options and Procedures*. Chicago: American Library Association, 1987.

Services and Resources for Young Adults in Public Libraries. U.S. Department of Education, Office of Educational Research and Improvement, National Center for Education Statistics. Washington: Government Printing Office, July 1988.

PART TWO: YOUNG ADULT PSYCHOLOGY/ CULTURE

Benson, Peter. *The Quicksilver Years: The Hopes and Fears of Early Adolesence*. San Francisco: Harper & Row, 1987.

Elkind, David. *All Grown Up and No Place to Go: Teenagers in Crisis*. Reading, MA: Addison-Wesley, 1984.

———— *The Hurried Child: Growing Up Too Fast Too Soon*. Reading, MA: Addison-Wesley, 1988.

Fuhrman, Barbara Schneider. *Adolesence. Adolescents*. Boston: Little Brown, 1986.

Larson, Reed and Mihaly Csikszentimahalyi. *Being Adolescent: Conflict and Growth in the Teenage Years*. New York: Basic Books, 1984.

"New Teens: What Makes Them Different." *Newsweek* special edition (Summer/Fall 1990).

Nielsen. Linda. *Adolescent Psychology: A Contemporary View*. New York: Holt, Rinehart and Winston, 1987.

Teens: A Fresh Look, edited by Anne Pedersen and Peggy O'Mara. Sante Fe, NM: John Muir Publications, 1991.

Youth Indicators 1991. Washington: Government Printing Office, 1991.

PART THREE: YOUNG ADULT LITERATURE

Overviews/Texts:

Campbell, Patricia. "Perplexing Young Adult Books: A Retrospective." *Wilson Library Bulletin* (April 1988): 20+.

Carlsen, G. Robert. *Books and the Teen-Age Reader,* 2nd ed. New York: Harper & Row, 1980.

Cline, Ruth and William McBride. *A Guide to Literature for Young Adults: Background, Selection and Use.* Glenview, IL: Scott, Foresman and Company, 1983.

Donelson, Kenneth L. and Alleen Pace Nilsen. *Literature for Today's Young Adults,* 3rd ed. Glenview, IL: Scott, Foresman and Company, 1989.

Fader, Daniel. *New Hooked on Books.* New York: Berkley, 1976.

Gallagher, Mary Elizabeth. *Young Adult Literature: Issues and Perspectives.* Haverford, PA: Catholic Library Association, 1988.

Reed, Arthrea J.S. Reed. *Comics to Classics: A Parent's Guide to Books for Teens and Parents.* Newark, DE: International Reading Association, 1988.

——— *Reaching Adolescents: The Young Adult Book and the School.* New York: Holt, Rinehart and Winston, 1985.

Shapiro, Lillian. *Fiction for Youth,* 2nd ed. New York: Neal-Schuman, 1986.

White, Valerie. "Selection and Development of a Young Adult Collection in the Public Library," in *Meeting the Challenge*: 131-146.

Young Adult Literature: Background and Criticism, edited by Millicent Lenz and Ramona Mahood. Chicago: American Libary Association, 1980.

Young Adult Literature: A Guide for Selection, Teaching and Services, edited by Beverly Youree. Boston: G.K. Hall, 1991

Young Adult Literature in the Seventies, edited by Jana Varlejs. Metuchen, NJ: Scarecrow Press, 1978.

Fiction/Paperbacks:

Broderick, Dorothy and Mary Kay Chelton. *Librarian's Guide: Young Adult Paperbacks*. New York: New American Library, 1986.

Eaglan, Audrey. "New Blood for Young Readers" (thrillers). *School Library Journal* (August 1990): 105.

Genco, Barbara, Eleanor MacDonald and Betsy Hearne. "Juggling Popularity and Quality." *School Library Journal* (March 1991): 115-119.

Gerhardt, Lillian. "Taking Trash Lightly." *School Library Journal* (January 1982): 28+.

Green, Sigrid. "Reading Teen Fiction Can Help Girls Develop a Healthy Self-Image." *School Libraries in Canada* (Spring 1990): 27+.

Huntwork, Mary. "Why Girls Flock to Sweet Valley High." *School Library Journal* (March 1990): 137-40.

Nilsen, Aleen Pace and Kenneth Donelson. "The New Realism Comes of Age." *Journal of Youth Services* (Spring 1988): 275-282.

Sutton, Roger. "Hard Times at Sweet Valley." *School Library Journal* (November 1990): 50.

———— "Libraries and the Paperback Romance." *School Library Journal* (November 1985): 25+

Nonfiction:

Carter, Betty and Richard F. Abrahamson. *Nonfiction for Young Adults: From Delight to Wisdom*. Phoenix: Oryx Press, 1990.

"Contemporary Nonfiction for Young Adults." *Booklist* (January 1, 1986): 678-81.

Comic Books/Graphic Novels:

Cartoons and Comics in the Classroom: A Reference for Teachers and Librarians, edited by James L. Thomas. Littleton, CO: Libraries Unlimited, 1982.

DeCandido, Keith. "Picture This: Graphic Novels in Libraries." *Library Journal* (March 15, 1990): 50-55.

Dorrell, Larry. "Why Comics Books?" *School Library Journal* (November 1987): 30-32.

Jones, Patrick. "Getting Serious About Comics." *Voice of Youth Advocates* (April 1988): 15-16.

Reid, Calvin. "Picture This: Comics' Success in All Markets." *Publishers Weekly* (October 12, 1990): 17-19.

Nonprint:

Caywood, Caroline. "Nonprint Media Selection Guidelines." *Journal of Youth Services* (Fall 1988): 90-94.

Gallant, Jennifer Jung. *Best Videos for Children and Young Adults*. Santa Barbara, CA: AMC-Clio, 1990.

Muzzerall, Darla. "Rock & Rebellion." *YA Hotline* (Issue 34).

Magazines:

Edmondson, Brad. "Teen Mags Dive In." *American Demographics* (June 1987): 23+

Jones, Patrick. "Wrestling with Young Adult Magazines." *Voice of Youth Advocates* (April 1989): 10-12.

Lewis, Sue. "Fashion Plus: Magazines for Young Women." *YA Hotline* (Issue 34): 25-30.

Payne, Sandra. "Periodicals Power," in *High/Low Handbook*, 3rd ed. New York: Bowker, 1990: 77-84.

"YA Magazines." *YA Hotline* (Issue 6/7).

Reluctant Readers:

Edmonds, Leslie. "Selling Reading: Library Services to Reluctant Adolescent Readers." *Illinois Libraries* (June 1986): 374-7.

High/Low Handbook: Encouraging Literacy in the 1990's, 3rd ed, edited by Ellen LiBretto. New York: Bowker, 1990.

Motivating Children and Young Adults to Read - 2, edited by James Thomas and Ruth Loring. Phoenix: Oryx Press, 1983.

PART FOUR: YOUNG ADULT SERVICES

Reference/Reader's Advisory:

Arent, Jeri. "Homework Assignments: We Can Help!" *Ohio Media Spectrum* (Fall 1989): 43-48.

Amey, L. "Neglected Enthusiasts: Adolescent Information Seekers," in *Meeting the Challenge*: 43-54.

Black, Nancy. "School Assignments: A Public Library Responsibility." *Emergency Librarian* (May-June 1986): 25-26.

Boylan, Patricia. "Young Adult Reference Services in the Public Library." *Top of the News* (Summer 1984): 415-17.

Chelton, Mary Kay. "Young Adult Reference Services in the Public Library." *Reference Services for Children and Young Adults*: 31-46.

Harmon, Charles and Frances Bradburn. "Realizing the Reading and Information Needs of Youth." *Library Trends* (Summer 1988): 19-27.

Kuhlthau, Carol. "Meeting the Information Needs of Children and Young Adults." *Journal of Youth Services* (Fall 1988): 51-57.

Matthews, Avis. "Breaking the Ice with YAs." *Voice of Youth Advocates* (June 1987): 72-73.

Reference Services for Children and Young Adults, edited by Bill Katz and Ruth Fraley. New York: Haworth Press, 1983.

Smith, Duncan, et al. "Homework Help: Problem-solving through Communication." *North Carolina Libraries* (Spring 1988): 33-37.

Steinmetz, Carol. "Creating Positive Reactions toward Reference Services among Young Adults." *Top of the News* (Fall 1981): 57-59.

Wallace, Mildred. "Viewing Problems as Challenges." *Voice of Youth Advocates* (August 1990): 147-8.

Wilson, Evie. "Reference Needs of Children and Young Adults in Public Libraries," in *Reference Services for Children and Young Adults*: 151-6.

Library Instruction/Orientation:

Breivik, Patricia. *Planning the Library Instruction Program*. Chicago: American Library Association, 1982.

Czopek, Vanessa. "Terra Incognita: Public Library Tours for Students." *Emergency Librarian* (November-December 1990): 18-23.

Eadie, Tom. "User Instruction Does Not Work." *Library Journal* (October 1, 1990): 42-45

Educating the Public Library User, edited by John Lubans. Chicago: American Library Association, 1983.

Gavryck, Jacquelyn. "Information Research Skills: Sharing the Burden." *Wilson Library Bulletin* (May 1986): 22-24.

Jweid, Rosann and Margaret Rizzo. *The Library-Classroom Partnership: Teaching Library Media Skills to Middle and Junior High Students.* Metuchen, NJ: Scarecrow Press, 1988.

Library Instruction and Reference Services, edited by Bill Katz and Ruth Fraley. New York: Haworth Press, 1984.

LIRT Library Instruction Handbook, edited by May Brottman and Mary Loe. Englewood, CO: Libraries Unlimited, 1990.

Payne, Patricia. "Narrowing the Gap Between Library Instruction and Functional Library Literacy," in *Reference Services for Children and Young Adults*: 115-122.

Booktalking:

Bodart, Joni. "Booktalks Do Work!" *Illinois Libraries* (June 1986): 378-81.

Chelton, Mary K. "Booktalking: You Can Do It." *School Library Journal* (April 1976): 39-43.

Goodman, Rhonna. "Booktalking," in *New Direction for Young Adult Services*: 93-102.

Jones, Patrick. "Booktalking Boosters." *Emergency Librarian* (November-December 1990): 28-30.

———— "Don't Tell, Sell." *The Booktalker* in *Wilson Library Bulletin* (September 1990, insert).

Klause, Annette Curtis. "Booktalking Science Fiction to Young Adults." *Journal of Youth Services* (Winter 1990): 102-116.

Ristau, Holly. "Defining the Young Adult and Describing the Effect of Book Talking." *Minnesota Libraries* (Summer-Autumn 1988): 48-49.

PART FIVE: MAKING CONNECTIONS

Billman, Betty and Patricia Owens. "School and Public Library Cooperation." *Collection Management* (Fall 1985): 183-95.

"Branching Out in Youth Services," edited by Carol Iffland. *Illinois Libraries* (January 1985).

Callison, Daniel. "A Survey of Cooperation and Communication Between Public and School Libraries." *Indiana Libraries* 8:2: 78-86.

Hart, Karen. "Using Each Other—A Necessity: School-Public Library Cooperation." *Colorado Libraries* (December 1986): 12-13.

Haycock, Ken. "Beyond Courtesy: School and Public Library Relationships." *Emergency Librarian* (May-June 1989): 27-30.

Jay, Hilda. *Developing Library-Museum Partnerships to Serve Young People.* Hamden, CN: Library Professional, 1984.

Look, Listen, Explain: Developing Community Library Services for Young Adults. Chicago: American Library Association, 1975.

Razzano, Barbara. "Public Library/School Library Cooperation: Applications for Reference Service." *Reference Librarian* (Spring/Summer 1983): 123-28.

Sullivan, Peggy. "Library Cooperation to Serve Youth," in *Libraries and Young Adults*: 113-18.

Tyson, Christy. "Coalition-Building: Maybe Tomorrow? Maybe Today!" in *Managers and Missionaries*: 41-54.

Wilson, Evie. "The Librarian in the Youth Services Network," in *New Directions for Young Adult Services*: 103-116.

"Workout Book: Getting In Shape to Cooperate." *Public Libraries* (Summer 1985): 71-73.

"Youth Services Cooperating Into the '90's," edited by Todd Morning. *Illinois Libraries* (February 1990).

PART SIX: PROGRAMMING

Planning:

Amey, L. "The Special Case for YA Programming." *Emergency Librarian* (January/February 1985): 25-26.

Courtly Love in the Shopping Mall: Humanities Based Programming for Young Adults. Chicago: American Library Association, 1991.

Greenberg, Marilyn. "Developmental Needs of Young Adults and Library Services," in *Libraries and Young Adults*: 90-99.

Jones, Patrick. "Know Your P's and Q's: A Planning Process for Young Adult Programs." *Journal of Youth Services* (Fall 1988): 95-100.

———— and Anne Prusha. "Young Adult Programming: Identifying the Elements of Success." *Voice of Youth Advocates* (June 1991): 83-85.

Moeller-Pfeiffer, Kathi. "After School Programming: You Can Do It!" *Voice of Youth Advocates* (February 1985): 184-5.

Rosenzweig, Susan, et al. "After School Programming for Early Adolescence." *Top of the News* (Fall 1983): 37-47.

White, Valerie. "Can't I Just Wing It?" *Emergency Librarian* (May-June 1986): 17-18.

YA Advisory Groups:

"Guidelines for Youth Participation in Library Decision Making," in *New Directions for Young Adult Services*: 203-4.

Tuccillo, Diane. "A Young Adult Advisory Council Can Work For You Too." *Emergency Librarian* (May-June 1986): 15-16.

Varlejis, Jana. "Youth Participation in Library Decision Making," in *New Directions for Young Adult Services*: 31-48.

Wigg, Ristina. "Would Teens Run Riot in the Library?: Youth Participation in Public Libraries." *Bookmark* (Spring 1985): 127-9.

Wilson, Evie. "The Young Adult Advisory Board: How to Make it Work." *Voice of Youth Advocates* (April 1979): 11-14.

"Youth Participation Guidelines." *VOYA Reader*: 45-48.

Youth Participation in Libraries: A Training Manual. Chicago: American Library Association, 1991.

Youth Participation in School and Public Libraries. National Commission on Resources for Youth with the Young Adult Services Division, American Library Association. Chicago: American Library Association, 1983.

Book Discussion Groups:

Kruse, Ginny Moore and Kathleen Horning. "Guidelines for Book Discussions," in *Evaluation Strategies and Techniques for Public Library Children's Services*, edited by Jane Robbins. Madison: University of Wisconsin, 1990.

Scales, Pat. *Communicating Through Young Adult Books*. New York: Bantam Books, 1989.

Yaconelli. Mike. *Get 'Em Talking: 104 Great Discussion Starters for Youth Groups*. Youth Specialties, 1989.

Summer Reading Programs:

Bacon, D. "Springfield's YA Reading Program." *Show-Me- Libraries* (October/November 1987): 31-33.

Blubaugh, Penny. "The Peace Safari: A Summer Reading Program." *Voice of Youth Advocates* (June 1990): 97+

Edgerton, Cathi. "We Spent Our Summer Chasing Unicorns: A Young Adult Reading Game Update." *Top of the News* (Spring 1986): 97+

―――― "Young Adult Summer Reading Games." *Voice of Youth Advocates* (August 1983): 134-141+.

Nagle, Ann. "YA Summer Reading Plan." *Voice of Youth Advocates* (June 1987): 71+.

Literary Magazines:

Bichel, Betty. "Lakewood YAs are Bibliomaniacs." *Voice of Youth Advocates* (February 1988): 268-70.

Dickey, Janet and Jean Delaney. "Teen Reflections." *School Library Journal*. (June 1988): 60.

Moron, Rosmeary. "Young Adult Creative Writing Contest." *Voice of Youth Advocates* (February 1988): 271-2.

Smith, Jayne. "How to Put Out a Literary Magazine." *English Journal* (January 1986): 29+.

Vernerder, Gloria. "Publication of a Literary Magazine." *Illinois Libraries* (January 1988): 68-72.

Williams, Gene. "The Public Library as Publisher: Some Scissors, Rubber Cement and Time." *Wilson Library Bulletin* (June 1987): 34-35.

PART SEVEN: MARKETING AND MERCHANDISING

Baker, S. "The Display Phenomenon: An Exploration into Factors Causing the Increase Circulation of Displayed Books." *Library Quarterly* (July 1986): 237+.

Carey, Cathy. "It's Not Totally Dreamland Quiz: Public Library Teen Area Self Evaluation." *Voice of Youth Advocates* (June 1990): 95-96.

Green, Sylvia. "Merchandising Techniques and Libraries." *School Library Journal* (September 1981): 35-39.

Hippenhammer, Craighton. "Marketing Youth Services: A User Approach," in *Managers and Missionaries*: 79-88.

Jones, Patrick. "Mall Things Considered." *School Library Journal* (July 1989): 40.

Kies, Cosette. *Marketing and Public Relations for Libraries*. Metuchen, NJ: Scarecrow Press, 1987.

Langhorne, Mary Jo. "Marketing Books in the School Library." *School Library Journal* (January 1987): 31-33.

LiBretto, Ellen. "Merchandising Collections and Services," in *New Directions for Young Adult Services*: 49-62.

Marketing: A Planned Approach for the Public Library (video). Chicago: ALA Video, 1989.

Schaeffer, Mark. *Library Displays Handbook*. New York: H.W. Wilson, 1990.

Setterington, Kenneth. "The Physical Layout and Set-up of the Young Adult Area," in *Meeting the Challenge*: 77-86.

Sivilich, Kenneth. "Merchandising Your Library." *Public Libraries* (March-April 1989): 97-100.

Strasser, Todd. "Lending Ambiance to Libraries." *School Library Journal* (June/July 1988): 59.

PART EIGHT: ISSUES AND CONCERNS

Confidentality/Privacy:

"Confidentality of Library Records in School Library Media Centers." *North Carolina Libraries* (Fall 1987): 142.

Hildebrand, Janet. "Is Privacy Reserved for Adults?" *School Library Journal* (January 1991): 21-25.

Stover, Mark. "Confidentality and Privacy in Reference Service." RQ (Winter 1987): 240-4.

Vandergrift, Kay. "Privacy, Schooling and Minors." *School Library Journal* (January 1991): 26-30.

Social Responsibility/Intellectual Freedom:

Freedom of Information and Youth, edited by Jana Varlejs. Jefferson, NC: McFarland, 1986.

Hit List: Frequently Challenged Young Adult Titles. Chicago: American Library Association, 1989.

"Intellectual Freedom," edited by Diane Woodward. *Library Trends* (Summer/Fall 1990).

Intellectual Freedom Manual. Chicago: American Library Association, 1989.

Waddle, Linda. "School Media Matters: Against the Practice of Self-Censorship." *Wilson Library Bulletin* (May 1988): 66-67.

Woods, L. "Self-Censorship in Collection Development by High School Library Media Specialists." *School Library Media Quarterly* (Winter 1981): 102-8.

Restricted Access:

Chelton, Mary K. "Issues in Youth Access to Library Services." *School Library Media Quarterly* (Fall 1985): 21-25.

McDonald, Frances. "Access to Information: Professional Responsbility and Personal Response," in *Managers and Missionaries*: 55-64.

———— "Information Access for Youth: Issues and Concerns." *Library Trends* (Summer 1988): 28-42.

Latchkey children/YAs:

Dowd, Frances Smardo. *Latchkey Children in the Library and Community.* Phoenix: Oryx Press, 1991.

Fuqua, Christopher. "Unattended Children: An Engagement Policy That Works." *Wilson Library Bulletin* (June 1988): 88-90.

"Latchkey Children in the Public Library." *Public Libraries* (Winter 1988): 196-8.

Rome, Linda. "Service to Latchkey Kids and the Public Library: Dealing with the Real Issues." *Wilson Library Bulletin* (April 1990): 34-37.

Out of school/Non-college-bound YAs:

Howery, Mary, et al. "Girls as Winners: A Personal and Career Development Program for At-Risk Adolescents." *Illinois Libraries* (February 1990): 171-75.

William T. Grant Commission on Work, Family and Citizenship. *The Forgotten Half: Non-College Youth in America.* Washington: The Commission, 1988.

Youth At Risk: A Resource for Counselors, Teachers and Parents, edited by David Capuzzi and Douglas Gross. Alexandria, VA: American Asssociation for Counseling and Development, 1989.

Lack of diversity in the literature:

Allen, Adela Artola. "Library Services to Hispanic Young Adults." *Library Trends* (Summer 1988): 81-99.

Beilke, Patricia and Frank Sciara. *Selecting Materials For and About Hispanic and East Asian Children and Young People.* Hamden, CT: Library Professional, 1984.

Jenkins, Christine. "Being Gay: Gay/Lesbian Characters and Concerns in Young Adult Books." *Booklist* (September 1, 1990): 39-41.

Schon, Isabel. *Books in Spanish for Children and Young Adults.* Metuchen, NJ: Scarecrow Press, 1989.

———— "Recent Books About Hispanics." *Voice of Youth Advocates* (February 1990): 28-30.

———— "A Selection of Hispanic Nonfiction." *Journal of Youth Services* (Summer 1990): 309-12.

Taylor, Deb. "Black Experience in Books for Young Adults." *Booklist* (December 1, 1989): 737-9.

Defining YAs/YA services:

Eaglen, Audrey. "An Immodest Proposal." *School Library Journal* (August 1989): 92.

Hakala-Ausperk, Catherine. "Are Young Adults Getting Younger?" Master's Research Paper. Kent State University School of Library Science, April 1991.

Harding, Margaret. "Where Have All the Children Gone: The Seventh Grader as Public Library Dropout." *Public Libraries* (Fall 1983): 92-96.

Tyson, Christy. "What's In a Name?" *School Library Journal* (December 1990): 47.

INDEX

Patrick Jones is a Branch Manager with the Allen County Public Library in Fort Wayne, Indiana. He was previously a Young Adult Regional Manager in the Cuyahoga County Public Library System in Cleveland, Ohio. He has written and spoken at conferences frequently on the subject of services to YAs.

Dr. Bill Katz is Professor at the School of Library and Information Science, State University of New York at Albany. He is the author of many distinguished works in library science.

Book design: Gloria Brown
Cover design: Gregory Apicella
Typography: Roberts/Churcher